TEXTS FOR ENGLISH AND AMERICAN STUDIES

edited by

Peter Freese

20

Canada

— Regions and Literature —

edited and annotated

by

Gerhard Düsterhaus

and

Rolf Franzbecker

STUDENTS' BOOK

Best.- Nr. 41 093 8

Ferdinand Schöningh

Unterrichtsmaterialien für die Sekundarstufe II

Dr. Gerhard Düsterhaus is *Akademischer Oberrat* in the English Department of Bonn University.

Dr. Rolf Franzbecker is *Akademischer Oberrat* in the *Fachbereich Sprach- und Literaturwissenschaften (Anglistik/Amerikanistik)* at the Universität/Gesamthochschule, Paderborn.

Detailed analyses of the texts in this Reader, didactic reflections, and methodological instructions can be found in the accompanying
TEACHER'S BOOK,
Schöninghbuch 41 0946

This book was produced with the help and support of the Canadian Embassy in Bonn to whom we extend our very grateful thanks.

(Verlag Ferdinand Schöningh, Jühenplatz 1, D 4790 Paderborn)

Printed in Germany. Gesamtherstellung Ferdinand Schöningh.

ISBN 3-506-41093-8

Contents

Titles marked * are provided by the editors.

Preface

Canada's ten provinces and two territories can easily be grouped into six distinct regions: the Atlantic Provinces, Québec, Ontario, the Prairies, the West Coast and the North. Three of them coincide with the boundaries of provinces, the rest transcend them and thus reveal the artificiality of frontiers.

Although geography constitutes a binding element for these regions it is not the primary means for defining them. The history of settlement, the experiences of a homogeneous population (e.g. in Québec, which, nevertheless, since World War II has become ethnically more diverse), economic developments, political struggles and common religious persuasions have contributed to the emergence of distinct regional feelings in Canada and to a considerable degree of self-awareness in each region, which has found expression in all genres of literature.

Regionalism is an important element in Candian literature, which is not to say that Canadian literature is entirely limited to rural subject matter, nor that it lacks wider interest. Admittedly, regionalism in literature is a controversial topic, as the line of distinction between sentimental provincialism and true fiction–which, though rooted in a region, transcends it in form and meaning and never precludes universal truths–is sometimes difficult to draw. For a good regional writer a region is a framework which offers themes, places, characters and events to identify with and to elaborate on. It is up to each author to decide about the degree of regional elements in his writing and the importance of local ideas for a universal readership.

This book is an attempt to present some of the outstanding Canadian writers whose works contain elements that link each of them with one of the six regions mentioned above.

---

1 *group* (v.): to form into a number of people or things – 3 *coincide* (v.): to be in agreement – 4 *transcend* (v.): to go beyond – 5 *constitute* (v.): to form – 7 *homogeneous* (adj.) /həumə'dʒinɪəs/: formed of parts of the same kind – 8 **ethnically** (adv.): related to a national, racial or tribal group – 8 *diverse* (adj.): different, various – 9 *persuasion* (n.): a particular religious belief – 10 *ermergence* (n.): the act of appearing from somewhere – 11 **self-awareness** (n.): having or showing consciousness of oneself – 12 **genre** (n.): a type of literature – 13 **regionalism** (n.): the use of a particular part of a country as the setting of stories, plays etc. representing it as affecting the lives of the characters – 15 *admittedly* (adv.): it must be stated true – 15 *controversial* (adj.): likely to cause much argument – 16 **topic** (n.): subject – 16 *sentimental* (adj.): showing too much tender feelings – 16 **provincialism** (n.): the state of showing limited or old-fashioned customs, ideas etc. – 17 **fiction** (n.): literature – 18 *preclude* (v.): to prevent – 19 *framework* (n.): a frame of reference – 20 *elaborate* (v.): to add more detail to – 22 **readership** (n.): a number of readers – 23 **outstanding** (adj.): very good

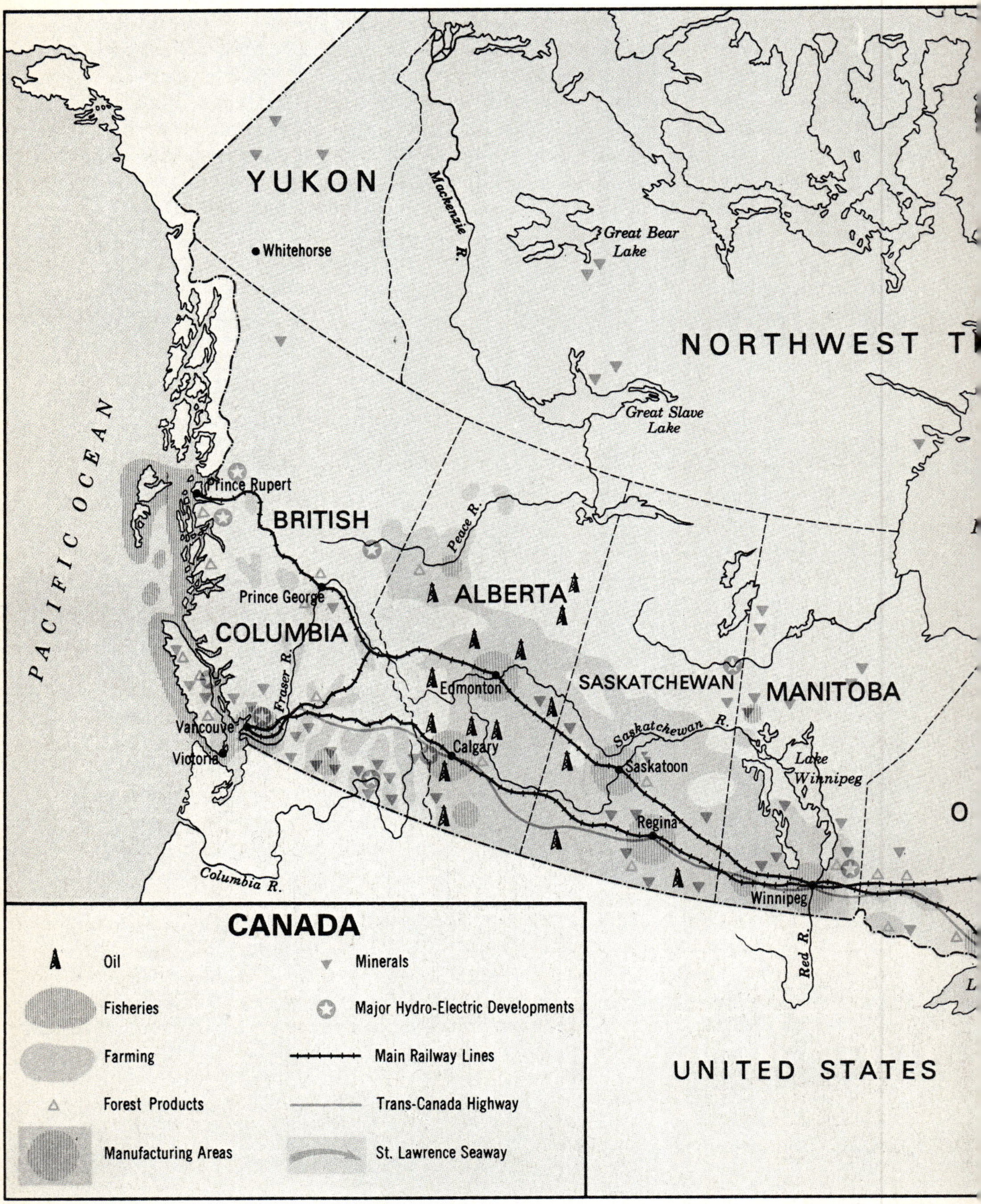

YUKON
Whitehorse
Mackenzie R.
Great Bear Lake
NORTHWEST T
Great Slave Lake
PACIFIC OCEAN
Prince Rupert
BRITISH
COLUMBIA
Prince George
Peace R.
ALBERTA
Fraser R.
Edmonton
SASKATCHEWAN
MANITOBA
Vancouver
Victoria
Calgary
Saskatchewan R.
Saskatoon
Lake Winnipeg
Regina
O
Columbia R.
Winnipeg
Red R.
UNITED STATES
CANADA
Oil
Minerals
Fisheries
Major Hydro-Electric Developments
Farming
Main Railway Lines
Forest Products
Trans-Canada Highway
Manufacturing Areas
St. Lawrence Seaway

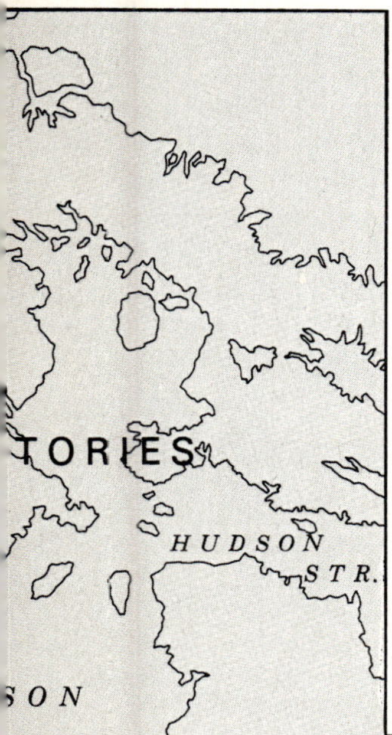
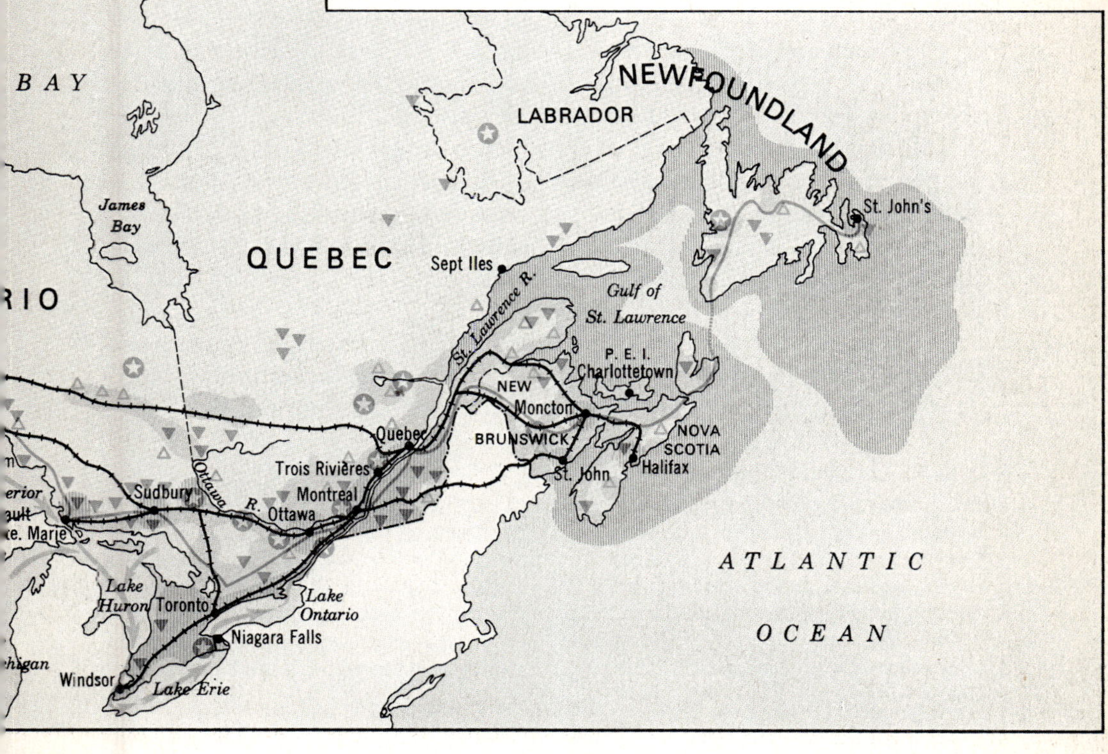

Geographically Canada is the second largest country in the world. Economically it is one of the most industrialized and enjoys one of the highest standards of living. Socially it is one of the most diverse, for the Canadian people have come from every land on the globe. Historically Canada has been part of the French and British Empires, and, like many other countries, has achieved its complete independence only in this century. Politically it has enjoyed democratic institutions for well over one hundred years. It is not an easy country to understand, even for Canadians.

From: John Saywell, *Canada Past and Present*, Toronto, Clarke Irwin, rev. ed. 1984, p. 4.

diverse (adj.): different – *achieve* (v.): to gain

I Introduction

1: JOHN SAYWELL: The Land and the People

John Tupper Saywell, a writer and university professor, was born in Saskatchewan in 1929. He attended the University of British Columbia and took his Ph.D. from Harvard University. Later he became Professor of History and Environmental Studies at York University in Toronto where he still teaches. From 1974–1979 he was head of an Economic Planning project in Kenya and spent the years from 1979–1981 in Japan where he developed Canadian studies at various universities. His writings include *The Office of Lieutenant-Governor* (1957), *The Canadian Journal of Lady Aberdeen* (1960) als well as dramas and documentaries for television and radio. Besides, he has written numerous magazine and newspaper articles. In "The Land and the People", published here in an abridged version, Saywell introduces Canada, in particular its regions and its history of settlement.

The text is taken from:
John Saywell, *Canada Past and Present*, Toronto, Clarke Irwin, rev. ed. 1984, pp. 4–11.

The sheer size of Canada is overwhelming. Smaller only than the Soviet Union, it sprawls from the Pacific to the Atlantic. Its northern boundary is the frozen Arctic, and its southern, the American border.

This size has always been a threat to its existence. Most of its 23 500 000 people are stretched out in a ribbon along the length of its southern boundary. The traveller can only marvel that the nation exists; for crossing the country he sees not one Canada but many. Geography does not divide Canada from the United States nearly so much as it divides sections of the country from one another.

The four Atlantic provinces are the northern-most extension of the Appalachian Mountains which run along most of the Atlantic seabord of North America. They have been little affected by modern immigration. Most of the

---

Ph. D.: Doctor of Philosophy – *Lieutenant-Governor:* the representative of the Queen of England in each Canadian province – *Lady Aberdeen:* the wife of Canada's Governor-General from 1893–1898 – **abridge** (v.): to shorten – 1 *sheer* (adj.): pure, unmixed with anything else – 1 *overwhelming* (adj.): very large – 2 *sprawl* (v.): to stretch out – 10 *Appalachian Mountains* /æpə'lætʃən/: the principal mountain system of the eastern United States and Canada, roughly paralleling the Atlantic coast from Newfoundland to Alabama – 12 **immigration** (n.) /ɪmɪ'greɪʃn/: coming into a country to make one's life and home there –

inhabitants are offspring of people from the British Isles and have lived in the region for generations or centuries. Poorer than the average Canadian, the people of the Atlantic provinces have a strong sense of independence, a distinctive oulook and loyalty and a distaste for the hustle and bustle of much of Northern American society.

United by geography, but divided by language the provinces of Québec and Ontario form two distinctive Canadian regions and societies. The people of both are concentrated along the banks of the St. Lawrence-Great Lakes waterway.

Eighty per cent of the people in Québec are French-speaking. While most now live in the industrial cities which produce almost one third of Canada's manufactures, the quiet villages and farms and the white towers of the parish church constantly reveal what the province was like for several centuries, and what for some it still is.

Over the border in Ontario, the most populous province, the floor of the St. Lawrence Valley broadens. The farms become larger, and settlement runs many miles north from the river. Prosperous farmers and dairymen, and fruit growers in the Niagara Peninsula, produce one third of the nation's agricultural wealth. In the bleak wilderness of the Shield, towns and cities like Sudbury, the nickel capital of the world, live off the rich yield of the forests and mines. But the pulse of the province comes from the large manufacturing cities that sweep around Lake Ontario. This "golden horseshoe" is the largest manufacturing region in Canada and one of the fastest growing centres in the world. At one time Ontario was basically Anglo-Saxon in composition. But particularly since the end of the Second World War it has been radically changed by the vast influx of immigrants who came to man the factories and build the growing cities of southern Ontario.

The southwestern portion of the Canadian Shield gradually disappears into the wheatlands of the Canadian prairies, one of the great granaries of the world. The prairies were largely settled in the early years of this century. Part of the population is made up of descendants of British, French and American

---

13 *offspring* (n.): children, descendents – 16 **outlook** (n.): view, opinion – 16 *loyalty* (n.): a connection which binds a person to someone – 16 *distaste* (n.): dislike, displeasure – 16 *hustle and bustle* /'hʌsl ən 'bʌsl/: hurried activity – 19 **distinctive** (adj.): clearly different from others – 20 *St. Lawrence-Great Lakes:* the St. Lawrence-Great Lakes Seaway allows ocean-going vessels to travel from the Atlantic up to Lake Superior – 24 *manufacture* (n.): something that has been manufactured – 24 **parish** (n.) /'pærɪʃ/: an area in the care of a single priest – 27 *populous* (adj.): having a large population – 29 *dairyman* (n.): milk farmer – 30 *Niagara Peninsula* /naɪ'ægrə pə'nɪnsjulə/: part of Ontario which lies between Lakes Erie and Ontario – 31 *bleak* (adj.) /blik/: without shelter, uninviting – 31 *Shield* (n.): The Canadian Shield forms an incomplete ring around Hudson Bay and covers about half the total area of Canada. It is largely unsuitable for agriculture – 32 *yield* (n.): that which is produced – 33 *pulse* (n.) /'pʌls/: the regular beating of blood in the vessels – 34 *sweep* (v.) here: to be in a curve across land – 34 *horseshoe* (n.): a curved piece of iron nailed on under a horse's foot – 36 **basically** (adv.): fundamentally – 36 *composition* (n.): mixture, combination – 38 *influx* (n.): arrival of large numbers – 41 **granary** (n.) /'grænərɪ/: a place which grows a lot of wheat, especially for other countries, G. Kornkammer.

settlers, but the descendants of the myriad of central European peoples who came to build the railways and open the land for settlement now make up half the prairie population. Today the three prairie provinces—Manitoba, Saskatchewan and Alberta—are no longer completely dependent on farming and ranching. Oil in Alberta, and to a lesser extent in the other provinces, potash and uranium in Saskatchewan, and gold and nickel in Manitoba have broadened the economy of the region and provided greater prosperity.

Beyond the Rockies lies British Columbia, a province extremely rich in the products of its forests, waters and mines. With an abundance of hydro-electric power, much of it exported to the United States, it boasts of a rapidly growing manufacturing industry based on its raw materials. While the capital city of Victoria retains a quiet old-world charm, much of the province's activity is on the edge of the frontier where life is vigorous and dynamic. Many British Columbians tend to regard their beautiful province as an empire in itself.

Stretching across the top of the four western provinces are the giant Northwest Territories and the Yukon. Governed largely from Ottawa but hoping someday to become provinces, the north makes up forty per cent of Canada's area, but has only about 65 000 inhabitants. Many of the people are Inuit and Indian, although increasing numbers of whites live in the north as prospectors, engineers, oilmen, merchants, government officials, and operators of radar lines and air bases that guard the northern approaches to the continent.

Less than half the population of Canada is of British stock. Of those who are, many emigrated from Britain and the United States in colonial days. Others arrived among the flood of immigrants in the first decade of the twentieth century and in the years since the end of the Second World War. They are scattered all over the country, but form the bulk of the population in the Atlantic provinces, rural Ontario and parts of the prairies and British Columbia.

One quarter of the Canadian population is of neither French nor British origin. Most of these Canadians have come from the countries of Europe, seeking escape from tyranny, war or poverty. Almost three million came in the decade and a half before 1914—from Germany, Poland, the Ukraine, Scandinavia, Italy and the United States—to break the virgin soil of the Canadian west, man the rapidly expanding factories in the east, or develop the mineral and forest resources on the northern frontier. More came in the 1920's, but the Great Depression and the Second World War effectively stopped immigration between 1930 and 1945.

---

44 *myriad* (n.) /'mɪrɪəd/: a great number – 48 *ranching* (n.): growing sheep, cattle or horses – 48 *potash* (n.): G. Pottasche – 52 *hydro-electric power:* electricity produced by the power of falling water – 56 **frontier** (n.): /frʌn'tɪə(r)/: the area between settled and wild country – 56 *vigorous* (adj.) /'vɪgərəs/: active – 59 **giant** (adj.): very large – 63 *prospector* (n.): a person who examines land to find gold, silver, oil etc. – 64 *operator* (n.): a person who works a machine etc. – 65 *radar lines:* radar stations – 65 *approaches* (n.): ways of entering – 66 **stock** (n.): origin – 68 **decade** (n.): a period of ten years – 70 *bulk* (n.): a great mass or quantity – 71 **rural** (adj.): referring to the countryside – 76 **virgin** (adj.): fresh, unspoiled, unchanged – 78 **mineral resources**: referring to substances that are formed naturally in the earth.

Then came the massive postwar immigration. Most of the immigrants—there were almost 5000000 between 1945 and 1980—headed for the cities of eastern Canada or British Columbia where the skilled found their place in the booming industries and expanding classrooms and offices, and the unskilled became the labour force of the postwar construction boom. A million of the immigrants were from the United Kingdom and almost half a million were from Italy.

Today more than one Canadian in twenty is of German origin. One in thirty is of Italian, one in forty of Ukranian, and one in fifty of Dutch descent. Contributing to the rich Canadian cultural mosaic are from 100000 to half a million people who trace their origins to Austria or Greece, Hungary or Poland, Russia, Sweden, Norway, Portugal, Yugoslavia, and China. Thousands from every other country in Europe mingle in Canadian cities with families from South America, the Caribbian, the length and breadth of Africa, the middle East, India and all of South East Asia. Canada has continued to be a haven for refugees like the thousands of Vietnamese "boat people" who survived the onslaught of storms and pirates and are now making their new homes in Canada.

---

81 *massive* (adj.): large – 84 *booming* (adj.): growing rapidly – 90 *mosaic* (n.): the fitting together of small pieces of coloured stone, glass etc. to form a pattern – 91 **trace** (v.): to find the origins – 96 *haven* (n.): a place of safety – 97 *onslaught* (n.): a fierce attack.

2: O Canada

A NATIONAL SONG FOR THE DOMINION

National Anthem—Hymne national

Published under authority of the Speaker of the House of Commons by the Queen's Printer for Canada

Publié en conformité de l'autorité de l'Orateur de la Chambre des communes par l'Imprimeur de la Reine pour le Canada

Available from the Canadian Government Publishing Centre, Supply and Services Canada, Hull, Québec, Canada K1A 0S9

En vente: Centre d'édition du gouvernement du Canada, Approvisionnements et Services Canada, Hull, Québec, Canada K1A 0S9

Dominion (n.): the Dominion of Canada was formed by three British North American colonies in 1867 – *thee* (pron.): arch. for you.

"The land of forests grand ..." Maligne Lake in the Canadian Rockies

3: ALEXANDER McLACHLAN: Young Canada

Alexander McLachlan (1818–1896) was born in Scotland, which he left for Canada at the age of 22. There he worked as a farmer and tailor, trying his best to support his wife and 11 children.

In his days McLachlan was known as "the Burns of Canada". He showed a keen interest in the common man and in country life. Between 1846 and 1874 he published 5 volumes of poems.

From: *Literature in Canada*, Vol. 1, ed. Douglas Daymond and Leslie Monkman, Toronto, Gage Educational Publishing Ltd., 1978, p. 187.

Burns: Robert Burns (1759–1796), a famous Scottish poet – *Jack:* collective name for any male servant – 3 *roam* (v.): to wander with no very clear aim – 5 *moil* (v.): (obs.) to work very hard – 5 *strain* (v.): to make great efforts – 5 **toil** (v.): to work hard – 6 **snob** (n.): a person who dislikes or keeps away from those he feels to be of lower social class – 6 *thrive* (v.): to develop well – 9 *knave* (n.): a dishonest man – 10 *idle* (v.): to waste time doing nothing – 11 *caste* (n.) /kast/: division of society based on class differences – 17 *aristocracy* (n.): the people of the highest social class – 19 *nobles* (n.): nobility – 19 *forge* (n.): a building containing a large apparatus with a fire inside, used for beating and shaping metal objects, G. Schmiede – 20 *pedigree* (n.): a list or drawing showing the families from which one is descended – 29 *'tis:* it is.

Young Canada

Or, Jack's as Good's his Master

I love this land of forest grand,
The land where labor's free;
Let others roam away from home,
Be this the land for me!
Where no one moils and strains and toils
That snobs may thrive the faster,
But all are free as men should be,
And Jack's as good's his master!

Where none are slaves that lordly knaves
May idle all the year;
For rank and caste are of the past—
They'll never flourish here!
And Jew or Turk, if he'll but work,
Need never fear disaster;
He reaps the crop he sowed in hope,
For Jack's as good's his master.

Our aristocracy of toil
Have made us what you see,
The nobles of the forge and soil,
With ne'er a pedigree.
It makes one feel himself a man,
His very blood leaps faster,
Where wit or worth's preferr'd to birth,
And Jack's as good's his master.

Here's to the land of forests grand,
The land where labor's free;
Let others roam away from home,
Be this the land for me!
For here 'tis plain the heart and brain,
The very soul, grow vaster,
Where men are free as they should be,
And Jack's as good's his master.

(1900)

4: BEN WICKS: Is There a Typical Canadian?

From: *Ben Wick's Canada*, Toronto, McClelland and Stewart, 1976, p.63.

Is there a typical Canadian?

There is.

He watches from 8 to 29 hours of television a week, and spends an average of 7 hours a week listening to the radio.

He shuns an active part in sports and doesn't work on arts and crafts.

The typical Canadian has a 39.3 hour-a-week manufacturing job and is married.

He has 1.7 children; .7 of whom are having their teeth straightened.

He is an overweight, unilingual smoker who is likely to die of circulatory ailments at the age of 69 years and 21 weeks.

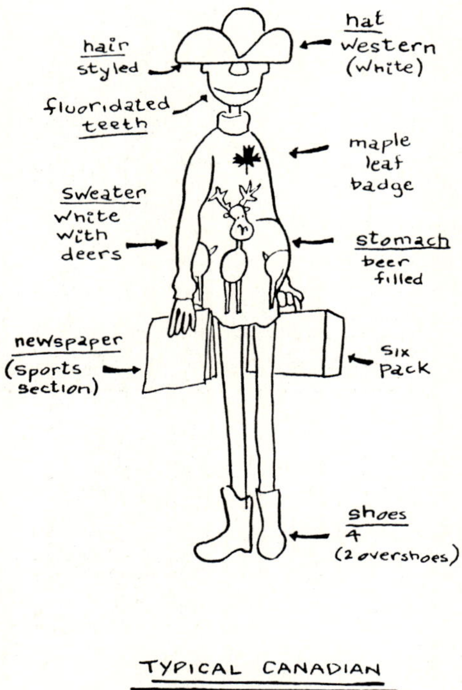

TYPICAL CANADIAN

---

5 *shun* (v.): to avoid, to stay away from – 6 *arts and crafts:* the arts that are concerned with making objects by hand – 10 *overweight* (adj.): weighing too much – 10 *unilingual* (adj.): speaking only one language – 11 *circulatory ailments* /'sɜkjulətərɪ 'eɪlmənts /: illnesses affecting the movement of blood round the body – *fluoridate* (v.): to add Fluoride to the water in order to protect the teeth – *six pack:* six bottles or cans of beer.

5: MIRIAM WADDINGTON: Canadians

Miriam Waddington was born in Winnipeg in 1917 and received her education there and in Ottawa. She took degrees from the University of Toronto and from the University of Pennsylvania School of Social Work. In the forties and fifties she worked at various jobs (hospitals, prisons) and was a teacher of social work at McGill University in Montreal. In Toronto she taught English and Canadian literature at York University and in 1983 she became "professor emeritus".

Ms. Waddington ist best known as a poet. Her first collection of verse was *Green World*, published in 1945. Other important titles are *The Season's Lovers* (1958), *The Glass Trumpet* (1966), *Call Them Canadians* (1968) and *Driving Home: Poems New and Selected* (1972) and *Collected Poems* (1986). Her main lyrical subjects are the Canadian landscape and human relationships, often expressed in a mixture of sadness and happiness.

The text is taken from: *Canadian Myths and Legends*, ed. Michael O. Nowlen, Toronto, Macmillan of Canada, 1977, pp. 111–112.

Canadians

Here are
our signatures:
geese, fish, eskimo
faces, girl-guide
cookies, ink-drawings
tree-plantings, summer
storms and winter
emanations.

We look
like a geography but
just scratch us
and we bleed
history, are full
of modest misery

are sensitive
to double-talk double-take
(and double-cross)
in a country
too wide
to be single in.

---

emeritus (adj.): retired, no longer holding office but keeping one's title – **landscape** (n.): open country – 2 **signature** (n.): a person's name written by his own hand – 5 *cookie* (n.): biscuit – 8 *emanation* (n.): that which comes out of s. th. (e.g. gases, smells) – 11 *scratch* (v.): to rub (a surface) with s. th. pointed or rough (as with claws or fingernails) – 15 **sensitive** (adj.): quick to feel the effect of s. th.

Are we real or
did someone invent
us, was it Henry
Hudson Etienne Brûlé
or a carnival
of village girls?
Was it
a flock of nuns
a pity of indians
a gravyboat of
fur-traders, professional
explorers or those
amateur map-makers
our Fathers
of Confederation?

Wherever you are
Charles Tupper Alexander
Galt D'Arcy McGee George
Cartier Ambrose Shea
Henry Crout Father
Ragueneau Lord Selkirk
and John A.–however
far into northness
you have walked–
when we call you
turn around please and
don't look so
surprised.

---

23 *Henry Hudson:* (1550–1611) English navigator (ship's officer) who, in search for a passage to Asia by way of the North Pole, discovered in 1610 what is now called Hudson Bay. In 1670 a trading-company known as the Hudson's Bay Company was founded – 24 *Etienne Brûlé:* (1592–1633) French pioneer who came to Québec with Samuel de Champlain in 1608 and who travelled widely among the Indians – 28 *flock* (n.): group, large number – 30 *gravyboat* (n.): a small deep long-shaped container with a handle, from which sauce can be poured at a meal – 31 **trader** (n.): a person who buys and sells goods – 32 **explorer** (n.): a person who travels into a new place with the aim of discovery – 35 **Confederation**: the union of 3 British North American provinces to form the "Dominion of Canada" in 1867 – 37–40 *Charles Tupper* (1821–1915); *Sir Alexander T. Galt* (1817–93); *Darcy McGee* (1825–68); *Sir George-Etienne Cartier* (1814–73); *Sir Ambrose Shea* (1815–1905): Canadian politicians and ministers who helped to found and shape the "Dominion of Canada" – 40 *Henry Crout*: settler in the first English colony in Nfdl. (around 1612–1617) – 40–41 *Father (Paul) Ragueneau:* (1608–80) Jesuit priest among the Indians in Québec, sent to teach his religion there – 41 *Lord Selkirk:* (1771–1820) a Scottish settler (in Canada), founder of the Red River Colony – 42 *John A.: Sir John Alexander Macdonald* (1815–91), first prime minister of the "Dominion of Canada".

6: JOHN ROBERT COLOMBO: A Canadian is Somebody Who

John Robert Colombo was born in Kitchener, Ont., in 1936 and graduated from the University of Toronto. He has worked as an editor, teacher, essayist, book-reviewer, translator and poet. In 1966 he published his first book of "found" poetry, *The Mackenzie Poems*. Colombo makes use of collages, creates "witty juxtapositions" and enjoys making fun of all kinds of material in prose and verse form.

From: *The Maple Laugh Forever: An Anthology of Canadian Comic Poetry*, ed. Douglas Barbour and Stephen Scobie, Edmonton, Hurtig Publishers, 1981, p.31.

A Canadian is Somebody Who

Thinks he knows how to make love in a canoe
Bets on the Toronto Maple Leafs
Enjoys Air Canada dinners, desserts and all
Distinguishes between Wayne and Shuster
Attends the concerts of Anne Murray and Liona Boyd
Boasts Donald Sutherland was born in New Brunswick
Possesses "a sound sense of the possible"
Is sesquilingual (speaks one and a half languages)
Has become North American without becoming
Either American or Mexican
Knows what the references in this poem are all about

---

graduate (v.): to take one's academic degree(s) – *reviewer* (n.): a person who writes short critical comments – *collage* (n.) /kə'laʒ/: an artistic composition of various materials and techniques – **witty** (adj.): showing a clever mind – *juxtaposition* (n.): (the act of) placing side by side – 1 *canoe* (n.) /kə'nu/: long narrow boat, moved by paddles – 2 *bet* (v.): to risk money – 2 *Toronto Maple Leafs:* a Toronto ice-hockey team (maple: G. Ahorn) – 3 *Air Canada:* Canada's national airline – 3 *dessert* (n.) /dɪ'zɜt/: sweet food served at the end of a meal – 4 *Wayne and Shuster:* a famous Canadian comedy duo – 5 *Anne Murray:* Canada's most successful pop performer of the 1970s – 5 *Liona Boyd:* a Canadian classical guitarist – 6 *Donald Sutherland:* Canada's best-known film-actor.

II Atlantic Provinces

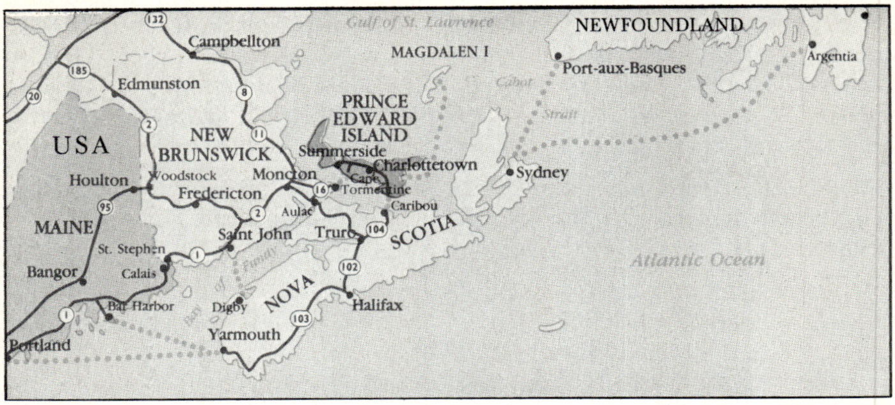

Newfoundland, first of the seven regions, is an island not merely physically. It had its own separate history from the late sixteenth century until 1949, for much of that period as a self-governing colony. During this time it developed linguistic patterns based on an ethnic mixture of Irish, West English and Acadian peoples that was unique in Canada, and an oral and written literature recording an austere way of life different even from that of the nearby Maritime provinces, though their existence also was based largely on fishing and seamanship.

The Maritime provinces of Prince Edward Island, Nova Scotia and New Brunswick share a great deal of history, in terms of French settlement, British conquest, Loyalist settlement, maritime prosperity and subsequent decline, which is markedly different from that of Newfoundland. Culturally they are distiguished by their special mingling of English-speaking Loyalist and French-speaking Acadian traditions, and by their early development of political autonomy and of a genuine local literary culture, both of which emerged before the middle of the nineteenth century.

The text is taken from:
George Woodcock, *The Meeting of Time and Space: Regionalism in Canadian Literature*,
Edmonton, Ne West Institute for Western Canadian Studies, 1981, p. 12.

---

1 *seven:* Woodcock treats Newfoundland as an extra region; in this book it remains part of the Atlantic region – 4 **ethnic** (adj.): of or related to a racial, national or tribal group – 5 *Acadia* (n.): an area within the present boundaries of Nova Scotia, New Brunswick, and Maine, USA, over which England and France struggled between 1613 and 1713, when France left Acadia to Britain – 5 **unique** (adj.): being the only one of its type – 5 **oral** (adj.): spoken – 6 *austere* (adj.): hard, lacking comfort – 6 *Maritime* /'mærɪtaɪm/: living or existing near the sea – 11 *subsequent* (adj.): coming after s. th. else, sometimes as a result of it – 13 **Loyalist** (n.): The Loyalists were American colonists who moved to Canada after the War of Independence in order to remain under British rule – 14 **autonomy** (n.): self-government – 15 **emerge** (v.): appear.

George Woodcock was born in Winnipeg in 1912, yet brought up in England where he became a poet and a pacifist. He returned to Canada in 1949 and settled in Vancouver, pursuing his career as a writer. His works include travel books, history books, books on Canada and biographical studies. Woodcock is also known as a literary critic. As an anarchist he has declined most awards offered to him by state authorities. In *The Meeting of Time and Space* he discusses aspects of literary regionalism in Canada.

---

pacifist (n.): a person who refuses to fight in a war – **critic** (n.): a person expressing judgements about the good or bad qualities of something – *anarchist* (n.): a person who wishes to destroy all forms of government and control – *decline* (v.): to refuse – *award* (n.): something given as a prize – **aspect** (n.): a particular side – **regionalism** (n.): the use of a particular part of a country as the setting of stories, plays etc. representing it as affecting the lives of the characters.

Coats of Arms of the four Atlantic Provinces

New Brunswick

Nova Scotia

Prince Edward Island

Newfoundland

1: The Discovery of Newfoundland*

The text is taken from:
Richard Hakluyt, *The Principal Navigations, Voyages, Traffiques and Discoveries of the English Nation* (1589),
repr. Glasgow, 1904 by James MacLehose and Sons, vol. VII, p. 146.

In the yere of our Lord 1497 John Cabot a Venetian, and his sonne Sebastian (with an English fleet set out from Bristoll) discovered that land which no man before that time had attempted, on the 24 of June, about five of the clocke early in the morning. This land he called Prima vista, that is to say, First seene, because as I suppose it was that part whereof they had the first sight from sea. That Island which lieth out before the land, he called the Island of S. John upon this occasion, as I thinke, because it was discovered upon the day of John the Baptist. The inhabitants of this Island use to weare beasts' skinnes, and have them in as great estimation as bowes, arrowes, pikes, darts, woodden clubs, and slings. The soile is barren in some places, & yeeldeth litle fruit, but it is full of white beares, and stagges farre greater then ours. It yeeldeth plenty of fish.

---

1 *John Cabot:* Giovanni Caboto (1455–98), an Italian in English service, who, accompanied by his son Sebastiano, discovered the North American Continent (Labrador and St. John's) in 1497 – 8 *John the Baptist:* forerunner of Christ, who baptized him in the River Jordan, later a Christian saint – 9 *pike* (n.): a type of long-handled spear, G. Pike – 10 *dart* (n.): a sharp-pointed object to be thrown or shot (used as a weapon or in games) – 10 *club* (n.): G. Keule – 10 *sling* (n.) G. Schleuder – 10 **barren** (adj.): bearing no fruit or seed – 10 *yeeldeth* arch.: yields, produces – 11 *stag* (n.): male deer.

John Cabot

2: JACQUES CARTIER: The First Relation

From: Jacques Cartier, *Two Navigations to Newe Fraunce*, London, 1580. Amsterdam, Theatrum Orbis Terrarum Ltd., 1975 and Norwood, N.J., Walter J. Johnson Inc., 1975, p. 1.

¶ The firſt relation of Iames Carthier *of the new land called* New Fraunce, nevvly diſcouered in the yeare of oure Lorde, 1534.

¶ How Maiſter Iames Carthier departed from the Port of *S. Malo*, with two Ships, and came to the new land, and howe he entred into the Porte of *Buona Viſta*.

After that Sir Charles of *Mouy*, Knight, Lord of *Meyleray*, & Vice-admirall of *Fraunce*, had cauſed all the Captaines, Maiſters, and Mariners of the Shippes to be ſworne to behaue themſelues truely and faithfully in the ſeruice of the moſt Chriſtian King of *France*, vnder the charge of the ſayde Carthier, vpon the 20. day of Aprill. 1534. we departed from the Porte of *S. Malo* with two Ships of thrée ſcore tun apéece burden, and by well appointed men in eche one, and with ſuche proſperous weather, we ſailed onwardes, that vppon the 10. of May we came to the newe found land, where we entred into the cape of *Buona Viſta*, which is in Latitude 48. degrées and a halfe, and in Longitude. * . But bicauſe of the great ſtore of Ice that was alongeſt the ſayde lande, we were conſtrayned to enter into a Hauen called, Saint Katherins Hauen, diſtaunt from the other Porte aboute fiue leagues towarde South ſoutheaſt: there did we ſtay ten daies, looking for faire weather, and in the meane while we mended and dreſſed our boates.

---

1 *James Cartier, Jacques Cartier* (1491–1557): Frenchman who sailed to North America in 1534 and, in 1535–36, went up the St.-Lawrence-River as far as the Indian village of Hochelaga (which later was to become Montreal) – 1 *relation* (n.): story – 6 *S. Malo:* a port in northern France – 7 *Buona Vista:* good sight (lit.), port on the west coast of Nfdl. (see map on p. 20) – 16 *charge* (n.): command – 16 *sayde* arch.: said – 18 *three score tun apeece burden:* each carrying a load of 3 times 20 (60) tons – 19 *eche* /ætʃə/: arch. each – 19 *prosperous* (adj.): very favourable – 22 *latitude* (n.): the distance north or south of the Equator measured in degrees – 23 *longitude* (n.): the position on the earth east or west of Greenwich – 24 *constrain* (v.): to force – 25 *hauen* (n.): arch. haven, rare for harbour – 25 *Saint Katherins Hauen:* today Catalina, port in Nfdl., a few miles south of Bonavista – 26 *league* (n.): obs. a measure of distance (3 miles).

3: THOMAS CHANDLER HALIBURTON: The Clockmaker

Thomas Chandler Haliburton was born in Windsor, N.S., in 1796. He was educated at King's College there and was called to the bar of Nova Scotia in 1820. He practised law in the Annapolis Valley for some years and became a judge of the Court of Common Pleas in 1829. In 1841 he was made a judge of the Supreme Court of N. S. Besides three books on the political and legal problems of the time Haliburton is best remembered for his humorous pieces about a Yankee clockpedlar, which were later published in book form as *The Clockmaker* series (1836–1840). Haliburton retired in 1856 and moved to England where he was a Member of Parliament until his death in 1865.

At the beginning of the 19th century Nova Scotia suffered from serious economic difficulties. Instead of making full profit of the land and building up an industry, the province relied mainly on government support. In order to awaken the people of Nova Scotia from their indolence, Haliburton wrote *The Clockmaker*, a number of satirical sketches in the picaresque tradition. They centre around Sam Slick, the clockpedlar, who accompanies the narrator, a visiting English gentleman, on a tour of the colony. Haliburton expresses his never-ending criticism of his compatriots and the weakness of human nature in general through Sam Slick's long monologues.

The Englishman and Sam Slick himself are ridiculed, too, the first for his attitude of superiority, the latter for his total lack of refinement.

The text is taken from:
Thomas Ch. Haliburton, *The Clockmaker*, Paris, Bandry's European Library, 1839, pp. 4–7. (Also in paperback edition in the New Canadian Library, No. 6, Toronto, 1958, repr. 1986, pp. 8–11.)

I had heard of Yankee clock pedlars, tin pedlars, and Bible pedlars, especially of him who sold Polyglot Bibles *(all in English)* to the amount of sixteen thousand pounds. The house of every substantial farmer had three substantial ornaments: a wooden clock, a tin reflector, and a Polyglot Bible. How is it that an American can sell his wares, at whatever price he pleases, where a blue-nose would fail to make a sale at all? I will inquire of the Clockmaker the secret of his success.

'What a pity it is, Mr Slick'—for such was his name—'what a pity it is,' said I, 'that you, who are so successful in teaching these people the value of *clocks*, could not also teach them the value of *time*.'

Court of Common Pleas: small claims court – **humorous** (adj.): funny, that makes people laugh – *pedlar* (n.): a person who goes from place to place trying to sell articles – *awake (n)* (v.): to cease sleeping – *indolence* (n.): the state of not liking to be active – *picaresque* (adj.): dealing with the adventures of a character of whom one thinks not well but who is not really wicked – *compatriot* (n.): person who was born in or who is a citizen of the same country as another – **monologue** (n.): rather long speech by one person – *ridicule* (v.): to laugh unkindly at – *superiority* (n.): the thinking of oneself as better than others – *refinement* (n.): quality of showing good education and gentleness of manners – 2 *Polyglot Bibles:* bibles composed of passages in several different languages – 3 *substantial* (adj.): important, of some size or value – 4 *reflector* (n.): s. th. which reflects light – 6 *blue-nose* coll: a name given to Nova Scotians.

'I guess,' said he, 'they have got that ring to grow on their horns yet, which every four-year-old has in our country. We reckon hours and minutes to be dollars and cents. They do nothing in these parts but eat, drink, smoke, sleep, ride about, lounge at taverns, make speeches at temperance meetings, and talk about "House of Assembly". If a man don't hoe his corn, and he don't get a crop, he says it is all owing to the bank; and if he runs into debt and is sued, why he says the lawyers are a curse to the country. They are a most idle set of folks, I tell you.'

'But how is it,' said I, 'that you manage to sell such an immense number of clocks, which certainly cannot be called necessary articles, among a people with whom there seems to be so great a scarcity of money?'

Mr Slick paused, as if considering the propriety of answering the question, and looking me in the face, said in a confidential tone, 'Why, I don't care if I do tell you, for the market is glutted, and I shall quit this circuit. It is done by a knowledge of *soft sawder* and *human natur*. But here is Deacon Flint's,' said he; 'I have but one clock left, and I guess I will sell it to him.'

At the gate of a most comfortable-looking farmhouse stood Deacon Flint, a respectable old man who had understood the value of time better than most of his neighbours, if one might judge from the appearance of everything about him. After the usual salutation, an invitation to 'alight' was accepted by Mr Slick, who said he wished to take leave of Mrs Flint before he left Colchester.

We had hardly entered the house, before the Clockmaker pointed to the view from the window, and addressing himself to me, said, 'If I was to tell them in Connecticut there was such a farm as this away down east here in Nova Scotia, they wouldn't believe me. Why there ain't such a location in all New England. The Deacon has a hundred acres of dyke–'

'Seventy,' said the Deacon, 'only seventy.'

'Well, seventy; but then there is your fine deep bottom, why I could run a ramrod into it–'

'Interval, we call it,' said the Deacon, who though evidently pleased at this eulogium, seemed to wish the experiment of the ramrod to be tried in the right place.

---

12 *reckon* (v.): to consider – 14 *lounge* (v.) /laundʒ/: to pass time in a lazy manner – 14 *tavern* (n.): inn – 14 *temperance* (n.): self-control in the drinking of alcohol – 15 *hoe* (v.) /həu/: G. hacken – 17 *sue* (v.): to bring a claim in law – 18 *set* (n.): G. Sippschaft – 21 *scarcity* (n.): lack – 22 *propriety* (n.): rightness of behaviour – 23 *confidential* (adj.): spoken in secret – 24 *glut* (v.): to supply with too much, overfill – 24 *circuit* (n.) /'sɜkɪt/: area – 25 *soft sawder* (n.): flattering speeches – 25 *deacon* (n.): rank of a clergyman, below a priest – 30 *salutation* (n.): expression of greeting – 30 *alight* (v.): to get down from the wagon and come in – 31 *take leave of* (v.): to say goodbye to – 35 *Connecticut* /kə'netɪkət/: a north-eastern state of the USA – 36 *ain't:* isn't – 36 **location** (n.): place – 37 *New England:* the north-eastern states of the USA – 37 *acre* (n.): G. ca. 2 Morgen – 37 *dyke* (n.): dike, a dam built to prevent flooding, here: land protected by dikes – 40 *ramrod* (n.): a stick for putting gunpowder into old guns – 42 *eulogium* (n.) obs. eulogy /ju'ləudʒjəm/: high praise.

'Well, interval if you please–though Professor Eleazer Cumstick, in his work on Ohio, calls them bottoms–is just as good as dyke. Then there is that water privilege, worth three or four thousand dollars, twice as good as what Governor Cass paid fifteen thousand dollars for. I wonder, Deacon, you don't put up a carding mill on it: the same works would carry a turning lathe, a shingle machine, a circular saw, grind bark, and–'

'Too old,' said the Deacon, 'too old for all those speculations–'

'Old,' repeated the Clockmaker, 'not you; why you are worth half a dozen of the young men we see nowadays. You are young enough to have–' Here he said something in a lower tone of voice, which I did not distinctly hear; but whatever it was, the Deacon was pleased. He smiled and said he did not think of such things now.

'But your beasts, dear me, your beasts must be put in and have a feed'; saying which, he went out to order them to be taken to the stable.

As the old gentleman closed the door after him, Mr Slick drew near to me and said in an under tone, 'That is what I call *"soft sawder"*. An Englishman would pass that man as a sheep passes a hog in a pasture, without looking at him; or,' said he, looking rather archly, 'if he was mounted on a pretty smart horse, I guess he'd trot away, if he could. Now I find–' Here his lecture on *"soft sawder"* was cut short by the entrance of Mrs Flint.

'Jist come to say good-bye, Mrs Flint.'

'What, have you sold all your clocks?'

'Yes, and very low, too, for money is scarce, and I wished to close the concarn; no, I am wrong in saying all, for I have just one left. Neighbour Steel's wife asked to have the refusal of it, but I guess I won't sell it; I had but two of them, this one and the feller of it that I sold Governor Lincoln. General Green, the Secretary of State for Maine, said he'd give me fifty dollars for this here one–it has composition wheels and patent axles; it is a beautiful article, a real first chop, no mistake, genuine superfine–but I guess I'll take it back; and besides, Squire Hawk might think kinder harder that I did not give him the offer.'

'Dear me,' said Mrs Flint, 'I should like to see it; where is it?'

'It is in a chest of mine over the way, at Tom Tape's store. I guess he can ship it on to Eastport.'

---

44 *Eleazer* /ˈelɪˈza(r)/: a first name – 48 *carding mill* (n.): G. Krempelmaschine (f. Textilien) – 48 *turning lathe* (n.) /leɪð/: G. Drehbank – 49 *shingle* (n.): thin piece of material (e.g. wood) for covering roofs – 49 *grind* (v.): G. zermalmen, "grinding bark" is a process in which bark from certain trees is ground up for kindling (= small pieces of wood used for starting fires) – 49 *bark* (n.): G. Rinde – 59 *under tone:* low voice – 60 *hog* (n.): a (fat) pig – 61 *arch* (adj.) /ɑtʃ/: amused, G. schelmisch – 61 *smart* (adj.): good-looking – 62 **guess** (v.) AE: to suppose, to consider likely – 62 *trot* (v.): of a horse, to move fairly quickly (between walk and gallop) – 63 *cut short* (v.): to cause to finish suddenly – 68 *the first refusal:* the right of deciding whether to buy s.th. before it is offered to other people – 69 *feller:* fellow – 70 *Maine:* a state in the north-eastern USA – 71 *composition wheels:* G. Kompositionsräder (aus einer Metallegierung) – 71 *(patent) axles:* s.th. on which a wheel turns round, G. patent(iert)e Achsen – 72 *first chop:* top quality – 73 *kinder* (coll.): kind of.

'That's a good man,' said Mrs Flint, 'jist let's look at it.'

Mr Slick, willing to oblige, yielded to these entreaties and soon produced the clock—a gawdy, highly varnished, trumpery-looking affair. He placed it on the chimney-piece where its beauties were pointed out and duly appreciated by Mrs Flint, whose admiration was about ending in a proposal when Mr Flint returned from giving his directions about the care of the horses. The Deacon praised the clock; he too thought it a handsome one. But the Deacon was a prudent man; he had a watch—he was sorry, but he had no occasion for a clock.

'I guess you're in the wrong furrow this time, Deacon. It ain't for sale,' said Mr Slick; 'and if it was, I reckon neighbour Steel's wife would have it, for she gives me no peace about it.' Mrs Flint said that Mr Steel had enough to do, poor man, to pay his interest, without buying clocks for his wife.

'It's no concarn of mine,' said Mr Slick, 'so long as he pays me, what he has to do, but I guess I don't want to sell it, and besides it comes too high; that clock can't be made at Rhode Island under forty dollars. Why it ain't possible,' said the Clockmaker, in apparent surprise, looking at his watch, 'why as I'm alive it is four o'clock, and if I haven't been two hours here. How on airth shall I reach River Philip tonight? I'll tell you what, Mrs Flint, I'll leave the clock in your care till I return on my way to the States. I'll set it a-going and put it to the right time.'

As soon as this operation was performed, he delivered the key to the Deacon with a sort of serio-comic injunction to wind up the clock every Saturday night, which Mrs Flint said she would take care should be done, and promised to remind her husband of it in case he should chance to forget it.

'That,' said the Clockmaker, as soon as we were mounted, 'that I call "*human natur*"! Now that clock is sold for forty dollars; it cost me just six dollars and fifty cents. Mrs Flint will never let Mrs Steel have the refusal, nor will the Deacon learn until I call for the clock that having once indulged in the use of a superfluity, how difficult it is to give it up. We can do without any article of luxury we have never had, but when once obtained, it is not "*in human natur*" to surrender it voluntarily. Of fifteen thousand sold by myself and partners in this Province, twelve thousand were left in this manner, and only ten clocks were ever returned; when we called for them they invariably bought them. We trust to "*soft sawder*" to get them into the house, and to "*human natur*" that they never come out of it.'

---

79 *entreaty* (n.): begging humbly or seriously – 80 *gawdy* (adj.) /'gɔdɪ/: bright and showy – 80 *varnish* (v.): to cover with a final, shining paint – 80 *trumpery* (adj.): showy but of little value – 81 *chimneypiece* (n.): G. Kaminsims – 85 *prudent* (adj.): sensible and wise – 86 *be in the wrong furrow:* to be wrong, mistaken (furrow lit.: a long narrow track cut by a plough) – 89 **interest** (n.): money paid for the use of money – 92 *Rhode Island:* a state in the north-eastern USA – 95 *airth:* earth – 99 *serio-comic* (adj.): half serious, half comic – 99 *injunction* (n.): order – 101 *chance* (v.): to take place by chance – 105 *call for* (v.): to collect – 106 *superfluity* (n.): a greater amount than is needed – 106 *do without* (v.) to live without – 108 **voluntarily** (adv.): willingly – 110 *invariably* (adv.): as a never-changing rule.

4: AL PITTMAN: The Day I Became a Canadian

Al Pittman was born in St. Leonard's, Newfoundland, in 1940. He received his education at the Universities of St. Thomas, Salem State and New Brunswick. Having been a high school teacher first he is now a professor at Memorial University, Corner Brook, Nfld. He has written plays (aired on CBC), poetry and stories which have often been anthologized. His published works include: *Seaweed and Rosaries* (1969), *Down by Jim Long's Stage* (1970) and *Once When I Was Drowning* (1978). His latest book of short stories is: *The Boughenwolf* (1984).

The following text is taken from:
Easterly: 60 Atlantic Writers, ed. B. E. Hatt, Don Mills, Ontario, Academic Press Canada, 1983, pp. 130–132.
(It was originally published in *Weekend Magazine*, March 31, 1979.)

It is April, finally, and 11 days from now I will be 9. Breakfast is over and I am in an awful hurry to get outdoors. Before I can escape from the kitchen, my father, standing in the doorways, says to me, "From now on you can call yourself a Canadian." It is April Fool's Day, and I have to be careful.

"What's a Canadian, Dad?"

"A Canadian is someone who lives in Canada."

"Do we live in Canada, Dad?"

"We do now. Yesterday we didn't. But today we do. And that's why from now on you can call yourself a Canadian."

"How come we still live in the same house, if we moved to Canada?"

"Well, we didn't move at all. Come here and I'll try to explain to you."

And he did. I'm not sure I understood, but I remember walking away from the conversation that morning feeling different. Different like you felt walking out of church on Confirmation Day, or different like you felt later on when you climbed all the way to the top of the Red Scrape without anyone around to watch. That kind of difference.

On April 1, 1949, Newfoundland became Canada's 10th province. Whatever it meant inside my nine-year-old mind, there seemed to be little evidence around the neighborhood that anything momentous had happened. Later on I heard about people hanging black flags on the window and wearing black armbands in protest, and other people gathering in halls to celebrate. But where I lived, it seemed to me that my father had shared a solemn secret with me. And what a secret to have hold of, to reveal or conceal according to my will.

I went off to find Johnny Moynahan. He beat me in every subject in school, and here he was, a Canadian, and didn't even know it. I've seldom felt such a delightful sense of triumph. Johnny denied it, of course. He was

---

aired (p. p.): transmitted – *CBC*: Canadian Broadcasting Corporation – *anthologize* (v.): to collect in an anthology – 4 *April Fool's Day:* 1st of April – 15 *Red Scrape:* a quasi-cliff in Nfdl. – 19 *momentous* (adj.) /mə'mentəs/: of great importance – 23 *conceal* (v.): to keep from being known –

good in geography and he knew all about Canada and he certainly was not a Canadian. Off he went to his father to confirm my stupidity. Poor old Johnny! I don't think he ever lived it down. He was a Canadian, of course, and had been for half a day. And so was Margaret, and Eddie, and Mom, and my brothers, and my sister Alice. And the rocks and the trees and the sky. Even the sky was Canadian now. And this ground I stood upon, this brown slope at the edge of the woods, this was Canada. Yesterday I had stood on this very spot and I was only in Newfoundland. Today I was in Canada.

Other people had other considerations, no doubt, but to me it was a miracle of time and space. I looked up that morning to watch a flock of Canadian snowbirds pitch in the Canadian trees above my head. I suppose only someone just about to be 9 could be so amazed.

Today, 30 years later, I have other recollections, other realizations. [...]

Newfoundland families were large families. A family of 12 was not considered overly large and the promise of an allowance for each child, no matter how small, added up to a substantial amount of money.

In 1949 Newfoundlanders had little but patriotism to be patriotic about. Conditions for most people were poor by any standard. Tuberculosis was on the rampage. There was a shortage of schools, hospitals, roads and jobs. The fishery was in a desperate state of disrepair, and it was all the Commission of Government could do to dig the country out of the ruins of bankruptcy [...]

Canada was a most foreign place to us in 1949. Until then, and until we got used to the fact that the border had been lifted between us and the Canadians, our familiar North American neighbors were the French islands of St. Pierre and Miquelon and the Boston States (which is what we called the United States of America). Until then Canada had been, for the most part, an unknown country to us.

We knew Halifax because it was a frequent port of call for ships enroute to Boston. [...] But of Canada we knew little else. One older friend of mine recalls he knew Canada then only "as that place on the Bay of Fundy" because he used to "run rum up there in prohibition years." Another friend tells me his concept of Canada was "a place up there that had Montreal in it." Because of our involvement in the foreign fish trade, many Newfoundlanders were

---

29 *stupidity* (n.): the state of being silly or foolish – 30 *live down* (v.): to cause to be forgotten – 37 *flock* (n.): group – 38 *pitch* (v.): to fly down and land – 40 *recollection* (n.): s. th. in one's memory (of the past) – 40 *realization* (n.): experience of understanding – 42 *overly* (adv.): too – 42 *allowance* (n.): money, provided regularly – 43 *add up to* (v.): to amount to – 43 **substantial** (adj.): big enough to be satisfactory – 46 *(be on the) rampage* (n.): violent behaviour – 46 *shortage* (n.): condition of having less than needed – 47 *disrepair* (n.): the state of being in need of repair – 48 *bankruptcy* (n.): the state of being unable to pay one's debts – 51 *St. Pierre, Miquelon:* two islands off the south-eastern coast of Nfdl., which still belong to France – 55 *Halifax:* the capital of Nova Scotia – 55 *enroute* (adv.): Fr. on the way – 57 **recall** (v.): to remember – 57 *Bay of Fundy:* the water passage between N. S. and N. B. (see map on p. 20) – 58 *run rum:* to distribute rum secretly, illegaly – 58 *prohibition years:* the period of years after 1918 when laws were in effect which forbade the making or sale of alcoholic drinks – 59 **concept** (n.): understanding, idea – 60 *involvement* (n.): the state of being connected with –

more familiar with the European ports of Cadiz and Oporto and the islands of the West Indies than they were with most of Canada. This was not idle ignorance on our part. We simply did not need to know. [...]

Confederation changed all that. In time we got used to thinking of Toronto as the new mecca, and in time we got used to Canadian money, Canadian stamps, Canadian cigarettes and candy and the rest. But it took many of us a lot longer to get used to being Canadian. To this day, most people of my own and older generations think of themselves as Newfoundlanders. [...]

Our images of the mainland were, of course, mostly American because they were inspired by American movies and magazines, with little help from Eaton's catalogue. Those were the days when [...] the latest American fashion or fad was adopted unanimously with a rapid passion unknown to urban Canadians [...]

Those were sad years. Sad because so many Newfoundlanders had such negative opinions of themselves. They thought, too often and with too much conviction, that they were an inferior people exiled by history to live inferior lives on an ugly rock in the Atlantic Ocean. They rejected their own music, their dances, their speech, their occupations, their customs, their history and their heritage.

It is only in recent years that the trend has reversed itself. Today you are more likely to encounter a young Newfoundlander proclaiming his origins with arrogant assurance than you are to encounter any of the apologetic attitudes so prevalent such a short time ago. The gospel in Newfoundland now is the gospel of pride and patriotism. This is perhaps more apparent in the arts than anywhere else. [...]

For hundreds of years before Confederation almost nothing had changed in Newfoundland. In 1949 the place was essentially the same as it had been for hundreds of years past. Then suddenly we became part of a country we hardly knew, and just as suddenly the government exhorted the people to abandon their old ways and adopt the new, to come out of their fishing boats to work in factories, to leave their homes on the islands and in the coves to take up residence in the "growth centres" of the new industrial Newfoundland. The change was sudden and shocking, and the shock waves have not yet faded. [...]

---

61 *Cadiz:* a seaport in south west Spain – 61 *Oporto:* a city in north west Portugal – 63 *on s. o.'s part:* shown or done by s. o. – 64 **Confederation:** the union of 3 British North American provinces to form the "Dominion of Canada" in 1867 – 65 *mecca* (n.): a place that many people wish to reach – 66 *candy* (n.) AE: a very sweet, soft, sugary food; BE sweets, chocolate – 69 *mainland* (n.): a land without its islands – 70 *inspire* (v.): to influence – 70 **movie** (n.) AE: film – 70 *Eaton's:* a large department store chain in Canada – 71 *fad* (n.): a short-lived but keenly followed interest or practice – 72 *unanimous* (adj.) /ju'nænɪməs/: all agreeing – 72 **urban** (adj.): of a town or city – 75 *exile* (v): to force to leave one's country – 76 **reject** (v.): to refuse to accept – 78 *heritage* (n.): family traditions – 79 *trend* (n.): tendency – 80 *encounter* (v.): to meet – 81 *apologetic* (adj.): excusing oneself – 82 *prevalent* (adj.) /'prevələnt/: existing widely – 82 *Gospel* (n.): the first 4 books of the New Testament; here: gospel: a principle which should be followed – 88 *exhort* (v.): to urge or advise strongly to do s.th. – 90 *cove* (n.): a small bay –

It will continue, at least, until we find a way to defend ourselves against those who would have us deny what we are. After 30 years of living with the constant threat of being swamped in a culture essentially foreign to our own, the threat remains. We're a little shy of change, the way we've known it, but there is a change taking place within us, a change in our attitude about ourselves, a change that permits us now to hang on to our heritage without forfeiting our aspirations for the future.

One of my friends told me recently that the only thing he remembers about Confederation is his sorrow that his younger brother was born in May of '49 because if he had been born a few weeks earlier he would have been a Newfoundlander instead of a Canadian. I think it safe to say that his younger brother is probably very much a Newfoundlander. Ray Guy calls Newfoundland "this dear and fine country" and lovingly declares, "There is no place else." This Newfoundlander, who's been a Canadian for 30 years now, couldn't agree more.

---

94 *deny* (v.): to refuse to accept — 95 *swamp* (v.): to fill with water causing to sink, destroy — 98 *hang on to* (v.): to try to keep — 98 *forfeit* (v.) /fɔfɪt/: to give up — 99 *aspiration* (n.): a strong desire to do s. th. great.

Newfie Jokes, painting by William Kurelek, 1974

5: FRED COGSWELL: The Uniqueness of Atlantic Literature

Fred Cogswell was born in East Centreville, New Brunswick, in 1917. He studied at the Universities of New Brunswick and Edinburgh. During World War II he served in the Canadian Army. Cogswell now lives in Frederictown where he is "professor emeritus".

He has written very many articles and reviews, and his poems have been printed in several anthologies, magazines and collections. Being a translator and a critic, too, he is regarded as a major figure in Canadian literature. His published works include *The Stunted Strong* (1954), *Descent from Eden* (1959), *Star People* (1968), *Immortal Ploughman* (1969), *Against Perspective* (1978), *A Long Apprenticeship* (1980), *Pearls* (1983), *The Atlantic Anthology* (2 vols., 1984/1985, as editor) and *Charles Mair* (1986).

The text is taken from: *Easterly: 60 Atlantic writers*,
ed. B. E. Hatt, Don Mills, Ont., Academic Press Canada, 1983, pp. 31–33.

Regional literature is any literature that places universal human problems and values in the context of the customs, beliefs, and background of a particular region. In the broadest sense all literature is regional, but because the conditions of city life are conducive to standardization and ready adaptation to change, the term "regional" has come to be applied to literature that deals specifically with areas where people, living together in relative isolation for generations, have evolved a distinctive style of speech, habit and character. In this sense, the literature of Nova Scotia, New Brunswick, Prince Edward Island and Newfoundland, may, until fairly recently, be considered a prime example of regionalism.

Creators of regional literature enjoy certain advantages over writers living in metropolitan areas. To begin with, their world is smaller, less varied in the ways people behave and earn a living, and more stable in its customs and morality. In this world, unlike that of the city, humankind must always share the stage with nature. The great theme of regional literature is how people must come to terms with the ways of their community, and with the vagaries of nature, in order to establish themselves. There has been little in regional literature, until very recently, of the kind of "navel-gazing" that is one of the

---

uniqueness (n.): The state of being unequalled – *emeritus* (adj.): retired, no longer holding office but keeping one's title – **review** (n.) /ri'vju/: an article that critically examines a new book – **anthology** (n.): a collection of poems or pieces of prose, or of both, by one or several writers – *major* (adj.): greater or more important – 4 *conducive* (adj.) /kən'djusɪv/: fml. likely to produce – 4 *standardization* (n.): the force fitting s. th. into a single standard of language – 4 *adaptation* (n.): the ability to change or be changed for new needs or conditions – 6 *specifically* (adv.): particularly – 6 **area** (n.): region – 7 *evolve* (v.): to develop gradually – 9 *prime* (adj.): first in rank, importance – 11 **creator** (n.): a person who produces (creates) s. th. – 12 *metropolitan* (adj.): referring to a chief city – 12 *varied* (adj.): of different kinds – 13 *stable* (adj.): steady, firm – 14 *humankind* (n.): mankind – 15 **theme** (n.): subject – 16 *vagary* (n.) /'veɪgərɪ/: (often pl. -ries) a wild or fantastic action – 18 "*navel-gazing*" (n.): being only concentrated on oneself.

hallmarks of urban literature. During almost the complete history of the Atlantic provinces, men and women have been engaged, directly or indirectly in such tasks as farming, fishing, lumbering and mining—activities which have changed relatively little through the years. Furthermore, immigration to the Atlantic region not only took place at an earlier date—Québec excepted—than immigration to more western regions of Canada, but it was also more homogeneous in its nature. Consequently, the literature of the Atlantic provinces reflects a basic stability that is rooted in common origins, traditions and pursuits, and in its more pure state it is apt to emphasize an attitude toward nature in which the prime virtues are patience and a stubborn refusal to quit in the struggle to extract a living from the forest, the soil, the sea, and the mine. Self aggrandizement and the achievement of individual desire at any cost are deemphasized—sublimated for the sake of family or community, or both.

Nothing, however, exists in a pure state, and certainly not regional literature. George Frederick Clarke entitled his history of New Brunswick *Too Small a World* and this title is symbolic not only of New Brunswick but of a great universal truth. Humankind has always found any world that it possessed too small; hence the spread from Eden, or a small enclave in Africa, to encompass the globe and to set foot on the moon. And where we cannot go in person we will try to go in the imagination. So, throughout the history of the Atlantic region, men and women, tied to their communities by poverty, by the difficulties of travel, or by personal commitments too strong to be broken, have escaped to other times and lands through literature, and have been strongly influenced by what they have discovered there. So, the genres, the devices, and to some degree the attitudes of regional writers have never been completely home-grown. They reflect the classics, past and contemporary, and invariably they are a response to pressures applied by contemporary scholars of taste in larger metropolitan centres.

In this process of cultural borrowing by regional writers, the degree to which the region is homogeneous and the degree of attachment the writer

---

19 *hallmark* (n.): a characteristic feature – 19 **urban** (adj.): of a town or city – 21 **lumbering** (n.) AE: cutting trees or wood into timber – 22 *furthermore* (adv.): in addition – 22 **immigration** (n.): coming into a country to make one's life and home there – 24 *homogeneous* (adj.) /'həumə'dʒinɪəs/: formed of parts of the same kind – 26 *basic* (adj.): fundamental – 27 *pursuit* (n.) /pə'sjut/: any activity to which one gives one's time – 27 *apt* (adj.): likely – 27 **emphasize** (v.): to place special force on – 28 *stubborn* (adj.): with a strong will – 28 **refusal** (n.): a case of not accepting s. th. – 28 **quit** (v.): to stop – 29 *extract* (v.): to take out with difficulty – 30 *aggrandizement* (n.) /ə'grændɪzmənt/ often derog.: increase in size, power, rank – 30 **achievement** (n.): successful gaining of s.th. – 31 *sublimate* (v.): to replace with socially acceptable activities – 37 *hence* (adv.): therefore – 37 *Eden:* Paradise – 37 *enclave* (n.) /'enkleɪv/: outlying part of a country, mostly surrounded by another country – 37 *encompass* (v.): to form a circle about and possess – 41 *commitment* (n.): obligation, loyalty – 43 **genre** (n.) /ʒõr/: class of works of literature – 43 *device* (n.): s. th. (e.g. words) intended to produce a particular artistic effect – 45 *classic* (n.): piece of literature or art of the first rank and lasting importance – 46 *invariable* (adj.): which cannot change – 49 *attachment* (n.): the feeling of being bound to s.th.

feels for the region and its values are all-important. If the author has no faith in the region, its institutions, and what it has to offer, then he may in his own writing simply borrow the trappings of urban writers who capture his imagination, without considering whether or not these fit his experience or talent. Or he may find himself wavering between two worlds without ever resolving the problem of divided loyalties to either his or his audience's satisfaction. Cultural borrowing can only be fruitful when it is balanced by a belief in the value and coherence of one's own culture. The uniqueness of the literature of the Atlantic region lies in the fact that the best Atlantic authors have been able to give weight to the people, ways, traditions and natural features of the land from which they have come, or in which they still reside.

In this way, what are considered by some people to be cultural defects—a life of primitive community, isolation from cultural centres, an habitual severe struggle with nature—can be turned by the regional writer into an advantage. Struggle is an epic thing, and it is essentially to primitive communities engaged in the struggle against nature that the world owes its myths and its religions—models upon which all subsequent human art and thought have been founded.

Regional writers retain many of these advantages over their urban contemporaries. Surrounded by less in the way of distracting detail, they are able to focus on issues which are universal precisely because they have a particular, recognizable human context. Regional writers come to grips with their surroundings because they have no choice—the environment is too insistent, too pressing to be ignored. And in so doing they find their voices—voices which speak directly, with purpose, and about real things in the real world.

"Immersed in Atlantic literature ..."

---

50 **faith** (n.): trust – 52 *trappings* (n.) pl: features (of artistic creation) (fig.) – 52 *capture* (v.): to win, take control of – 54 *waver* (v.): to be unsteady – 55 *loyalty* (n.): the state of being faithful to s. o. – 56 *balanced* (adj.): accompanied, compensated, neutralized – 57 *coherence* (n.) /'kəu'hɪərns/: being naturally, or reasonably connected – 61 *defect* (n.) /'difekt/: s. th. lacking – 64 **epic** (adj.): full of brave action and excitement – 66 *subsequent* (adj.) /'sʌbsɪkwənt/: coming as a result of s. th. – 69 *retain* (v.): to avoid losing – 71 **contemporary** (n.): a person living at the same time as another – 72 *distract* (v.): to take a person's mind off s. th. – 73 *focus* (v.): to direct one's attention to – 74 **issue** (n.) /'ɪʃu/ (important) point – 77 *come to grips with:* to deal seriously with – 80 *insistent* (adj.): repeatedly insisting or making demands – 81 **ignore** (v.) /ɪg'nɔ(r)/ not to take notice of.

III Québec

The French language and a *canadien* culture dating from the sixteenth century have distinguished Québec from the beginning [...]

There has never been any doubt of Québec's regional uniqueness within Canada.

George Woodcock: *The Meeting of Time and Space*, p. 12.

---

canadien (adj.): Fr. referring to the French settlers – *uniqueness* (n.): quality or state of being without a like or equal.

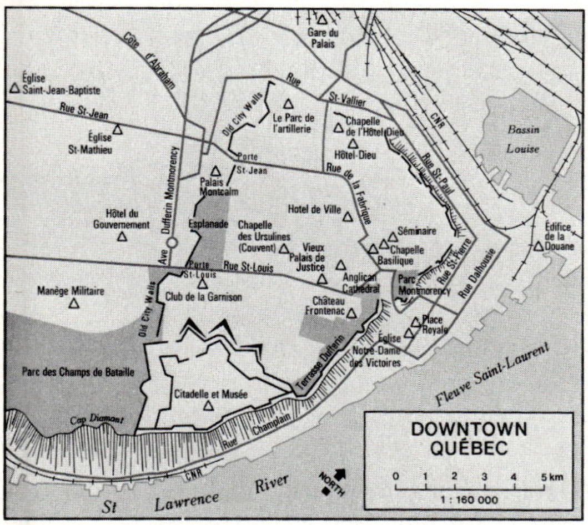

The Meeting of Two Worlds, painting by Eugène Hamel, 1890

1: FRANCES BROOKE: An Englishwoman's First Encounter with the Indians and the French in Canada*

Frances Brooke was born in 1724 in Lincolnshire, England. In 1756 she married the Reverend John Brooke, whom she followed to Canada in 1763 when he was appointed chaplain of the British garrison at Québec. Except for one voyage back to England, Mrs. Brooke supposedly remained with her husband in Québec until 1768, when the couple returned to England. Mrs. Brooke died there in 1789.

Frances Brooke is said to be the first novelist to live and write in Canada. In 1769 her main work, *The History of Emily Montague*, was published in London; it was reprinted in 1777 and 1784 and also translated into French.

This epistolary romance is seminal to the Canadian literary tradition in that it places two worlds, Old and New, in direct confrontation. In addition, the author uses typically Canadian opposites and sets society against nature, the urbane against the rustic, civilization against savagery and male against female. Thus this often amusing document is of high historical significance for Canadians.

The text is taken from: Frances Brooke, *The History of Emily Montague*, Toronto, New Canadian Library No. 27, 1961, pp. 39–42, 59–60, 166–167.

Letter 11—Quebec, September 10:

I find, my dear, that absence and amusement are the best remedies for a beginning passion; I have passed a fortnight at the Indian village of Lorette, where the novelty of the scene, and the enquiries I have been led to make into their ancient religion and manners, have been of a thousand times more service to me than all the reflection in the world would have been. [...]

But to my savages: other nations talk of liberty, they possess it; nothing can be more astonishing than to see a little village of about thirty or forty families, the small remains of the Hurons, almost exterminated by long and continual war with the Iroquoise, preserve their independence in the midst of an European colony consisting of seventy thousand inhabitants; [...] they are not only free as a people, but every individual is perfectly so. Lord of himself, at once subject and master, a savage knows no superior. [...]

---

chaplain (n.): a priest (here: of the Church of England) – *garrison* (n.): a group of soldiers living in a town and defending it – *supposedly* (adv.): as believed – *reprint* (v.): to print again (when supplies have run out) – *epistolary* (adj.): in the form of letters – *romance* (n.) /rə'mæns/: a light story of love and adventure (often unreal or improbable) – *seminal* (adj.): containing the seeds of later development and influencing others – *opposite* (n.): things that are totally different – *urbane* (adj.) /ɜ'beɪn/: having good social manners – *rustic* (adj.): simple and rough – *savagery* (n.): the quality of being uncivilized – **significance** (n.): importance – 3 *fortnight* (n.): two weeks – 8 **astonishing** (adj.): producing surprise – 9 *remains* (n.): s.th. which is left – 9 *Hurons:* Indian tribe occupying southern Ontario in the early 17th century – 9 *exterminate* (v.): get rid of (as by killing) – 10 *Iroquois* /'ɪrəkwɔɪ(z)/: 5 Indian peoples originally inhabiting the northern and central part of New York State – 10 **independence** (n.): the quality or state of being independent, not subject to control by others – 13 *superior* (n.): s.o. of higher rank –

I have taken some pains to develop their present, as well as past, religious sentiments, because the Jesuit missionaries have boasted so much of their conversion; and find they have rather engrafted a few of the most plain and simple truths of Christianity on their ancient superstitions, than exchanged one faith for another. [...]

They anciently believed in one God, the ruler and creator of the universe, whom they called the *Great Spirit* and the *Master of Life*; in the sun as his image and representative; in a multitude of inferior spirits and demons; and in a future state of rewards and punishments, or, to use their own phrase, in *a country of souls*. They reverenced the spirits of their departed heroes, but it does not appear that they paid them any religious adoration. Their morals were more pure, their manners more simple, than those of polished nations, except in what regarded the intercourse of the sexes. [...]

The sex we have so unjustly excluded from power in Europe have a great share in the Huron government; the chief is chose by the matrons. [...]

Their language is at once sublime and melodious; but, having much fewer ideas, it is impossible it can be so copious as those of Europe. [...] Their style even in speaking French is bold and metaphorical. [...]

They have no idea of letters, no alphabet, nor is their language reducible to rules: 'tis by painting they preserve the memory of the only events which interest them, or that they think worth recording, the conquests gained over their enemies in war. [...]

Their general character is difficult to describe; made up of contrary and even contradictory qualities; they are indolent, tranquil, quiet, humane in peace; active, restless, cruel, ferocious in war: courteous, attentive, hospitable, and even polite, when kindly treated; haughty, stern, vindictive, when they are not; and their resentment is the more to be dreaded, as they hold it a point of honour to dissemble their sense of an injury till they find an opportunity to revenge it.

They are patient of cold and heat, of hunger and thirst [...]; yet indulging themselves in their feasts even to the most brutal degree of intemperance.

---

14 *develop* (v.): to explain step by step and in all detail – 16 *conversion* (n.): change of religion – 16 *engraft* (v.): G. aufpropfen – 17 *superstition* (n.): belief not based on reason or fact but on phantasy – 19 **creator** (n.): a person who causes s.th. to exist – 19 **universe** (n.) /'junɪvɜs/: the whole world – 21 *image* (n.): likeness, copy – 21 *multitude* (n.): large number – 21 *demon* (n.) /'dimən/: evil spirit – 23 *reverence* (v.): worship – 23 *departed* (adj.): dead – 24 *adoration* (n.): religious worship – 25 *polished* (adj.): civilized – 26 *intercourse* (n.): relationship – 28 *chose* = chosen – 28 *matron* (n.) /'meɪtrən/: an older married woman – 29 *sublime* (adj.): very noble – 30 *copious* (adj.) /'kəupɪəs/: abundant – 31 *metaphorical* (adj.): full of figures of speech – 32 *reducible* (adj.): limited to or defined by – 37 *contradictory* (adj.): directly opposed – 37 *indolent* (adj.): lazy – 37 *tranquil* (adj.): calm – 37 *humane* (adj.) /hju'meɪn/: showing qualities of a civilized person – 38 *ferocious* (adj.) /fə'rəuʃəs/: cruel, violent – 38 *courteous* (adj.) /'kɜtɪəs/: polite and kind – 38 *hospitable* (adj.): giving a generous welcome to guests or strangers – 39 *haughty* (adj.): appearing proud – 39 *vindictive* (adj.): unwilling to forgive and looking for revenge – 40 *resentment* (n.): feeling of anger or bitterness – 41 *dissemble* (v.): to hide one's feelings or intentions – 43 *indulge* (v.): to allow o.s. to enjoy s.th. – 44 *intemperance* (n.): the strong indulgence of a natural appetite or passion –

They despise death, and suffer the most excruciating tortures not only without a groan, but with an air of triumph; singing their death song, deriding their tormentors [...]

Letter 22–Silleri, Sept. 25:

The Canadians live a good deal like the ancient patriarchs; the lands were originally settled by the troops, every officer became a seigneur, or lord of the manor, every soldier took lands under his commander; but, as avarice is natural to mankind, the soldiers took a great deal more than they could cultivate, by way of providing for a family: which is the reason so much land is now waste in the finest part of the province: those who had children, and in general they have a great number, portioned out their lands amongst them as they married, and lived in the midst of a little world of their descendents.

There are whole villages [...] where the inhabitants are all the descendents of one pair. [...]

Idleness is the reigning passion here, from the peasant to his lord; the gentlemen never either ride on horseback or walk, but are driven about like women, for they never drive themselves, lolling at their ease in a calash. [...]

I should tell you, they are so indolent as never to manure their lands, or even their gardens; and that, till the English came, all the manure of Quebec was thrown into the river. [...]

Letter 117–Silleri, April 8:

The winter is passed in a mixture of festivity and inaction; dancing and feasting in their gayer hours; in their graver smoking, and drinking brandy, by the side of a warm stove: and when obliged to cultivate the ground in spring to procure the means of subsistence, you see them just turn the turf once lightly over. [...]

I must, however, observe, as some alleviation, that there is something in the climate which strongly inclines both the body and mind, but rather the latter, to indolence: the heat of the summer, though pleasing, enervates the very soul, and gives a certain lassitude unfavourable to industry; and the winter, at its extreme, binds up and chills all the active faculties of the soul. [...]

---

45 *excruciating* (p. p.): very bad (pains) – 46 *groan* (n.): loud sound of suffering – 46 *air* (n.): appearance – 46 *deride* (v.): to laugh at – 47 *tormentor* (n.): s.o. who causes a person to suffer great pain – 49 *Canadians*: here: the French – 49 *patriarch* (n.) /'pəɪtrɪɑk, US: 'pæt-/: an old and much respected man – 50 *seigneur:* Fr. nobleman or landowner – 51 *manor* (n.): land belonging to a nobleman – 51 *avarice* (n.) /'ævərɪs/: great desire to get or keep wealth – 55 *portion* (v.): to divide into parts – 59 *idleness* (n.): lazy behaviour – 61 *loll* (v.): to be in a lazy position – 61 *calash* (n.): a light, low-wheeled carriage – 62 *manure* (v.) /mə'njuə(r)/: to treat land with waste matter from animals – 66 *festivity* (n.): celebrating – 67 *brandy* (n.): a strong alcoholic drink made from wine – 69 *subsistence* (n.): living (with little money or food) – 69 *turf* (n.): suface of the soil (with the grass and roots growing in it) – 71 *alleviation* (n.): lessening (here: of criticism) – 72 *incline* (v.): to tend to encourage – 73 *enervate* (v.): to make weak – 74 *lassitude* (n.): tiredness of body and mind – 74 *unfavourable* (adj.): showing no advantage – 75 *bind up* (v.): to cause to stop – 75 **faculty** (n.): natural power or ability.

Breaking the Lent, painting by Cornelius Krieghoff (1848)

Their religion, to which they are extremely bigoted, is another great bar, as well to industry as population: their numerous festivals inure them to idleness; their religious houses rob the state of many subjects who might be highly useful at present, and at the same time retard the increase of the colony. Sloth and superstition equally counter-work providence, and render the bounty of Heaven of no effect.

I am surprized the French, who generally make their religion subservient to the purpose of policy, do not discourage convents, and lessen the number of festivals, in the colonies, where both are so peculiarly pernicious.

It is to this circumstance one may in great measure attribute the superior increase of the British American settlements compared to those of France: a religion which encourages idleness, and makes a virtue of celibacy, is particularly unfavourable to colonization.

---

76 *bigoted* (adj.) /'bɪgətɪd/: blindly attached – 76 *bar* (n.): s. th. that makes things difficult to do, anything that hinders – 77 *festival* (n.): time for being gay and celebrating – 77 *inure to* (v.) /ɪ'njuə(r)/: to accustom s. o. by experience to – 79 *retard* (v.): to delay – 80 *sloth* (n.): laziness – 80 *counter-work* (v.): work against – 81 *bounty* (n.): gift, generous attitude – 82 *subservient* (adj.): useful in gaining a purpose – 83 *convent* (n.): a house in which religious sisters live – 84 **peculiarly** (adv.): in an unusual way – 84 *pernicious* (adj.): having an evil effect, full of harm – 87 *celibacy* (n.): state of being unmarried.

2: HUGH MacLENNAN: Two Solitudes

Hugh MacLennan was born in Cape Breton Island, N.S., in 1907. The family moved to Halifax in 1914, where they witnessed the great explosion in Halifax harbour in 1917 which killed 3,000 people. (This event was later worked into MacLennan's first novel *Barometer Rising*, 1941.)

MacLennan received his academic degrees from Dalhousie, Oxford and Princeton Universities (1932 to 1935). After that he was a teacher in Montreal and started writing novels. His second book, *Two Solitudes*, appeared in 1945 and remained perhaps his most famous achievement. Other novels are: *Each Man's Son* (1951), *The Watch That Ends the Night* (1959), *Return of the Sphinx* (1967) and *Voices in Time* (1980).

In 1951 MacLennan was appointed to the Department of English at McGill University (Montreal), where he taught until recently. He still lives in Montreal as "professor emeritus".

Two Solitudes is structured in 4 parts covering the years 1917 to 1921 and 1934 to 1939. In the first half the figure of Athanase Tallard is presented, a French Canadian rural "seigneur" who cooperates with the English Canadian capitalists from Montreal to develop the natural (water) resources of Québec. He comes under attack from his nationalist compatriots, who see him as a traitor. When his persistence brings him into conflict with the parish priest and the whole French community, Tallard loses his influence and is eventually dropped by his English-speaking business colleagues.

The second half of the novel is about Tallard's two sons, Marius, a fanatical French Canadian nationalist, and Paul, who finishes his education in English schools in Montreal. Paul, the novel's main character, marries Heather Methuen from Westmont. By symbolically uniting the two protagonists MacLennan suggests a successful fusion of the French and English cultures in Québec.

The text is taken from: Hugh MacLennan, *Two Solitudes*,
Toronto, Laurentian Library 1, 1967, repr. 1970, pp. 1–2.

Northwest of Montreal, through a valley always in sight of the low mountains of the Laurentian Shield, the Ottawa River flows out of Protestant Ontario into Catholic Quebec. It comes down broad and ale-coloured and joins the Saint Lawrence, the two streams embrace the pan of Montreal Island, the Ottawa merges and loses itself, and the mainstream moves northeastward a thousand miles to the sea.

Halifax: the capital of N. S. – *Dalhousie:* a small town in northern N. B. – *Princeton:* a town in New Jersey, USA, with one of the country's best universities – **achievement** (n.): the successful finishing of s. th. – *emeritus* (adj.): s. o. who is no longer holding office but keeps his title – **rural** (adj.): concerning country life – *seigneur* (n.): Fr. a nobleman or landowner – *resources* (n.): a country's possessions in the form of wealth and goods (e.g. minerals) – **compatriot** (n.): a citizen of the same country as another – *persistence* (n.): the act of continuing firmly in s. th. (in spite of opposition or warning) – **parish** (n.): an area in the care of a priest – *eventually* (adv.): finally – *colleague* (n.) /'kolig/: a fellow worker, friend in a profession – *Westmount:* the wealthy English-speaking neighbourhood in Montreal – **protagonist** (n.): the chief character in a play or novel – *fusion* (n.): joining together by melting – 3 *ale* (n.): English type of beer – 4 *pan of* ...: Montreal island has the form of a pan – 5 *merge* (v.): to become part of s. th. else –

Nowhere has nature wasted herself as she has here. There is enough water in the Saint Lawrence alone to irrigate half of Europe, but the river pours right out of the continent into the sea. No amount of water can irrigate stones, and most of Quebec is solid rock. It is as though millions of years back in geologic time a sword had been plunged through the rock from the Atlantic to the Great Lakes and savagely wrenched out again, and the pure water of the continental reservoir, unmuddied and almost useless to farmers, drains untouchably away. In summer the cloud packs pass over it in soft, cumulus, pacific towers, endlessly forming and dissolving to make a welter of movement about the sun. In winter when there is no storm the sky is generally empty, blue and glittering over the ice and snow, and the sun stares out of it like a cyclop's eye.

All the narrow plain between the Saint Lawrence and the hills is worked hard. From the Ontario border down to the beginning of the estuary, the farmland runs in two delicate bands along the shores, with roads like a pair of village main streets a thousand miles long, each parallel to the river. All the good land was broken long ago, occupied and divided among seigneurs and their sons, and then among tenants and their sons. Bleak wooden fences separate each strip of farm from its neighbour, running straight as rulers set at right angles to the river to form long narrow rectangles pointing inland. The ploughed land looks like the course of a gigantic and empty steeplechase where all motion has been frozen. Every inch of it is measured, and brooded over by notaries, and blessed by priests.

You can look north across the plain from the river and see the farms between their fences tilting towards the forest, and beyond them the line of trees crawling shaggily up the slope of the hills. The forest crosses the watershed into an evergreen bush that spreads far to the north, lake-dotted and mostly unknown, until it reaches the tundra. The tundra goes to the lower straits of the Arctic Ocean. Nothing lives on it but a few prospectors and hard-rock miners and Mounted Policemen and animals and the flies that brood over the

---

8 *irrigate* (v.): to supply water to (dry land) – 12 *wrench* (v.): to pull hard with sharp turning – 13 *reservoir* (n.): a place where water is stored, sources – 13 *unmuddied* (adj.): not made dirty, without mud – 14 *cumulus* (adj.): a type of thick white feathery cloud – 15 *pacific* (adj.): showing calmness, helping to cause peace – 15 *welter* (n.): disordered mixture – 18 *cyclops* (n.) /'saɪklɔps/: a one-eyed giant (in Greek stories) – 20 *estuary* (n.): the wide mouth of a river – 21 *delicate* (adj.): finely made, drawn – 23 *broken* (p.p.): opened, for use as farmland – 23 *seigneur* (n.) /'seɪnjə(r)/: Fr. landowner, nobleman – 24 *tenant* (n.): a farmer who pays rent for the use of land – 24 *bleak:* cold, uninviting, joyless – 25 *strip* (n.): a narrow piece – 26 *rectangle* (n.): a figure with 4 right angles – 27 *steeplechase* (n.): a place for (horse-, foot-) races with so many jumps – 28 *brood* (v.): to continue to think (sadly, intensely) about – 29 *notary* (n.): a person with the legal power to witness the signing of statements – 31 *tilt* (v.): to form a slope – 32 *shaggy* (adj.): having a rough surface – 32 *watershed* (n.): high land separating 2 river systems – 33 *dotted* (p.p.): covered (with small spots, here: lakes) – 34 *strait* (n.): a narrow passage of water – 35 *prospector* (n.): a person examining the land for gold, oil, etc. – 36 *brood* (v.): to sit on eggs to give birth to, bring forth new beings.

barrens in summer like haze. Winters make it a universe of snow with a terrible wind keening over it, and beyond its horizons the northern lights flare into walls of shifting electric colours that crack and roar like the gods of a dead planet talking to each other out of the dark.

But down in the angle at Montreal, on the island about which the two rivers join, there is little of this sense of new and endless space. Two old races and religions meet here and live their separate legends, side by side. If this sprawling half-continent has a heart, here it is. Its pulse throbs out along the rivers and railroads; slow, reluctant and rarely simple, a double beat, a self-moved reciprocation.

---

37 *barren* (n.): the region of poor, almost uninhabited land (tundra) – 37 *haze* (n.): a sort of light mist – 38 *keen* (v.): to make bad sounds like howling – 38 *flare* (v.): to burn with a bright but uncertain flame – 39 *roar* (v.): to make a loud noise (e.g. like a lion) – 43 *sprawl* (v.): to spread irregularly – 44 *throb* (v.): to beat strongly – 45 *reluctant* (adj.): unwilling, slow to act – 45 *reciprocation* (n.): mutual exchange between two races, peoples.

3: MORDECAI RICHLER: The Apprenticeship of Duddy Kravitz

Mordecai Richler was born in Montreal in 1931 and spent his youth in that city's Jewish section (St. Urbain Street), situated between the French Canadians in the East End and the economically dominant English Canadian districts of western Montreal. He left Canada before he was twenty in order to live in Spain, in Paris, and esp. in London. In England, where he lived for more than 12 years, he wrote film scripts, e.g. for *Life at the Top* (by John Braine). In 1955 Mordecai Richler published *Son of a Smaller Hero*, set in the Montreal Jewish ghetto. After *The Apprenticeship of Duddy Kravitz* (1959), which many critics consider to be his best work, Richler wrote the novels *The Incomparable Atuk* (1963) and *St. Urbain's Horseman* (1971). *The Street*, published in 1969, is a collection of autobiographical short stories. Besides fiction, Richler has written two volumes of essays and articles, a lot of film scripts and TV-plays, and has worked as a journalist.

Richler returned to Canada in 1972 and has mainly lived in Montreal since then, teaching occasionally at Carleton University (Ottawa) as a visiting professor.

The text is taken from: Mordecai Richler, *The Apprenticeship of Duddy Kravitz*, Markham, Ont., Penguin Books Canada Ltd., pp. 67–77, 280–281.

---

apprenticeship (n.): the period of learning a trade – *Jewish* (adj.): G. jüdisch – *script* (n.): the written form of a speech, play, film, etc. – **autobiographical** (adj.): concerning the facts of one's own life – **fiction** (n.): novels and stories.

The novel traces Duddy Kravitz' progress out of high school and through several adventures in the Jewish immigrant section around St. Urbain Street, Montreal.

It is Duddy's drive for land that is the central theme of the novel.

Duddy found the land he wanted quite by accident.

That summer, the year he graduated from FFHS, he went to work as a waiter in an hotel in the Laurentian mountains. Rubin's Hotel Lac des Sables was in Ste Agathe des Monts and of all the waiters taken on for the summer only Duddy was not a college boy. The others were first and second year McGill boys, none had ever been to FFHS—they came from more prosperous families—and Duddy found it difficult. Some of the other employees, like Cuckoo Kaplan, the recreation director, and the boys in Artie Bloom's band, had their own rooms, but all the waiters slept in the same dormitory over the recreation hall that extended above the lake. After a long day's work they often shared a bottle of rye. [...] On other nights, when the boys went on midnight swims or to drink beer in Val Morin, Duddy was not invited.

Duddy, alone among the boys, was not rattled by the heat and the hurry, the quarrels and the sometimes spiteful squalor, of the kitchen. The gift of a bottle of rum insured the cook's goodwill—Duddy had no trouble getting his orders. In fact he was so quick in the dining room that after two weeks Mr Rubin gave him three extra tables. This seemed to antagonize the other boys even more and, provoked by Irwin Shubert, they began to ride Duddy hard.

'It's the cretinous little money-grubbers like Kravitz that cause anti-semitism,' Irwin told the boys. [...]

Shunned by the college boy waiters, Duddy began to investigate Ste Agathe on his own when he had time off.

Some sixty miles from Montreal, set high in the Laurentian hills on the shore of a splendid blue lake, Ste Agathe des Monts had been made the middle-class Jewish community's own resort town many years ago. Here, as they prospered, the Jews came from Outremont to build summer cottages and hotels and children's camps. Here, as in the winter in Montreal, they lived largely with their neighbours. Friends and relatives bought plots of land and built their

---

trace (v.): to follow the course of – **immigrant** (n.): a person coming into a country to make his home there – *drive* (n.): an important need that urges a person to act.

2 **graduate** (v.): to complete an educational course – 2 *FFHS:* Fletcher's Field High School – 3 *Laurentians:* a scenic mountainous region north of the St. Lawrence – 6 *McGill:* one of Montreal's 4 universities (English) – 6 *prosperous* (adj.): wealthy – 7 **employee** (n.) /'emplɔ'i/: a person who is employed – 8 *recreation* (n.): amusement, way of spending free time – 9 *dormitory* (n.): a large room for sleeping – 11 *rye* (n.): G. Roggen, AE whisky made from rye – 13 *rattle* (v.): to make nervous or anxious – 14 *spiteful* (adj.): full of dislike, ugly – 14 *squalor* (n.): the condition of being very dirty – 17 *antagonize* (v.) /'æn'tægənaɪz/: to cause to become an enemy – 18 *ride* (v.): to annoy – 20 *cretinous* (adj.) /'kretɪnəs/: stupid, foolish – 20 *money grubber* (n.): G. Geldscheffler – 22 *shun* (v.): to avoid, keep away from – 26 *resort* (n.): a holiday place – 27 *Outremont:* a higher-class (French, partly Jewish) neighbourhood in Montreal.

cottages and boat houses competitively, but side by side. There were still some pockets of Gentile resistance, it's true. Neither of the two hotels that were still in their hands admitted Jews [...]

Rubin's was not the only Jewish resort in Ste Agathe, either. There were many others. But Rubin had, in the shape of Cuckoo Kaplan, Ste Agathe's undisputed number one comic. [...]

Duddy told Cuckoo about some of his business ideas.

Next summer, he thought, he might try to set up in the movie rental business. All he needed was a truck, a projector, and a *goy* to run the camera, and with a good movie, playing a different resort each night, he would rake in no fortune, but ... Another idea he had was to make colour movies of weddings and *barmitzvahs*. There might be a gold mine in this, he told Cuckoo, and he was thinking of calling himself Dudley Kane Productions. Who knows, but if the idea caught on, five-six years from now he might be able to make a feature-length comedy right here in Montreal, starring Cuckoo Kaplan. But, to begin with, he needed that truck and projector and a *goy* to operate it. Maybe the Boy Wonder who was an intimate of his father would stake him. Duddy said that he would see about that in the autumn. [...]

Yet another business idea Duddy told Cuckoo about was his plan for a Ste Agathe newspaper. There were nine hotels in town, he said, and each one must have a list as long as your arm of addresses for all over the States. Wouldn't it be smart publicity for them to keep Americans in touch. [...] He thought he might call it the *Laurentian Liner*, because it would travel everywhere, and Cuckoo agreed the name was a catchy one. Duddy said he would speak to the Boy Wonder about it in the autumn.

Duddy had been putting money in the bank since he was eleven and in his first month at Rubin's he had earned nearly three hundred dollars in tips, but what he needed was a real stake.

At night, lying exhausted on his cot, Duddy realized how little money he had in big business terms and he dreamed about his future. He knew what he wanted, and that was to own his own land and to be rich, a somebody, but he was not sure of the smartest way to go about it. He was confident. But there had been other comers before him. South America, for instance, could no longer be discovered. It had been found. Toni Home Permanent had been

---

30 *competitively* (adv.): in an effort to outdo the others — 31 *pocket:* a nest, small group that exists separated from others — 31 *gentile* (adj.) /'dʒentaɪl/: a person who is not Jewish — 35 *undisputed* (p. p.): s. th. that cannot be called into question — 35 *comic* (n.): a funny person — 37 *set up* (v.): to establish (oneself) in business — 37 *rental* (n.): money fixed to be paid regularly for the use of s. th. — 38 *truck* (n.): AE a large motor car for carrying goods — 38 *goy* (n.): Yiddish: not Jewish — 39 *rake in* (v.): to earn — 43 *catch on* (v.): to become popular — 43 *feature:* a full-length cinema film with an invented story — 44 *star* (v.): to have s. o. play the most important role — 46 *intimate* (n.): a close friend — 46 *stake* (v.): to support with money (to get started) — 51 *smart* (adj.): clever — 51 **publicity** (n.): the business of bringing s. o. or s. th. to favourable public notice — 53 *catchy* (adj.): catching the attention of — 58 *cot* (n.): a small kind of bed, usually for small children or babies — 59 *in ... terms:* with regard to — 62 *comer* (n.): infml. a successful person — 63 *Toni Home Permanent:* Firma für Haarfestiger.

invented. Another guy had already thought up Kleenex. But there was something out there, like let's say the atom bomb formula before it had been discovered, and Duddy dreamed that he would find it and make his fortune. He had his heroes. There was the stranger who had walked into the Coca Cola Company before it had made its name and said, 'I'll write down two words on a piece of paper, and if you use my idea I want a partnership in the company.' The two words were 'Bottle it'. Don't forget, either, the man who saved that salmon company from bankruptcy with the slogan, *this salmon is guaranteed not to turn pink in the can*. There was the founder of the *Reader's Digest*—he'd made his pile too. The man who thought up the super-market must have been another shnook of a small grocer once. There was a day when even the Boy Wonder gathered and sold streetcar transfers. Sure, everyone had to make a start, but it was getting late. Duddy was already seventeen and a half and sure as hell he didn't want to wait on tables for the rest of his life. He needed a stake. When he got back to Montreal in the autumn he would speak to his father and go to see the Boy Wonder.

'I'm not,' he once told Cuckoo, 'the kind of a jerk who walks around deaf and dumb. I keep my eyes peeled.' And already Duddy had plenty of ideas. He had even had letterheads printed—Dudley Kane, Sales Agent—and every week he marked the advertising section of the Sunday edition of the *New York Times* for novelties, bargains, and possible agencies. That was a hint he had picked up from Mr Cohen, whose family was staying at Rubin's for the entire summer.

Duddy watched all the businessmen who came to the hotel. He made sure they got to know him too, and that they made no mistake about his being a waiter. That was temporary. He watched the way they avoided their wives and the sun and sat around playing poker and talking about the market and the boom in real estate. Most of them ate too much and took pills. One, a Mr Farber, had summoned Duddy to his table on his first day at the hotel and torn a hundred dollar bill in two and given Duddy half of it. 'We're here for the season,' he said, 'and we want snappy service. You give it to us and the other half of this note is yours. O.K. kid?'

Duddy replied to several advertisements in the *Times*. He was, at one time, interested in a new soap that was guaranteed not to sting the eyes. Duddy dreamed, he planned, he lay awake nights smoking, and meanwhile Irwin continued to torment him. One night a bottle of ketchup was emptied on his sheets and another he discovered a dead mouse in his serving jacket pocket.

---

64 *formula* (n.): G. Formel – 69 *bottle* (v.): to fill into bottles – 70 *salmon* (n.) /'sæmən/: G. Lachs – 70 *bankruptcy* (n.): the state of being unable to pay one's debts – 70 **guarantee** (v.): to give promise of s. th. – 72 *pile* (n.): heap (e. g. of money) – 73 *shnook* (n.): schnook, sl.: a stupid person of no imporance who can easily be influenced – 74 *streetcar* (n.): AE tram – 74 *transfer* (n.): a ticket allowing a passenger to change from one tram to another – 79 *jerk* (n.): AE sl. a foolish person – 80 *keep one's eyes peeled:* infml. to be careful, watchful – 83 *agency* (n.): an establishment or company doing business for others – 90 **boom** (n.): rapid growth – 90 *real estate* (n.): land and buildings – 93 *snappy* (adj.): quick – 94 *kid* (n.): infml. AE young person – 98 *torment* (v.): to cause to suffer pain.

A small resort in the Laurentian Mountains

The other waiters began to feel badly. 'Aw, lay off,' Bernie Altman said. Another night Donald Levitt said, 'Take it easy, Irwin. I'm warning you. He's had enough.'

But Irwin couldn't stop and Duddy began to retaliate. When Irwin started to mock him in the dormitory with the others there, Duddy would begin to improvise songs. [...]

He enters into an affair with Yvette, a Québecois girl, with whose help he starts buying land at a nearby lake. In order to raise more money he engages in the movie business, producing films of Jewish weddings and "barmitzvahs".

He also swindles money out of Virgil, his crippled epileptic assistant and friend. He even scores against Jerry Dingleman, the "Boy Wonder", a rich criminal on the Jewish scene. Thus he obtains more and more land.

Duddy walked the length of the land he owned, tapping a tree here, picking up a piece of paper there. Lying on the grass he chewed on a weed and considered the topmost pine trees in the surrounding hills. The frogs began to croak. I could have salted the lake with trout, he thought. That would have been a fine attraction. He entered the cool damp woods and climbed to the top of the highest hill overlooking the lake and that land was his too. A natural ski-run, he thought. Around and around he could see all the land he owned

---

100 *lay off* (v.): infml. to stop – 103 *retaliate* (v.): to pay back evil with evil.
movie (n.) AE: film – *barmitzvah:* a Jewish religious ceremony that recognizes a boy of 13 as a responsible member of the community – *swindle* (v.): to cheat – *score* (v.) to make a successful point.
106 *tap* (v.): to strike lightly – 107 *chew* (v.): to crush with the teeth – 109 *croak* (v.): to make the deep noise typical of frogs – 109 *salt* (v.): infml. to put in some of its kind in order to raise many (usu. with the idea of fooling others) – 109 *trout* (n.): G. Forelle.

and the rest, a third maybe, that was still in other hands. Beyond the woods he could make out the highway and Ste Agathe. Wheat, potatoes, and barley was being grown on some of the fields between and here and there wretched, skinny cows wandered, but already ranch-style houses were encroaching on the countryside, drawing nearer. I was right, he thought. I knew what I was doing. Five years from now this land will be worth a fortune.

There could have been a real snazzy hotel and a camp, the finest ski-tow money could buy, canoes, cottages, dancing on the lake, bonfires, a movie, a skating rink, fireworks on Israeli Independence Day, a synagogue, a Western-style saloon, and people saying 'Good morning, sir,' adding in a whisper after he'd passed, 'That was Kravitz. He built the whole shebang. They used to say he was a dreamer and he'd never make it.'

There could have been his father, sitting on the porch and sucking sugar cubes maybe. 'My boy was broke,' he'd say. 'He hadn't made his name yet. He was just another kid at the time and he got this job as a waiter at Rubin's. But he wasn't going to be a waiter for long, you bet. All the while he's serving those *chazers* ideas are ticking over like bombs in his head. Tick-tock, tick-tock ... He sets up a roulette game, can you imagine? There he is not even eighteen yet, a St Urbain Street punk [...]

There could have been his grandfather on the farm and everybody saying how Duddy was the easiest touch in town, allowing ten St Urbain Street boys into the camp free each season [...]

Duddy started back through the woods as the sun began to sink and he stopped twice to rest and reflect on the long walk home. Yvette was waiting for him on the porch steps.

'Are you all right?' she asked.

'I went for a walk.'

'You've been crying.'

'Don't be crazy. Where's our fighting editor?'

'Duddy! He's asleep. Listen, I've got some news for you.'

'Bad?'

'The notary phoned me at the office. The rest of the land has gone up for sale. There are two different owners and—' [...]

In the end Duddy is the proud owner of all the land he had plotted for, but he has lost his friends and even the respect of his grandfather Simcha.

---

114 *barley* (n.): G. Gerste – 116 *skinny* (adj.): thin, without much flesh – 116 *encroach* (v.): to advance (more than welcome) – 119 *snazzy* (adj.): good-looking in a showy way – 119 *tow* (n.) /təu/: lift – 120 *bonfire* (n.): a large fire in the open air, for pleasure – 121 *skating rink:* G. Eislaufbahn – 122 *saloon* (n.) /sə'lun/: a large public drinking place – 123 *the whole shebang* (n.) /ʃə'bæŋ/: AE infml. the whole thing – 125 *porch* (n.): G. Veranda – 125 *suck* (v.): to draw into the mouth with the lips – 126 *cube* (n.): a solid object with 6 equal sides – 128 *you bet* (v.): sl. you can be sure – 129 *chazer* (n.): sl.: pig, swine (Hebrew) – 131 *punk* (n.): an unpleasant young boy, man, often fighting and breaking the law – 133 *touch* (n.): a person from whom it is easy to get money – 144 *notary* (n.): person with legal power to witness the signing of statements.
plot (v.): to plan (to get) s. th secretly.

4: GASTON MIRON: Poetic Voice of Québec Nationalism

From: The *New York Times*, Sunday, April 2, 1978.

By HENRY GINIGER
Special to The New York Times

MONTREAL—If Quebec had a poet laureate, he would probably be Gaston Miron, a forceful leader of its highly vocal and nationalist community of arts and letters.

Mr. Miron has been called Quebec's "national poet" at a time when Quebec is not yet a nation but has a government that is intent on making it one. [...]Observers of the Quebec scene are struck by the vigor of its cultural life and the nationalism that permeates it. "The majority of our creators—the novelists, playwrights, artists, poets and singers—are in favor of independence as well as a strong proportion of the intelligentsia, the scholars, university people, et cetera," Mr. Miron said.

Key Word Is 'Quebec'

Given this bent, it is not surprising to find in the literature and the songs strong expressions of bitterness and revolt against the more numerous and powerful English-speaking Canadians. These are accompanied by assertions of love for and pride in French Quebec and its past. [......] He and his fellow writers feel they are fighting for a specific Quebec culture that he defines as "an American culture of French expression." Such a culture, he contends, must have its own independent state to protect it.

In his book-cluttered home in a section of eastern Montreal where little English is heard, he was asked why it was important to a poet that Quebec be indepenent.

"Because any culture that does not have a political expression is destined sooner or later to retreat and become simply ethnic or folkloric," he said. "Every Quebec writer has always in mind this interrogation: 'In 50 or 60 years will there still be people to read my work? Am I writing for a culture with a death sentence hanging over it?' " [......]

Difference Praised and Defended

Mr. Miron [......]
said every work created in French in Quebec "is a subversive and revolutionary fact because it introduces difference into North America. Every Quebec work goes against all the forces of the American imperialist steamroller which seeks to level out, make uniform and homogenize the continent."

The question of whether Québec's flourishing culture is in danger within the present Canadian federation or within the wider North American context is one of the fundamental ones in the debate now raging in Quebec and throughout Canada.

Mr. Miron shares the feeling of the Parti Québécois, now in power, that this culture is indeed in danger to a large extent because French-speaking

---

2 *laureate* (adj.) /'lorɪət/: crowned with laurel (Lorbeer), specially distinguished – 4 *vocal* (adj.): connected with the voice, spoken, sung, expressed aloud – 5 *letters* (n. pl.): literature in general – 9 *intent on* (adj.): intending to do – 12 *permeate* (v.): to spread or pass through or into every part – 13 **majority** (n.): the greater number of (people) – 13 **creator** (n.): a person who creates s.th. – 14 **playwright** (n.): a writer of plays – 16 *proportion* (n.): part, share – 17 *intelligentsia* (n.): people in a society who concern themselves with ideas and new developments – 21 *bent* (n.): tendency of mind – 26 *assertion* (n.): a forceful statement – 33 *contend* (v.): to claim – 36 *clutter* (v.): to spread out in a disorderly fashion – 44 **ethnic** (adj.): of or related to a racial, national or tribal group – 46 *interrogation* (n.): a formal question – 54 *subversive* (adj.): which may cause the destruction of those in power – 58 *steamroller* (n.): infml. a force that destroys all opposition – 59 *level out* (v.): to stop rising, make flat or equal in position, rank etc. – 59 *uniform* (adj.): the same in every way – 60 *homogenize* (v.) /hə'modʒɪnaɪz/: to make the parts of a whole become equal – 63 *federation* (n.): a group of provinces united under one government – 64 *context* (n.): general conditions – 65 *fundamental* (adj.): deep, from which all else develops – 69 *Parti Québécois:* P. Q. a nationalist (and—at times—separatist) political party which came into power in 1976 with René Levesque as "premier ministre". It was replaced by the Liberals (Bourassa) in 1985.

Gaston Miron, Quebec poet

Quebecers constitute a diminishing minority in Canada and in time will be reduced to just another little-known ethnic group. Within Quebec's borders, French-speakers form about 80 percent of the people and thus constitute the majority culture. But in Canada, "we will always be outvoted and told in the name of democracy that we must submit to the Canadian majority," he said.

The 50-year-old writer, who also runs a small publishing house, has spent half his life working with others to raise the level of awareness of Quebecers to the need for independence. He even went to jail for two weeks in 1970 when the Federal Government rounded up nationalists right and left in its attempt to stamp out a wave of violence. But no poll has ever shown more than a minority of Quebecers in favor of independence. [......]

Miron's Creed in Verse

Following is the last stanza of "Octobre," a poem by Gaston Miron. Octobre refers to nationalist violence in October, 1970, which was suppressed by armed force and mass arrests.

Nous te ferons, terre de Québec
Lit des résurrections
Et des mille fulgurances de nos métamorphoses
De nos levains où lève le futur
De nos volontés sans concessions
Les hommes entendront battre ton pouls dans l'histoire
C'est nous ondulant dans l'automne d'Octobre
C'est le bruit roux, roux des chevreuils lumière
L'avenir dégagé, l'avenir engagé.

We shall make of you, land of Quebec
A bed of resurrections and of a thousand flashing metamorphoses
Of our leavening from which the future will arise
And of our uncompromising wills
Men will hear your pulse beating in history
It is we rippling through the October autumn
It is the russet noise of deer in the sunlight
With the future open, the future committed.

72 *constitute* (v.): to form – 72 *diminish* (v.) to become or seem smaller – 72 **minority** (n.): a smaller part of the population – 74 **reduce to** (v.): to make smaller, cheaper etc. – 79 *be outvoted* (v.): to be in the minority – 86 **awareness** (n.): state of knowledge or consciousness – 88 *jail* (n.): prison – 90 *round up* (v.): to gather together – 91 *stamp out* (v.): to put an end to completely – 92 *poll* (n.): a questioning of a number of people (as to their ideas).

95 *creed* (n.): a (short) statement of religious or political belief – 96 **stanza**: a group of lines in an poem, forming a division – 101 *resurrection* (n.) /'rezə'rekʃn/: the rising of hope, life; G. Auferstehung – 102 *metamorphosis* (n.) /'metə'mɔfəsɪs/: a complete change from one form to another – 104 *leavening* (n.) /'levnɪŋ/: G. hefeartiges Aufgehen – 106 *uncomprising* (adj.): refusing to change ideas, firm in beliefs, ways – 107 *pulse* (n.): the regular beating of blood in the main blood vessels carrying blood from the heart – 109 *ripple* (v.): to move in very small and gentle waves – 111 *russet* (adj.): esp. lit. of a reddish or golden brown colour – 114 *committed* (adj.): having given one's whole loyalty to a particular aim, job, way of life.

5: HUGH HOOD: Bicultural Angela

Hugh Hood was born in Toronto in 1928 of bilingual parents. He was educated there and graduated from the University of Toronto in 1950 (B. A.), 1952 (M.A.) and 1955 (Ph.D.). He then taught at the Department of English at Hartford in the USA (1955–1961) and currently teaches at Université de Montréal. In 1962 he published a first book of short stories, *Flying a Red Kite*. His most important works are *White Figure, White Ground* (1964), *A Game of Touch* (1970) and *The Swing in the Garden* (1975), the first volume of a projected 12-volume series of novels, entitled *The New Age/Le nouveau siècle* (*A New Athens* (1977) was part two of this series and *Reservoir Ravine* (1979) part three). Hood has published a second short story collection *Around the Mountain: Scenes from Montreal Life* (1967), from which "Bicultural Angela" is taken. (Toronto, Peter Martin Associates Ltd., 1976, pp. 35–48.)

Not so long ago, in her mid-teens, growing up in Stoverville seventy miles from the Québec border, Angela Mary Robinson heard her mother exclaim to a visitor from Montréal, 'I do so much want to know what is happening to you people. So exciting, everything one hears about the new Québec.'

Angela had not heard her mother express this view before.

'Is Westmount burning?' said Mrs. Robinson playfully.

The visitor, an elegant bond salesman spending a weekend on somebody's houseboat, raised an eyebrow with a polite air of one who has heard the tune before. 'Do you really want to know?' he said.

'I think it is my duty.'

'Why not subscribe to *Le Devoir*? They cover the province so fully that they hardly talk about anything else. It would cost you twenty dollars a year, but it's worth much more.'

Mrs. Robinson sighed. 'Ah, but you see, I don't read a word of French.'

Thinking this over afterwards, Angela decided that her mother's words implied several things: hypocrisy, frivolity, obstinate persistence in a dangerous prejudice. She was old enough to spot the tone in her mother's voice which meant that Mrs. Robinson was attempting to please by pretending an interest in an obscure, probably trivial, special subject.

---

bilingual (adj.): speaking two languages – **graduate** (v.): to take one's first academic degree – *B. A.:* Bachelor of Arts – *M. A.:* Master of Arts – *Ph. D.:* Doctor of Philosophy – *kite:* G. Flugdrachen – *projected* (adj.): planned – *bicultural* (adj.): related to two cultures – 1 *teens* (n.): the period of one's life between 13 and 19 years – 6 *Westmount:* the (rich) English quarter of Montreal – 7 *bond* (n.): G. Pfandbrief, festverzinsliches Wertpapier – 8 *air* (n.): appearance – 11 *subscribe* (v.): to pay regularly to receive a newspaper – 11 *Le Devoir:* a Montreal (French) newspaper – 16 *imply* (v.): express indirectly – 16 *hypocrisy* (n.) /hɪ'pokrəsɪ/: the act of pretending to have a character, belief, etc. that one does not possess – 16 *frivolity* (n.): the inability to take important matters seriously – 16 *obstinate* (adj.): not easy to change by argument – 16 *persistence* (n.): continuing firmly and unreasonably in s. th. (e. g. a habit) – 17 **prejudice** (n.): G. Vorurteil – 17 *spot* (v.): to recognize – 19 *obscure* (adj.): not clear –

Rejecting Queen's and the Conservatory, Angela went to Trinity College in the University of Toronto and wore pastel sweaters from Holt-Renfrew, oatmeal-tweed skirts and a single strand of pearls through freshman and sophomore year. After that, involved with the production of a fugitive film and learning French voraciously, she switched to coarsely knit Italian sweaters in bright reds and yellows fitting loosely around the hips. She discarded skirts for slacks, often rather tight. She had a smart, navy-blue duffle coat. In her last year, she subscribed to the international edition of *Le Monde* and acquired a startling expertise connected with the General Agreement on Tariffs and Trade.

She read the film quarterlies, having been deeply influenced by Marshall McLuhan, and had a vague notion of doing a Master's degree on one of the media. By graduation, Angela Mary knew definitively that the one place to be, in Canada in the mid-sixties, was French Montréal, not Westmount, which she knew well from weekends, nor the McGill campus, but *le vrai Montréal*, as she considered it, of the Bonsecours market, old picturesque restored Montréal. She also had the idea that there was a lot of activity at *l'Office National du Film* and *Radio-Canada*, and she went to a lot of trouble to get herself a job in CBC-Montréal. Not much of a job. She was a trainee program organizer in FM, and hoped that she might have a chance to get into French-language programming if she worked very hard on her spoken French and cultivated obvious French types around the studios.

---

20 **reject** (v.): to refuse to accept – 20 *Queen's:* name of the university at Kingston, Ont. – 20 *Conservatory:* a school where students are trained in music or acting (here: of the University of Toronto) – 21 *pastel* (adj.) /'pæstl, US: pæ'stel/: any soft light colour – 21 *sweater* (n.) /'swetə(r)/: a woolen garment for the top of the body – 21 *Holt-Renfrew:* a higher class department store – 21 *oatmeal* (n.): G. Hafermehl – 22 *tweed* (n.): a coarse woollen cloth woven from threads of different colours – 22 *strand* (n.): a thread – 22 *freshman* (n.): a 1st year student – 22 *sophomore* (n.): a 2nd year student – 23 *involved with* (adj.): closely connected with – 23 *fugitive* (adj.): not lasting, passing rapidly (in importance) – 24 *voracious* (adj.): showing a limitless hunger for s. th. – 24 *switch* (v.): to change – 25 *hip* (n.): G. Hüfte – 25 *discard* (v.): to get rid of – 26 *slacks* (n.): loosefitting trousers – 26 *smart* (adj.): neat and stylish in appearance – 26 *duffle-coat* (n.) /'dʌfl/: a loose coat made of a rough heavy woolen cloth often with a baglike headcover – 27 *Le Monde:* a French newspaper – 28 *expertise* (n.) /'ekspɜ'tiz/: skill in a particular field – 28 *General Agreement on Tariffs and Trade:* international treaty (GATT) – 30 **quarterly** (n.): a magazine appearing every 3 months – 30 *Marshall McLuhan* (1911–1982): a Canadian expert on communication and methods of information who won an international reputation with books like *The Medium is the Message* (1967) – 31 **vague** (adj.) /veɪg/: not clearly understood – 31 *Master's degree:* academic degree (e.g. MA or MSc) granted by a college and being above a B.A. – 32 **medium** (n.) /'midɪəm/: pl. -dia, a method for giving information – 32 *graduation* (n.): the time of getting one's degree – 32 *definite* (adj.): without any uncertainty – 34 *McGill:* one of Montreal's two English universities – 34 *campus:* (the grounds of a) university – 34 *le vrai:* Fr. the true, real – 35 *Bonsecours:* a market-place in Old Montreal – 35 *picturesque* (adj.): charming enough to be made into a picture – 36 *l'Office National du Film* (ONF): Fr. National Film Board, a national institution and agency for film activities – 38 *CBC:* Canadian Broadcasting Corporation – 38 *trainee* (n.): a person who is being trained – 39 *organizer* (n.): a person who arranges things – 39 *FM:* frequency modulation (G. UKW) – 41 *cultivate* (v.): to encourage the growth of friendship with s. o. –

She took to spending a lot of time in various Montréal cafés and bars. When her duties took her as far south as the main building on Dorchester West, she would spend an hour after the completion of her errand at that little place just west of Mackay where you never knew whom you might run into. She watched the French girls, the way they did their hair, their make-up, and began to experiment with her looks, with metallic green eyeshadow, at first very discreetly applied. She bought some hairpieces and began to tease the acquired hair and her own into extremely bouffant situations. Whether in this she was fully *dans le vent* remains an open question. She discarded slacks for dresses like Petula Clark's with narrow fit and short skirt.

Angela was a very pretty and agreeable young woman and not stupid, and as she made great efforts in these directions she made friends, mostly men friends, in radio at first and later among TV people. She met boys who had film to sell, film by the mile, sometimes hijacked out of ONF stock, sometimes paid for by an indulgent parent in Outremont. After a while she found that she was seeing more French boys than English, which made her excited, content and prettier than ever.

Maplewood Avenue unveiled its charms to her. The street is in effect the dormitory of *l'Université de Montréal*, since there is little residence accommodation on the campus. West from the *Centre Social* as far as Côte des Neiges, the street is a long row of apartments housing professors, students and functionaries associated with university business. There is a certain amount of subterranean political activity carried on, usually in basement apartments rented by three or four students, providing each with low rent. These students are not rich. Many are poor, sometimes even hungry. They are older than the students Angela was used to and their interests are most various. They do not much like to speak English, and an English girl who speaks French is likely to seem an anomaly, perhaps to be taken up and examined with curious care, perhaps then to be put down.

She got a second-floor apartment on Maplewood just west of the campus and started to submit program ideas to her producer which took her into the

---

43 *Dorchester:* one of the main streets in Montreal, with the CBC-building on it – 44 *completion* (n.): fulfillment – 44 *errand* (n.) /'erənd/: a short journey made to get s. th. – 45 *Mackay:* a street in the shopping centre of Montreal – 48 *discreet* (adj.) careful – 48 *hairpiece* (n.): a piece of false hair (used to make one's own hair seem thicker) – 48 *tease* (v.): to comb – 49 *bouffant* (adj.) /'bufoŋ/bu'fʌnt/: fancyful hair-style – 50 *dans le vent:* Fr. up-to-date – 51 *Petula Clark:* an international singer and show-star of British origin (born 1932) – 55 *hijack* (v.): to take control of (e.g. an aircraft) by force of arms, formerly for the purpose of stealing – 56 *indulgent* (adj.); too kind to s. o. – 56 *Outremont:* a higher-class (French, partly Jewish) neighbourhood in Montreal – 59 *Maplewood Ave.:* now called Boulevard Edouard Montpetit, a wide street running alongside the campus of Université de Montréal – 59 *unveil* (v.): to reveal – 60 *dormitory* (n.): a large room for sleeping, here: sleeping-area – 60 *accomodation* (n.): a place to live – 61 *Centre Social:* the student's social centre at a university – 61 *Côte des Neiges:* an important street connecting the shopping centre with the area around Université de Montréal – 62 *functionary* (n.): a person with official duties – 63 *subterranean* (adj.): underground – 64 *basement* (n.): rooms below street level – 69 *anomaly* (n.) /ə'nomalı/: unusual irregularity – 70 *put down* (v.): to abandon, lay aside – 72 *submit* (v.): to offer for consideration.

university *ambiance*. First one of her programs got aired, then another; she learned how to make an acceptable tape under difficult conditions, huddled under a speaker's platform or in the cloakroom after a violent *conférence*.

I used to see her where I work, standing among the coffee and sandwich machines, talking rapid inaccurate French to students her own age, sometimes to a *chargé d'enseignement junior*, a writer or critic. She became rather well-known as a young woman who had made great strides, who might in the end manage to get all the way across. Then I heard that she was involved in the production of a half-hour film documentary for French TV, in which she was the star, interviewed in depth over several weeks in coffee houses, at work, *après-ski* and the rest of it. When it was finally telecast the half-hour was called 'Miss Robinson', a Franglicism of the type which repels Général de Gaulle, like *le barman, le weekend*, prevalent in certain Parisian circles, and creeping into Montréal society.

I had the feeling that this title may have concealed immediately under the surface a certain puritanical, if playful, contempt, typical of many of the younger French intellectuals in the city. Sometime later I learned that Miss Robinson had changed her given names to 'Marie-Ange' pronounced with the strongly aspirated French 'r' which is almost an 'h'. Apart from stressing it like a French word, giving each syllable equal emphasis in an un-English way, she couldn't do much about 'Robinson'.

The TV film had a certain impact when it appeared on *Canal Deux*. Full of nuance, half mocking and half encouraging, it managed to suggest much of the ambiguity and pathos in the situation of the transformed Marie-Ange. She used that name in the interviews. Whether she had attempted something impossible was left an open question in the viewer's mind. She photographed beautifully; perhaps part of the joke was this vivid presentation of her new beauty which owed very much to, might indeed be said to derive from, purely French manners.

---

73 *ambiance* (n.): Fr. character, atmosphere of a place – 73 *air* (v.): to broadcast – 74 **tape** (n.): narrow plastic material for recording sound – 74 *huddle* (v.): to crowd together – 75 *platform* (n.): a raised floor of boards for speakers, performers – 75 *cloakroom* (n.): a room, as in a theatre, where coats, hats etc. may be left for some time – 75 *conférence* (n.): Fr. meeting – 77 *inaccurate* (adj.): not correct – 78 *chargé d'enseignement junior:* Fr. sort of teacher and tutor for younger students – 79 *make great strides* (phr.): to improve, to do well – 80 *involve* (v.): to become connected or concerned – 83 *telecast* (p.p.): broadcast on TV – 84 *Franglicism:* a word composed of French and English elements – 84 *repel* (v.): to cause feelings of dislike – 84 *Charles de Gaulle* (1890–1970): French general and statesman who, during a visit to Québec in 1967, ponounced the famous words: "Vive le Québec libre" – 85 *prevalent* (adj.): existing widely – 88 *puritanical* (adj.): like a Puritan (member of a religious group) – 91 *aspirate* (v.): to pronounce a consonant sound with a slight (burst of) air after it – 91 *apart from:* except for – 91 *stress* (v.): to give force to (a part of) a word – 92 *emphasis* (n.): special force given to certain words – 94 *impact* (n.): effect – 94 *Canal Deux:* Fr. Channel Two – 95 *nuance* (n.) /'njuəns, US: nu'æns/: a shade of meaning – 95 *mocking* (adj.): laughing at s. o. or s. th. – 96 **ambiguity** (n.): unclear condition – 96 *pathos* (n.) /'peɪθos/ quality that causes a feeling of pity and sorrow – 96 *transform* (v.): to change – 99 **vivid** (adj.): full of life and force – 99 *presentation* (n.): the way in which s. th. is shown to others –

Certainly her circle of men considered her a beauty. Stéphane Dérôme had been floating around film circles for a couple of years, working first in amateur film, then for a time for an independent producer, then as composer of the score for an expensive feature launched with much publicity which sank without trace. He took her up lovingly, on the waves of the 'Miss Robinson' furore. She had become the mode.

In those days I was spending a lot of time out at the Montrose Record Center on Bélanger, west of Montée Saint-Michel. [...]

Around the Montrose Center the buildings are drab new housing dating from the mid-fifties, with little to distinguish one from the next. It's surprising to find the record store in such a location because, as I once told the owner, George Tabah, it's 'the most exciting record store in town'.

He thought this over while I went through the Nonesuch bin, featured that day at a very good price.

'I may use that in an ad,' he said finally, 'I like it. "The most exciting record store in town".'

He never did use it though. [...]

Sometimes when I was idling away a chilly early spring afternoon talking to George about the complexities of record marketing, I would see Stéphane and Marie-Ange down at the end of the narrow aisle, holding up for inspection first one record then another. I could hear a continuous soft flow of critical comment from them.

'Not the real thing.'

'Too much arrangement, do you think?'

'No, he is simply a poor poet. The music is not bad.'

Marie-Ange took most of Stéphane's comments at face value, possibly because of his plan to become a *chansonnier* himself. You have to understand what this implies, and it's not simple. In French Canada, since the seventeenth century, there's been a great race of singers, a descending tradition, who compose their own songs—that's the most important thing. A Québec *chansonnier*

---

104 *composer* (n.): a person who writes music – 105 *score* (n.): a long piece or group of pieces of music for a film – 105 *feature* (n.): a full-length cinema film – 105 *launch* (v.) /lɔntʃ/ to set going, start off – 105 **publicity** (n.): the act of bringing s.th. to favourable public notice – 106 *trace* (n.): a sign showing the former presence of s.th. – 107 *furore* (n.) /fjuˈrɔrɪ/: a sudden excited interest among a large group of people – 107 *mode* (n.): style of dressing or doing s. th., model – 109 *Bélanger, Montée St.-Michel:* streets in Montreal – 110 *drab* (adj.): uninteresting, dull – 112 **location** (n.): place – 114 *Nonesuch bin:* a container holding cheap records of the firm Nonesuch – 114 *feature* (v.): to advertise as a special offer – 116 **ad.**: short for advertisement (n.): notice in a newspaper of s. th. for sale – 119 *idle* (v.): to waste time doing nothing – 119 *chilly* (adj.): noticeably cold – 120 *complexity* (n.): difficulty (in operating, running) – 120 *marketing* (n.): the various activities by which goods are supplied and sold – 121 *aisle* (n.) /aɪl/: a narrow passage between a row of shelves – 123 *comment* (n.): opinion – 127 *at face value:* without question – 128 *chansonnier* (n.): Fr. singer – 130 *descend* (v.): to come down from generation to generation.

is *not* a collector and performer of folk songs, nor is he a popular entertainer; there is nothing primitive about his work. He has to be a poet, a good musician, a performer on some instrument. Sometimes, like Gilles Vigneault, he recites and acts things out. He must be a leader and encourager of his people. In Québec now, there are three or four magnificent singers of this kind, not more, and plenty of would-bes.

In France the term means something a bit less serious, like 'singer-comedian-satirist', and here we move closer to the style of Aznavour, or Jacques Brel, who does what is really a night-club or theatre act. Brel sings, acts, writes, and in most respects resembles a Québec *chansonnier* with the one great difference that he doesn't have the responsibility to protect and encourage the national tradition of a resentful minority. He has real gifts, but not the same social commitment. 'Winter is my country', sings Gilles Vigneault, getting a strength that Jacques Brel can't quite manage; of course, there is a difference in their audiences. When Brel sings *'Ne me quitte pas'*, his impersonation of an anguished lover can be recognized and appreciated anywhere in the world. But this is nevertheless a commercial love song.

In my book Stéphane Dérôme had the talent of a minor film composer or a commercial songwriter, not that of a poet, an actor or leader. An accomplished pianist with plenty of formal musical training, certainly good-looking and pleasant to talk to, able to get through an acceptable evening on a guitar, he reeked of Paroisse Saint-Germain and of Stanislas, not at all of small isolated Natashquan-type villages eight hundred miles east. He played dates in small restaurants, made a record, was praised by his friends, by Marie-Ange, by Victorine Boucher who had starred in that doomed feature film he'd composed.

This group flocked to the Montrose Record Center like the swallows in March, picking up disc after disc, buying many, discarding the unauthentic ones. They all seemed to know each other intimately, with the exception of

---

132 *performer* (n.): a person that carries out (a piece of work) – 132 **folk song** (n.) /fəuk/: music which has grown up among country people – 133 **musician** (n.) a person who plays an instrument or who sings – 134 *Gilles Vigneault:* a famous singer from Québec – 134 **recite** (v.): to say s. th. aloud from memory – 137 *would-be* (adj., here n.): what one wishes to be but is not – 138 *comedian* (n.): an actor who tells jokes to make people laugh – 139 *satirist* (n.): a person who writes or speaks critically of things in an amusing way – 139 *Charles Aznavour, Jacques Brel:* famous French chansonniers; Brel died in 1978 – 143 *resentful* (adj.): feeling angry or bitter at s. th. or s. o. – 143 **minority** (n.): a small part of a population different from the rest – 144 *commitment* (n.): responsibility – 146 *Ne me quitte pas:* Fr. don't abandon me – 146 *impersonate* (v.): to copy the behaviour of s. o. – 147 *anguish* (n.): feeling great pain – 149 *minor* (adj.): of lesser importance – 153 *reek of* (v.): to smell strongly of – 153 *Paroisse Saint-Germain:* a large Catholic church in Outremont near Université de Montréal – 153 *Stanislas:* a French school (lycée) in Montreal – 153 *isolate* (v.): to cause to be separated from others – 154 *Natashquan:* a place in Québec where G. Vigneault was born – 154 *play dates:* to perform by appointment – 156 *star* (v.): to appear as a main performer – 156 *doom* (v.): to experience s. th. unpleasant, such as death – 158 *flock* (v.): to gather – 158 *swallow* (n.): G. Schwalbe – 159 *disc* (n.): record – 159 *unauthentic* (adj.): not of genuine origin.

Marie-Ange. She was always in the center of the group, forcing the pace of the chatter a little hysterically, flushed. [...] They were kind to her, I thought, letting her run on as she pleased, rarely interrupting.

Her full flow of talk was assuming obsessive proportions, it seemed to me. Towards the end of March, I got a little extra money quite unexpectedly, which meant that for once I had enough money to gratify my need to buy records. I hustled out east, arriving at the Montrose about two o'clock, figuring on spending most of the afternoon talking to George and slowly and happily picking out forty dollars worth of his bargains. I wasn't really happy to be interrupted in the middle of our conversation, which had developed through some long pauses over about an hour.

'Why don't you stock the Haydn Society reissues?'

Moments would pass slowly while he thought about this. He went next door and brought back a pear from the fruit store, which he began to eat slowly with relish.

'Well?'

'Why won't you pay more than two-fifty for a record?'

'Can't afford it. Get me Haydn Society at two-fifty or under and I'll gradually take the whole line.'

'Can't be done.'

'They do it in New York.'

We'd been over all this before, and we both started to laugh, and on the wave of our laughter Marie-Ange was carried in the door. She made straight for me and instantly began to talk as though we were the closest of friends, maybe even related, and as though in the middle of a sentence broken off seconds ago. Conversation with her was always exhausting for the first minutes, while you tried to figure out whom she was referring to and what was implied.

'... Couldn't stand pets, any pets, so they had to go, as I couldn't consider moving, not right now with so much happening downstairs.'

'Downstairs?'

'In our building, Victorine's apartment. She claims there has been a voyeur peeking in the bathroom windows, she's right in the basement you know, and thinks it may be dangerous. If you ask me, it's Gérard up to some trick or other.'

'Voyeurism doesn't sound like Gérard. Satyriasis, more likely.'

'I wish some of it would rub off on me,' she said gloomily.

---

161 *pace* (n.): speed – 162 *chatter* (n.): rapid informal unimportant conversation – 162 *flushed* (adj.): excited and eager – 164 *obsessive* (adj.) /əb'sesɪv/: filling s. o.'s mind continuously – 164 *proportion* (n.): here: great size – 166 *gratify* (v.): to give satisfaction to – 167 *hustle* (v.): to move fast – 167 *figure* (v.): to consider, believe – 172 *stock* (v.): to supply, to store – 172 *reissue* (n.): s. th. printed or produced again after some time – 175 *relish* (n.): a great deal of pleasure – 188 *pet* (n.): an animal kept in the house as a companion – 191 **claim** (v.): to declare (to be true) – 191 *voyeur* (n.) /vwa'jɜ(r)/: Fr. a person who watches the other sex in secret – 192 *peek* (v.): to look at s.th. when one should not – 193 *trick* (n.): a funny act, joke – 195 *satyriasis* /'sætə'rɪəsɪs/: an uncontrollable sexual desire in men.

'Oh, come on.'

'Then again it could be François, though he's still supposed to be in Québec.'

'I think it might, but then why go to all the trouble of peeking? He has full access to Victorine's apartment.'

'Oh?'

She had been just on the boiling point, simmering as it were, and now boiled over. 'Heaven knows I try,' she said, 'I do my best. *Je fais mon très petit possible, quoi?'*

'Evidemment.'

'What I have to put up with. I've been out with these guys every night in the week for months; it's affecting my skin. I've put them on the air. I want an AM show where I can do bilingual interviews and meet people and try to help. And then to be told that I can't really be part of the group because I can't understand their jokes, it's something else, really. *Pas gentille.'*

'It's very hard.'

'What?'

'To catch the jokes. I speak a fair French myself and ...'

'Pooh,' she said, 'pooh. A lot of it is smut, pure and simple, nothing but sex. Look at French theatre, intrigue, bare bosoms.'

'I'm in favor of that.'

'I can see you would be, but what woman can be bothered?' She glanced at George Tabah and moved to the back of the store; there was an unmistakable air of strain and ill-health about her. When I followed her back, she lowered her voice. 'There's something up that I don't know about, involving François and Gérard and Stéphane and Victorine, a plot of some kind, and I just can't keep up to what they're saying.'

'Not politics, surely?'

'No, no, nothing like that. You can't see Stéphane risking it, can you? No revolutions for him.' She had a Leo Ferré album in her hands and was examining his face with some bitterness.

'That's the stuff,' she said, 'Ferré, good and strong.'

'I find him a little hard to take.'

'You would.'

This was simply generalized resentment—at least I hope it was—and I let it pass.

---

200 *access* (n.) /'ækses/: the right of entering – 202 *simmer* (v.): to cook just below boiling heat, be filled with anger – 203 *je fais mon trés petit possible, quoi?:* Fr. I do what I can best, don't I? – 205 *evidemment:* Fr. obviously – 206 *put up with:* infml.: to suffer without complaining – 206 *guy* (n.): infml. AE fellow – 207 *put s. o. on the air:* infml. to start s. o. off on the radio – 208 *AM:* amplitude-modulation (G. MW) – 208 **bilingual** (adj.): in two languages – 210 *pas gentille:* Fr. not nice – 214 *smut* (n.): material for reading, hearing or seeing that is morally improper – 215 *intrigue* (n.) /'ɪntrig/: act of planning s. th. secretly – 217 *bother* (v.): to annoy – 218 *unmistakeable* (adj.): clearly recognizable – 219 *strain* (n.): the condition of being under physical (and emotional) stress – 221 **plot** (n.): a secret plan directed against s.o. – 225 *Leo Ferré:* a great French singer of France – 230 **generalize** (v.): to make a general statement – 230 *resentment* (n.): a feeling of anger, bitterness –

'I'm sorry,' she said, 'I'm not your responsibility, am I?'

That question always bothers me, and I didn't answer.

'I've been so miserable,' she said.

George had left the store for a moment. He was standing outside with his back to the window, looking at the sky. The March light was extremely ambiguous, very pale, chilly looking, yet with a peculiar tone in some way evocative of the approach of finer weather. It was still plenty cold out, but another few weeks would see us out of it. The equinoctial gales, very troublesome in Montréal, had just begun, and the wind was gusting to fifty. And yet there was this almost imperceptible promise of fineness to come. The end of winter makes me feel better, encourages a certain buoyancy of feeling. Perhaps it had the reverse effect on Marie-Ange, and she was simply expressing physical discomfort induced by the weather. I said, 'Tell me about it, if you like.'

She gave a faint smile. 'You don't want to hear.'

'I'm not sure.'

'I'll tell you something anyway. I love Stéphane.'

I sometimes wonder whether there are any girls here and there burdening other men with the tale of their hopeless passion for me. The man who hears this story is bound to feel considerable distaste for the love-object, from feelings of unacknowledged rivalry perhaps; few men really care for the role of confidant. When she said this, I was conscious of a sharp pang of dislike for Stéphane. I felt like making a callous and flippant answer like, 'Sorry about that, chief,' but repressed the impulse. I said, 'He's a very nice guy,' thinking that, on the whole, he wasn't much.

Naturally Marie-Ange, far from stupid, sensed this, and putting down the Ferré disc she went out of the store more quickly, if anything, than she'd entered. You're a cold fish, I told myself. You might have been nicer. Must be the change in the weather.

When I heard about Victorine and Stéphane going off to Paris together, I kept my ears open and was able to collect a pretty full impression of the end of Marie-Ange's affair. Victorine, dark, small, fragile of ankle and wrist, adorable, had innocently announced that she would be in Paris for the principal event

---

236 **ambiguous** (adj.): unclear – 237 *evocative* (adj.) /ɪ'vokətɪv/: s. th. that produces feelings – 239 *equinoctial* (adj.): occurring twice in the year when day and night are of the same length (March 21, September 22) – 239 *gale* (n.): storm, strong wind – 239 *troublesome* (adj.): causing trouble, annoying – 240 *gust* (v.): to blow with a sudden strong rush of air – 241 *imperceptible* (adj.): unable to be noticed – 242 *buoyancy* (n.) /'bɔɪənsɪ/: a cheerful state of mind – 243 *reverse* (adj.): opposite – 244 *induce* (v.): to cause – 248 *burden* (v.): to load, trouble – 250 *bound* (adj.): certain – 251 *unacknowledged* (adj.): not recognized, admitted – 251 *rivalry* (n.) /'raɪvlrɪ/: competition, condition of being rival – 252 *confidant* (n.): a person to whom one tells one's secrets – 252 *pang* (n.): a sharp feeling of pain of the mind – 253 *callous* (adj.) /'kæləs/: unkind – 253 *flippant* (adj.): lacking respect – 254 *chief:* sl. boss, or (infml.) polite form of address – 254 *repress* (v.): to control – 256 *sense* (v.): to feel – 262 *fragile* (adj.) /'frædʒaɪl/: weak, slight – 262 *ankle* (n.): G. Knöchel – 262 *adorable* (adj.) /ə'dɔrəbl/: worthy of being loved deeply.

of the year, the opening at the Olympia of Claude Gauthier and Monique Leyrac. To such bait more considerable men than Stéphane Dérôme would have risen. They booked seats together on the appropriate Air Canada flight, Stéphane including his banjo and guitar and little else in his weight allowance.

He had a final meeting with Marie-Ange out at the Montrose, just checking over the new releases, I suppose. She turned to him with bewildered tears in her eyes, certainly incapable of understanding why she hadn't reached him.

'Ne me quitte pas!' she said.

'Brel,' said Stéphane absently, and he turned away.

---

264 *Olympia:* a famous concert-hall for light music in Paris – 264 *Claude Gauthier:* a Québec singer and composer – 264 *Monique Leyrac:* a Québec singer – 265 *bait* (n.): s. th. (e. g. food) used to attract e.g. fish, animals, men which/who are then caught – 266 *appropriate* (adj.): suitable – 266 *Air Canada:* Canada's official airline – 267 *allowance* (n.): what is admitted, permitted – 268 *check over* (v.): to examine – 269 *release* (n.) here: a new record.

MON PAYS

Mon pays ce n'est pas un pays c'est l'hiver
Mon jardin ce n'est pas un jardin c'est la plaine
Mon chemin ce n'est pas un chemin c'est la neige
Mon pays ce n'est pas un pays c'est l'hiver

Dans la blanche cérémonie
Où la neige au vent se marie
Dans ce pays de poudrerie
Mon père a fait bâtir maison
Et je m'en vais être fidèle
A sa manière à son modèle
La chambre d'amis sera telle
Qu'on viendra des autres saisons
Pour se bâtir à côté d'elle

Gilles Vigneault,
Québec's most famous singer

"... chased out of Corriveau's house ..."

6: ROCH CARRIER: La Guerre, Yes Sir!

Roch Carrier was born in a small village in Québec in 1937. He studied classics at the Université de Montréal and then taught for two years at a Collège in Edmunston, N.B. After that he continued his studies at the Sorbonne in Paris, where he wrote a doctoral thesis. He has been a resident dramatist at the Théâtre du Nouveau Monde in Montreal and combines teaching with writing.

With Michel Tremblay, Roch Carrier is the best-known Québécois writer in both Québec and English Canada. The two authors share a humorous, ironic and sometimes sentimental view of Québec life. Carrier's first book was *Jolis deuils* (1964), a collection of fantastic and allegorical tales. The novel trilogy *La guerre, yes sir!* (1968), *Floralie, où es-tu* (1969) and *Il est par là le soleil* (1970) have been translated into English and seen a tremendous success in both languages.

Since 1972 Carrier has published several other novels, e.g., *Le jardin des délices* (1975, The Garden of Delights, 1978) and *La dame qui avait des chaînes aux chevilles* (1981). *Les enfants du bonhomme de la lune* (1979, transl. as *The Hockey sweater and other stories*) is the title of another collection of stories.

Carrier has also produced a dramatic version of *La guerre, yes sir!*, which has been made into a film.

La guerre, yes sir! is a comic though at times nightmarish account of how World War II intrudes on individuals and the community in a Québec village: Corriveau, a young soldier from the village, has been killed in the war and is brought home for burial by a group of English soldiers. The two following scenes take place during the wake in his parents' house.

The text is taken from: Roch Carrier, *La guerre, yes sir!* (translated by Sheila Fischman), Toronto, House of Anansi Press, 1970, pp. 81–83 and 89–90.

---

classics (n.): the languages and literature of ancient Greece and Rome – *thesis* (n.) /'θiːsɪs/: a long article/book written on a particular subject for a higher university degree – *resident* (adj.): living in a place; here: while working, carrying on official duties (e.g. writing plays) – *allegorical* (adj.): concerning a story in which the characters and actions represent good and bad qualities – *trilogy* (n.): a group of 3 related books – *tremendous* (adj.): very great in size, degree – **version** (n.): form, copy – *comic* (adj.): funny – *nightmarish* (adj.): having or causing unpleasant and terrible dreams – *intrude* (v.): to come when not wanted, uninvited – *wake* (n.): a gathering to watch over a dead person the night before the burial –

The candles on Corriveau's coffin had burned out. Now the living room was lit only by the light coming from the kitchen. The light was yellow, greasy looking. The soldiers had been present, imperturbable, at Arsène's massacre. They had looked impassively at the savage rites, drowned in heavy laughter, cider and greasy *tourtières*, but their lips were sealed by disgust.

What kind of animals *were* these French Canadians? They had the manners of pigs in a pigpen. Besides, if you looked at them carefully, objectively, French Canadians really looked like pigs too. The long thin Anglais looked at the French Canadians' double chins, their swollen bellies, the big flaccid breasts of their women; they scrutinized the French Canadians' eyes, floating inertly in the white fat of their faces—they were real pigs, these French Canadians, whose civilization consisted of drinking, eating, farting, belching. The soldiers had known for a long time that French Canadians were pigs. "Give them something to eat and a place to shit and we'll have peace in the country," they used to say. That night the soldiers had proof before their eyes that the French Canadians were pigs.

Corriveau, the French Canadian they had transported on their shoulders through snow so deep it made them want to stretch out and freeze they were so tired, Corriveau, this French Canadian sleeping under their flag, in a uniform like the one they were so proud of, this Corriveau was a pig too.

French Canadians were pigs. Where would it end? The sergeant decided that it was time to take the situation in hand. French Canadians were unmanageable, undisciplined, crazy pigs. The sergeant prepared a plan of attack in his head.

His subalterns remembered what they had learned in school: French Canadians were solitary, fearful, barely intelligent; they didn't have a talent for government or business or agriculture, but they made lots of babies.

When the English arrived in the colony the French Canadians were less civilized than the Indians. The French Canadians lived grouped in little villages

---

1 *coffin* (n.): a box in which a dead person is buried – 2 *greasy* (adj.): covered, filled with animal fat – 3 *imperturbable* (adj.) /ˈɪmpəˈtɜbəbl/: remaining calm in spite of confusion – 3 *Arsène:* the village's old gravedigger who, during the turbulent scenes in Corriveau's house, is brutally knocked down and made fun of by Bérube, a French soldier of the same village – 3 *massacre* (n.) /ˈmæsəkə(r)/: the killing of large numbers of people, animals; here: bad treatment (thrashing) – 4 *impassive* (adj.): showing no feelings – 4 *savage* (adj.): cruel or violent, uncivilized – 4 *rite* (n.): a form of (religious) behaviour with a fixed pattern – 4 *drown* (v.): to cover up (a sound) by making a loud noise – 5 *cider* (n.): an alcoholic drink made from apple juice – 5 *tourtière* (n.): Fr. a sort of meat pie – 5 *seal* (v.): to close as with a seal – 7 *pigpen* (n.): small piece of land enclosed by a fence for keeping pigs in – 8 *Anglais:* English Canadian – 9 *swell* (v.): to fill – 9 *belly* (n.): G. Bauch – 9 *flaccid* (adj.) /ˈflæksɪd/: not firm enough – 10 *scrutinize* (v.) /ˈskrutɪnaɪz/: to examine closely – 10 *inert* (adj.): slow, lazy – 12 *fart* (v.): to send out air from one's behind – 12 *belch* (v.): to pass wind noisily from the stomach out through the throat – 14 *shit* (v.): sl. to produce human waste (from one's behind) – 18 *stretch out* (v.): to lie down in full length – 21 *sergeant* (n.) /ˈsadʒənt/: G. Feldwebel – 22 *unmanageable* (adj.): not easy to control or deal with – 23 *undisciplined* (adj.): having no self-control, no order – 25 *subaltern* (n.) /ˈsʌbltən, AE: səˈbɔltərn/: a soldier in the army of lower rank.

along the shores of the St. Lawrence, in wooden cabins filled with dirty, sick, starving children, and lousy, dying old men. Every year English ships used to go up the St. Lawrence because England had decided to get involved in New France, which had been neglected and abandoned by the Frenchmen. The English ships were anchored in front of the villages, and the Englishmen got off to offer their protection to the French Canadians, to become friends with them. But as soon as they had seen the British flag waving on the St. Lawrence the French Canadians had gone and hidden in the woods. Real animals. They hadn't a vestige of politeness, these pigs. They didn't even think of defending themselves. What they left behind—their cabins, animals, furniture, clothes—were so dirty, so crawling with vermin, so smelly, that the English had had to burn it all in order to disinfect the area. If they hadn't destroyed it the vermin would have invaded the whole country.

Then the boats went away, but the French Canadians stayed in the woods until autumn. Then they got busy building new cabins.

Why did they not accept the help offered by the English? Because France had abandoned them, why would they not accept the privilege of becoming English? England would have civilized them. They wouldn't be French-Canadian pigs then. They would know how to understand a civilized language. They would speak a civilized language, not a *patois*.

Accustomed to obeying, the soldiers felt that they were being given an order. They turned their eyes towards the sergeant, who motioned with his head. The soldiers understood. They carried out the order fervently.

They went through the house picking up boots, coats, scarves and hats, and threw them outside. The villagers were invited to leave.

More preoccupied with finding their clothes than protesting the insult, they left, pushing each other as they went.

When the villagers found themselves in front of Anthyme Corriveau's house, their feet in the snow which was as sharp as splinters of glass, when they understood that they had been expelled from Anthyme Corriveau's house, that they had been thrown out into this icy sea where they were trembling in their soaking clothes, when they thought again that it was outsiders, Anglais, who had chased them out of Corriveau's house, a house that had come down through five generations of Corriveaus, all living in the village and in the same

---

30 **cabin** (n.): a small roughly built (often) wooden house – 31 *lousy* (adj.): G. verlaust – 32 *get involved* (v.): to interfere in – 34 *anchor* (v.): to stop sailing and lower the anchor – 38 *vestige* (n.) /'vestɪdʒ/: sign, mark – 38 **politeness** (n.): the showing of good manners for others – 40 *crawl with* (v.): here: to be completely covered by – 40 *vermin* (n.): any kind of unpleasant, biting insect, drawing blood – 40 *smelly* (adj.): unpleasant-smelling – 41 **area** (n.): region esp. that around one's home – 49 *patois:* Fr. nonstandard language spoken only in a small area – 51 *motion* (v.): to give a signal by means of a movement (e.g. hand) – 52 *fervent* (adj.): eager – 53 *scarf* (n.): pl. -ves, cloth for wearing around the neck or head – 55 *preoccupied* (adj.): with the mind fixed on s.th. else – 58 *splinter* (n.): a small sharp piece broken off s.th. – 59 *expel* (v.): to dismiss, chase – 61 *soaking* (adj.): very wet.

house on the same bit of land for more than a hundred years; when they reminded themselves that Corriveau, a little French-Canadian boy, a son of the village, had been killed in a war that the Anglais from England, the United States and Canada had declared on the Germans (Corriveau had been killed in the mud of the old country while the Anglais were sitting on cushions in their offices; the Anglais left their shelters sometimes, but only to go and bring a young French Canadian, dead in the war, back to his family); when the villagers realized that they had been sent out like dogs that had peed on the rug by the Anglais who weren't from their village or their county or their province, or even their country, Anglais who weren't even Canadians but only *maudits* Anglais then the villagers knew the depth of their humiliation.

Gesticulating, swearing, bickering, arguing, pushing and shoving, spitting, drunk, they swore inflammatory oaths against the Anglais who had settled themselves into Corriveau's house.

Joseph waved his stump, wrapped up in its bandages, and shouted louder than the others. "The *maudits* Anglais have taken everything away from us, but they haven't got our Corriveau. They won't get Corriveau's last night!"

---

71 *pee* (v.): sl. to pass yellow liquid from the body, urinate – 74 *maudit:* Fr. damned – 74 *humiliation* (n.): feeling of shame (after) losing the respect of others – 75 *gesticulate* (v.): to express s.th. with movements of the body – 75 *bicker* (v.): to quarrel – 75 *shove* (v.): to push in a rough way – 75 *spit* (v.): to force liquid from the mouth – 76 *inflammatory* (adj.) /ɪnˈflæmətrɪ/: likely to cause strong feelings to rise or violence to happen – 76 *oath* (n.): light use of the name of God or anything sacred – 78 *Joseph:* At the beginning of the novel Joseph, a villager, had cut off his hand to escape military service – 78 *stump* (n.): the remaining part of a limb which has been cut off – 78 *bandage* (n.): a long piece of cloth for dressing a wound.

The Montral Star, Saturday, April 23, 1977

IV Ontario

Ontario, the heir to Upper Canada, with its Loyalist and Regency English traditions, its memories of the war of 1812 that shaped its special self-awareness, its old communities of German sectarians, and its sharp geographical definition by lakefront and Shield, remains a distinct region even though its two greatest cities, Ottawa and Toronto, have become the foci of a political, economic and cultural centralism that goes entirely against the Canadian grain.

George Woodcock: *The Meeting of Time and Space*, p. 13.

---

1 **Loyalist** (n.): The Loyalists were American colonists who moved to Canada after the War of Independence in order to remain under British rule – 1 *Regency* (n.): referring to the period from 1811 to 1820 in Britain – 2 *the war of 1812:* the war between Canada and the USA, which the USA lost – 2 **self-awareness** (n.): having understanding of oneself, one's surroundings – 3 *sectarian* (n.): a member of a religious sect – 4 *lakefront* (n.): the area along Lake Ontario – 4 *Shield* (n.): The Canadian Shield forms an incomplete ring around Hudson Bay and covers about half the total area of Canada. It is largely unsuitable for agriculture. – 5 *foci* /ˈfəusaɪ/ pl. of focus (n.): the central points, places of greatest activity – 6 *it goes against the grain* (phr): here: it goes against the sense of regionalism that most Canadians support.

Toronto with CN Tower and Lake Ontario

1: WILLIAM KILBOURNE: In the Beginning

William Morley Kilbourne (born 1926) is Professor of History and Humanities at York University in Toronto. He received his school education at Upper Canada College and later attended the universities of Toronto, Harvard and Oxford. Kilbourne is particularly known for his work on William Lyon Mackenzie and the rebellion in Upper Canada in 1837. His other writings include *The Restless Church* (1966), *The Making of the Nation* (1966), *Religion in Canada* (1968), *Canada: A Guide to the Peacable Kingdom* (1970) etc. He is a member of various learned societies and takes a keen interest in cultural and political affairs in Toronto. In the first part of his article "In the Beginning" he sums up the early history of settlement in Upper Canada, later called Ontario.

The text is taken from:
William Kilbourne: 'In the Beginning'. In: *Ontario: A Bicentennial Tribute.* Toronto, Key Porter Books, 1983, pp. 9–10.

They were refugees and defeated soldiers, the settlers of 1784, looking for land and work and peace in what was left of British North America.

Among the American colonists who eventually found their way to the virgin forests of Ontario, there were a few well-to-do tories like the Robinsons of Virginia, persecuted for their loyalty by the revolutionary mobs; there were pacifists like the Mennonites and Quakers of Pennsylvania; but the great majority of that first six thousand who occupied the banks of the St. Lawrence and the Niagara and the Kingston-to-Quinte shore were simple farmers who had been on the losing side of what was essentially a New York civil war.

The old regiments were kept together: Colonel Butler's Rangers at Newark, Major Rogers' Corps west of Fort Cataraqui and Sir John Johnson's Royal Yorkers–Anglicans, Scottish Presbyterians, Gealic-speaking Catholic

---

Humanities (n.): studies such as literature, ancient languages, history and other Arts subjects – *Upper Canada College:* a private high school in Toronto – *William Lyon Mackenzie* (1795–1861): the leader of the rebellion in Upper Canada in 1837 – *learned* /'lɜnid/ societies: societies of scholars – 1 **refugee** (n.): a person who has been driven from his country – 3 **virgin** (adj.): unspoilt, unchanged by human activity – 4 *well-to-do* (adj.): rich – 4 **tory** (n.): here: a supporter of the British government during the American War of Independence (1775–1783) – 5 **persecute** (v.): to cause to suffer for political or religious reasons – 5 *loyalty* (n.): a connection which binds a person to someone – 5 *mob* (n.): a large noisy crowd – 6 *pacifist* (n.): a person who refuses to fight in a war – 6 *Mennonites* (n.): a German Protestant sect – 6 *Quakers* (n.): a Christian religious group which opposes violence and spends most of its religious services in silence – 8 *Kingston:* a city on Lake Ontario at the mouth of the Cataraqui river – 8 *Quinte:* a place west of Kingston/Ont., also on the Lake – 9 *a New York civil war:* referring to the American War of Independence (1775–1783) – 11 *colonel* (n.) /'kɜnl/: G. Oberst – 11 *Newark:* today called: Niagara-on-the-Lake – 12 *Fort Cataraqui:* a fort at the mouth of the Cataraqui river, built by the French (today Kingston/Ont.) – 13 *Anglicans:* members of the Church of England – 13 *Scottish Presbyterians:* members of the Church of Scotland – 13 *Gaelic* (n.): one of the Celtic languages, esp. that of Scotland or Ireland –

Cadets at Old Fort Henry, overlooking Kingston

Highlanders, German Lutherans and German Calvinists, each in their separate allotments—from Longueil to the Long Sault to the Thousand Islands.

To defend themselves against the assault of the seasons in their new homeland, they were each supplied by the British authorities with axe and saw, hammer, pick and crowbar, carpenter's tools, hoes, twine, ploughshares, seed and a few provisions. Land grants ranged from fifty acres for an ordinary civilian to two hundred for NCOs and a thousand for field officers. Some brought wives and children and animals, a few had servants and heirlooms.

The necessary land was purchased from the Mississaugas and other aboriginal peoples, including three million acres for the British allies Joseph Brant and the Six Nations to make their new home on the banks of the Grand.

Until then, the Great Lakes region had been the domain of a few migrant tribes, the merchants and *coureurs de bois* who traded with them, and a

---

14 *Highlander* (n.): a person from the mountainous area of Scotland – 15 *allotment* (n.): here: parts of land given to a person – 15 *Longueil:* a place on the south shore of Montreal Island, now a suburb of the city – 15 *the Long Sault* /'su/: a location on the St. Laurence river, south-west of Montreal – 15 *the Thousand Islands:* a large number of islands in the St. Laurence river near Kingston/Ont. – 16 *assault* (n.): a sudden violent attack – 18 *crowbar* (n.): G. Brecheisen – 18 *pick* (n.): G. Spitzhacke – 18 *hoe* (n.): G. Hacke – 18 *twine* (n.): strong cord or string – 18 *ploughshare* (n.): G. Pflugschar – 19 **grant** (n.): here: land given by a king or government – 19 *range* (v.): to vary – 19 *acre* (n.): G. ca. 2 Morgen – 19 **civilian** (n.): a person not of the armed forces – 20 *NCO:* a non-commissioned officer, G. Unteroffizier – 21 *heirloom* (n.): /'eəlum/: a valuable object given by older members of a family to younger ones over many years – 22 *the Mississaugas:* an Indian tribe – 22 *aboriginal* (adv.): native – 23 **ally** (n.): a person who helps to support one – 23 *Joseph Brant* (1742–1807): an American Indian chief who aided the British during the American Revolution – 24 *the Six Nations:* a confederacy of eastern North American Indian tribes – 24 *Grand* (n.): a river in southern Ontario which empties into Lake Erie – 25 *domain* (n.): living area – 25 *migrant* (adj.): moving from place to place – 26 *coureurs de bois:* Fr. fur traders –

sparse scattering of soldiers whose palisades and plumage symbolized the suzerainty of a European monarch.

The only settlements of any size in what is now Ontario were at the two extremities: the *habitants* placed along the river banks at Fort Detroit in the last years of the French regime, and the hive of storekeepers and craftsmen who had occupied the main Hudson's Bay Company post on the Moose River south of James Bay since the 17th century.

In 1791 the Loyalists were granted British institutions and laws in the new colony of Upper Canada. Expecting another American war, Governor Simcoe chose the protected harbour of Toronto for the site of a fort and his capital. He and his wife Elizabeth lived in a tent purchased from the effects of the explorer Captain Cook and, like Adam and Eve new-naming things in the Garden, set about creating a society.

Simcoe's British officials stayed on to become, along with a few educated Loyalists, the colony's governing class. Their children's tutor, John Strachan, who sailed from Scotland to New York in 1799, and thence walked through the forest to Kingston, became their spokesman during the American invasion of 1813, and after the war their political leader. George III, he told them, though he had never been to England, was a paragon of men and that democrat Jefferson the devil incarnate.

Strachan became the first bishop of Toronto but his goal was to "preach civilization" as well as the Gospel. The father of education in the province,

---

27 *sparse* (adj.): thin – 27 *scattering* (n.): a small number separated widely – 27 *palisade* (n.): a fence made of strong iron or wooden poles – 27 *plumages* (n.) /'plumɪdʒɪz/: feather decoration – 27 **symbolize** (v.): to represent a person, idea etc. – 28 *suzerainty* (n.) /'suzəreɪntɪ/: supremacy, highest power – 28 *monarch* (n.): a king or queen – 30 *extremity* (n.): the outermost point – 30 *habitants* (n.): the French farmers in Canada – 31 *regime* (n.): government, rule – 31 *hive* (n.): a busy crowd – 31 **craftsman** (n.): a highly skilled worker – 32 *Hudson's Bay Company:* an English trading company founded in 1670. It explored vast areas in western Canada and set up many trading posts. In 1867 the lands of the company became part of the Candian Confederation. – 33 *James Bay:* the southern arm of Hudson Bay – 34 **Loyalists** (n.): American colonists who moved to Canada after the War of Independence in order to remain under British rule – 35 *Upper Canada:* today called Ontario – 35 *Governor Simcoe:* John Graves Simcoe (1752–1806): first lieutenant governor of Upper Canada – 36 *site* (n.): a piece of ground for building – 36 *fort* (n.) /fɔt/ a strongly made building used for defence at some important place – 37 *effects* (n.): personal property – 38 **explorer** (n.): someone who travels into a place for the purpose of discovery – 38 *Captain Cook:* James Cook (1728–1779). The famous seaman and explorer of the Pacific Ocean and the shores of North America – 38 *new-name* (v.): to give a name to somebody or something – 39 *Garden* (n.): the Garden of Eden, Paradise – 39 *set about* (v): to begin – 41 *tutor* (n.): here teacher – 41 *John Strachan* (1778–1867): first Anglican Bishop of York (today Toronto) and a famous educator – 43 **spokesman** (n.): a person chosen to speak for others – 43 *George III:* King of England (1760–1820) – 45 *paragon* (n.): a perfect model to copy – 46 *Thomas Jefferson* (1743–1826): President of the United States and author of the Declaration of Independence – 46 *incarnate* (adj.): in bodily form – 47 **goal** (n.): aim – 48 **Gospel** (n.): any of the 4 accounts of Christ's life in the Bible –

he also created the Loyalist myth and guarded against the incursion of American democracy.

Upper Canada was in the path of the American migration west, however, and by 1812 the population was predominantly American. My ancestors crossed the Niagara River in 1794, to take up land in what is now London, and like most of their fellows, they were scarcely aware of being under a new allegiance and little inclined to serve a governing class. Their spokesman was another poor Scottish immigrant, the populist editor and agitator William Lyon Mackenzie. He eventually led them in an armed uprising, whose final defeat was planned in Strachan's parlour.

The upshot of 1837 was that neither opponent was to dominate again. Their ideals interfered with progress and prosperity. But they are still our best spiritual guides. Like the lion and the unicorn contending for the Crown, tory Strachan and radical Mackenzie are fixed forever in the still-motion dance of the monarch's Coat of Arms, augury and emblem of this royal province of the pioneers.

---

49 **myth** (n.): something invented, not real – 49 *guard against* (v.): to prevent by special care – 49 *incursion* (n.): a sudden attack – 51 **migration** (n.): the movement from one place to another – 52 **ancestor** (n.): a person from whom another is descended – 53 *take up* (v.): to occupy, to settle – 53 *London:* a city in western Ontario – 55 *allegiance* (n.) /ə'lidʒəns/: dutiful support to a king or country – 55 *inclined* (v.): feeling a wish to – 56 **immigrant** (n.): a person coming into a country from abroad to make his home there – 56 *populist* (adj.): referring to a person who believes in the good qualities of ordinary people, esp. in political matters – 56 *agitator* (n.): a person who excites and influences other people's feelings – 57 *eventually* (adv.): finally – 57 *uprising* (n.): an occasion of rising against the government – 59 *upshot* (n.): result – 59 *opponent* (n.): a person who takes the opposite side – 59 **dominate** (v.): to have or exercise controlling influence – 61 *guide* (n.): here: leading idea – 61 *unicorn* (n.): a horse-like animal with one horn on its forehead – 61 *contend* (v.): to compete as in a race. (the lion and the unicorn contend for the Crown in the arms of Ontario) – 62 **tory** (n.): conservative – 62 *still-motion* (adj.): without movement – 63 *Coat of Arms:* G. Wappen – 63 *augury* (n.) /'ɔgjurɪ/: a declaration telling what the future will be – 63 *emblem* (n.): an object which is the sign of something. G. Emblem

A settler might take three years to clear 30 acres. Trees were cut down or burned or girdled (killed by cutting a broad ring around the trunk, thus stopping the flow of sap).

2: SUSANNA MOODIE: Burning the Fallow

Susanna Moodie, 1803–1885, was born in Suffolk, England, and emigrated to Canada in 1832. Like her sisters she turned to writing early and published stories for young people, poems and magazine articles while still in England. In Canada she and her husband began farming 8 miles northwest of Cobourg. In 1834 they sold their property and moved to their original land grant north of Lakefield. *Roughing It In the Bush* describes their experiences in both places. When Mr. Moodie was appointed Sherriff of Hastings County they were able to leave the bush and quit farming. In Canada, too, Susanna Moodie wrote articles for literary magazines and finally had her autobiographical book published in London/England in 1852, followed by two additional volumes which make up a trilogy and various other writings. *Roughing It* is a frank account of pioneer life, full of humour, keen observation and realistic attitudes. 'Burning the Fallow', from which the following text is taken, is a chapter in the first edition of 1852 (chapter III of volume II, pp. 57–66, Richard Bentley, London).

From: *Roughing It In the Bush Or, Forest Life in Canada*. Toronto, Coles Publishing Company Ltd., repr. 1980, pp. 329–330. (repr. as facsimile of the 1913 edition by Bell and Cockburn, Toronto)

It is not my intention to give a regular history of our residence in the bush, but merely to present to my readers such events as may serve to illustrate a life in the woods.

The winter and spring of 1834 had passed away. The latter was uncommonly cold and backward; so much so that we had a very heavy fall of snow upon the 14th and 15th of May, and several gentlemen drove down to Cobourg in a sleigh, the snow lying upon the ground to the depth of several inches.

A late, cold spring in Canada is generally succeded by a burning hot summer; and the summer of '34 was the hottest I ever remember. No rain fell upon the earth for many weeks, till nature drooped and withered beneath one bright blaze of sunlight; and the ague and fever in the woods, and the cholera in the large towns and cities, spread death and sickness through the country.

---

fallow (n.): lit: land that has been cleared but left unplanted – *roughing it* (phr.): living in a simple and not very comfortable way – **emigrate** (v.): to leave one's own country in order to go and live in another – *Cobourg:* a city on Lake Ontario, between Kingston and Toronto – *Lakefield:* a place 10 km north of Peterborough/Ont. – *Hastings County:* a district in Ontario between Peterborough and Belville – **quit** (v.): to give up – **autobiographical** (adj.): concerning the facts of one's own life – **additional** (adj.): in addition – *trilogy* (n.): a group of three related books – **pioneer** (n.): one of the first settlers in a new land – 5 *backward* (adj.): behind in development – 7 *sleigh* (n.) /sleɪ/: a horse-drawn vehicle which slides on snow – 8 *inch* (n.): 0,025 m – 11 *droop* (v.): to lose strength – 12 *blaze* (n.): brightly shining light – 12 *ague* (n.) /'eɪgju/: fever – 13 *cholera* (n.) /'kolərə/: a disease which attacks the stomach –

Two English sisters, Catharine Parr Traill and Susanna Moodie came to Upper Canada with their husbands in 1832. Catharine in her books *The Backwoods of Canada* (1836) and *The Female Emigrant's Guide* (1854), gave practical advice—and warnings—to English emigrants. In *Roughing It in the Bush* (1852) Susanna told of feeling like a "criminal ... his only hope of escape being through the grave." But she escaped from a forest fire and a bear, and in 1853 produced a more optimistic book, *Life in the Clearings*.

Moodie had made during the winter a large clearing of twenty acres around the house. The progress of the workmen had been watched by me with the keenest interest. Every tree that reached the ground opened a wider gap in the dark wood, giving us a broader ray of light and a clearer glimpse of the blue sky. But when the dark cedar swamp fronting the house fell beneath the strokes of the axe, and we got a first view of the lake, my joy was complete; a new and beautiful object was now constantly before me, which gave me the greatest pleasure. By night and day, in sunshine or in storm, water is always the most sublime feature in a landscape, and no view can be truly grand in which it is wanting. From a child, it always had the most powerful effect upon my mind, from the green ocean rolling in majesty, to the tinkling forest rill, hidden by the flowers and rushes along its banks. Half the solitude of my forest home vanished when the lake unveiled its bright face to the blue heavens, and I saw sun, and moon, and stars, and waving trees reflected there. I would sit for hours at the window as the shades of evening deepened round me, watching the massy foliage of the forests pictured in the waters, till fancy transported me back to England, and the songs of birds and the lowing of cattle were sounding in my ears. It was long, very long, before I could discipline my mind to learn and practise all the menial employments which are necessary in a good settler's wife.

---

15 *Moodie:* Mr. Moodie, the author's husband — 15 *acre* (n.): G. ca. 2 Morgen — 18 **gap** (n.): an empty space between two objects — 19 *cedar* (n.) /'sidə/: G. Zeder — 19 *front* (v.): to face, to stand opposite to — 23 *sublime* (adj.): wonderful — 23 **landsape** (n.): open country — 25 *majesty* (n.): greatness — 25 *tinkle* (v.): to make a series of sounds like those of a small bell — 26 *rill* (n.): a small stream — 26 *rushes* (n.): G. Binsen — 26 *solitude* (n.): the state of being alone — 30 *massy* (adj.): heavy — 30 *foliage* (n.) /'fəʊlɪdʒ/: leaves in general — 32 *low* (v.): to produce deep tones — 33 *discipline* (v.): to train — 33 *menial* (adj.): low, fit for servants — 33 **employment** (n.): work, business

3: RICK SALUTIN: 1837: The Farmers' Revolt

Rick Salutin was born in Toronto in 1942 and won academic degrees at Brandeis University in Walthem, Mass., at Columbia University and the New School for Social Research in New York City (Ph.D.). Originally his aim had been to become a rabbi, but later he turned to the labour movement and became a union activist. Salutin has written various articles for magazines. His first play *Fanshen* was produced in Toronto in 1972, followed by others in which he showed deep concern for ordinary people. *Scenes From 1837: The Farmer's Revolt* was published in 1976, after it had been created together with a group of actors in 1972/73. The play takes sides with the rebels who fought against the oligarchy in Upper Canada, now Ontario, in 1837.

From: *1837. William Lyon Mackenzie and the Canadian Revolution.* Rick Salutin and Theatre Passe Muraille, Toronto, James Lorimer and Company, 1976, pp. 205–208.

Use your own dictionary for any unknown words.

(From Act I)

WALKING

A man is walking on the set. He carries an axe and a sack. He walks and walks, seeing the forests and the occasional cleared farm of Upper Canada pass by him as he goes. The audience are still entering. They are asking each other, Who is he? Where's he going? What's he got with him? *He keeps walking. This is a play about a time when people in Canada walked to get anywhere and do anything. Eventually two farmers enter, one stage left, and one stage right. They are taking a rest. They watch him go by their field.*

FIRST FARMER: Who is that fellow?

SECOND: Name's Thomas Campbell.

FIRST: Where's he from?

SECOND: Glasgow.

He walks. Enter two more farmers.

THIRD FARMER: Where's he going?

FOURTH: He's bought a plot of land near Coldwater.

They watch him awhile. They are all tired from hard work.

SECOND: How much did it cost him?

---

revolt (n.): a violent act against those in power – *academic degree:* a rank given by a university to a student – *Ph. D.:* Doctor of Philosophy – *rabbi* (n.): a teacher of the Jewish law – *labour movement:* the workers' movement – *union* (n.): an organization to protect the interests of the workers – *activist* (n.): a person taking an active part in a political or other movement – **take sides with** (v.): to be on one side or the other in a quarrel – *oligarchy* (n.): government or rule by a few.

16 *Coldwater:* a place in Ontario, between Lake Simcoe and Georgian Bay –

FIRST: Twenty dollars down—he'll work the rest out.

FOURTH: How long has be been walking?

THIRD: Four and a half days.

FIRST: *Feeling his own feet.* Ouch.

SECOND: Does he have any family?

FOURTH: Wife. Son. Three daughters. Younger brother. All back in Scotland. They'll be over later.

THIRD: What's he got with him?

FIRST: Everything he owns.

SECOND: Think he knows how to use that axe?

THIRD: If he doesn't, he'll learn.

FIRST: What does he see?

THIRD: Trees.

SECOND: Trees.

FOURTH: Trees.

FIRST: Trees and trees and trees and trees—

They all fill in the word "trees" as he speaks. They are planting a forest of trees with their voices. It mounts, then recedes and dies.

THIRD: What's he going to do when he gets there?

He gets there. He puts down his load, very weary. Looks around at the trees, up at the trees, tries to see through to the sky. He decides not to rest, raises his axe, and begins clearing his land.

BLACK

CLEARING

Grunts and sounds of straining in the dark. Lights up slowly. Four people working around a great (imaginary) stump, hacking and hauling at it. With one mighty heave it comes loose and they fall away from it, spent.

VOICE: *Offstage.* Hallooooo—
STEADMAN: *Panting.* Hallooo—

VOICE: *Offstage.* Is there a Peter Steadman there?

They lie there, too exhausted to respond. Enter Magistrate Thompson, obviously an official. He approaches one of them.

MAGISTRATE: Peter Steadman?

He is motioned toward Steadman.

MAGISTRATE: Magistrate Thompson, from Richmond Hill.

---

53 *Richmond Hill:* a small village north of Toronto, now a suburb of the city —

STEADMAN: Magistrate, how do you do? *With distaste, the Magistrate shakes Steadman's sweaty hand.* It's a long ride from Richmond Hill. Will you take something to drink? Sit down?

MAGISTRATE: Thank you, no.

STEADMAN'S WIFE: Can I get you anything?

MAGISTRATE: No. I was told I would find you here.

STEADMAN: We've been here a long time.

MAGISTRATE: How long, exactly?

STEADMAN: Close to two years.

MAGISTRATE: This is fine land. How much have you cleared?

STEADMAN: Eighteen acres.

STEADMAN'S BROTHER: Eighteen acres in two years!

STEADMAN'S WIFE: We've been working hard.

MAGISTRATE: Yes. Congratulations. That's a fine home.

STEADMAN'S WIFE: First one I've ever had that was my own.

STEADMAN: We were going to come up to Toronto to see you people pretty soon.

MAGISTRATE: Good, black, fertile soil.

STEADMAN: Yes, it's a good farm.

MAGISTRATE: Could I see your deed please, Mr. Steadman?

STEADMAN: I don't have a deed.

MAGISTRATE: Then your letter of license.

STEADMAN: Now I wouldn't have one of those without a deed, would I?

MAGISTRATE: Mr. Steadman, don't presume to tell me my business. *He unrolls a survey map, which looks to us like a Union Jack.* Your lot is number seventeen. On this government survey map, lot seventeen, here in this corner—I see no record whatever of the name Steadman. But it *is* part of a parcel of one thousand acres which was granted three weeks ago to Colonel Sparling of the Forty-Eighth Highlanders.

STEADMAN: Granted!

MAGISTRATE: By the Lieutenant-Governor.

STEADMAN'S SISTER-IN-LAW: This farm is not for sale!

STEADMAN'S BROTHER: You listen—we homesteaded this land.

MAGISTRATE: I choose to call it squatting.

---

77 *Union Jack:* the British flag – 81 *Forty-Eight Highlanders:* a Scottish regiment in the British army – 83 *Lieutenant-Governor:* the representative of the Queen of England in a Canadian province

STEADMAN'S BROTHER: Call it what you want. It's what everybody does when they don't have any money to start.

MAGISTRATE: And everybody who does it accepts the risk that something of this sort will happen.

STEADMAN: *Trying to be reasonable.* I'll be glad to go down to Toronto and talk to this Colonel and buy the land from him.

MAGISTRATE: Mr. Steadman, I know with certainty that he simply does not want you on his land. He is not however an ungenerous man, and if you approach him on the right footing, he might be willing to recompense you for your labour on his land.

STEADMAN'S BROTHER: How's he going to pay us for two years of clearing?

MAGISTRATE: He wants you off the land. You have one week, Steadman.

STEADMAN: *Burning.* You have one minute, Magistrate—to get off my farm.

Steadman's brother picks up his axe. The Magistrate beats a retreat.

MAGISTRATE: *As he goes.* One week Steadman—

STEADMAN: *Calling after him.* We'll be here a week from now, Magistrate. We'll be here long after you're dead—

Left alone again, the anger quickly drops away and doubt sets in.

STEADMAN'S WIFE: What do we do now?

STEADMAN: *Ponders, then*—Go back to work. Come on—

They set in around the stump again, straining and grunting. Lights down slowly to black.

An early settler's log cabin

4: ROBERTSON DAVIES: The Village of Deptford*

Robertson Davies was born in Thamesville, Ont., in 1913, which he later depicted as Deptford in three of his many novels, of which *Fifth Business* (1970) is perhaps the best known. He attended Upper Canada College (a private high school), Queen's University in Kingston, Ont. and Balliol College in Oxford. For two seasons he worked with the Old Vic Company in London. After his return to Canada he became a magazine and newspaper editor, a famous playwright, director, a widely read novelist and Master of Massey College, Toronto. He has been awarded many honours for his academic, literary, and theatrical achievements. Robertson Davies can be called the grand old man of Canadian letters.

In the third chapter of *Fifth Business* he introduces the village of Deptford, where the novel's principal character, the schoolmaster Dunstan Ramsay, was born. It is a true replica not only of Thamesville but also of the average village or small town in Ontario. The novel is Ramsay's alleged autobiography, beginning December 27th, 1908, when he evaded a snowball thrown at him by his friend Percy Boyd Staunton. It fatally hit Mrs. Mary Dempster's head instead.

The book, however, not only narrates the often unusual incidences in Ramsay's life, but also the roles that he played as Fifth Business (i. e. aș a minor part) in the life of others.

The text is taken from:
Robertson Davis: *Fifth Business*, New York, The Viking Press, 1970, pp. 15–18.

Thamesville: a town in western Ontario – **depict** (v.): to describe – *Old Vic Company:* a famous theatre company in London – *editor* (n.): a person who is responsible for the organization and opinions of a newspaper or magazine – **playwright** (n.): a writer of plays – *director* (n.): a person who is responsible for the production of plays – *award* (v.): to give as a prize – *letters* (n.): literature – *replica* (n.): a close copy – *allege* (v.): to state without proof – *evade* (v.): to get out of the way of – **narrate** (v.): to tell a story – **roles** (n.): parts – *minor* (adj.): smaller –

Village life has been so extensively explored by movies and television during recent years that you may shrink from hearing more about it. I shall be as brief as I can, for it is not by piling up detail that I hope to achieve my picture, but by putting the emphasis where I think it belongs.

Once it was the fashion to represent villages as places inhabited by laughable, lovable simpletons, unspotted by the worldliness of city life, though occasionally shrewd in rural concerns. Later it was the popular thing to show villages as rotten with vice, and especially such sexual vice as Krafft-Ebing might have been surprised to uncover in Vienna; incest, sodomy, bestiality, sadism, and masochism were supposed to rage behind the lace curtains and in the haylofts, while a rigid piety was professed in the streets. Our village never seemed to me to be like that. It was more varied in what it offered to the observer than people from bigger and more sophisticated places generally think, and if it had sins and follies and roughness, it also had much to show of virtue, dignity, and even of nobility.

It was called Deptford and lay on the Thames River about fifteen miles east of Pittstown, our county town and nearest big place. We had an official population of about five hundred, and the surrounding farms probably brought the district up to eight hundred souls. We had five churches: the Anglican, poor but believed to have some mysterious social supremacy; the Presbyterian, solvent and thought—chiefly by itself—to be intellectual; the Methodist, insolvent and fervent; the Baptist, insolvent and saved; the Roman Catholic, mysterious to most of us but clearly solvent, as it was frequently and, so we thought, quite needlessly repainted. We supported one lawyer, who was also the magistrate, and one banker in a private bank, as such things

---

4 *emphasis* (n.): special force given to words, ideas etc. — 5 *laughable* (adj.): causing laughter, funny — 6 *lovable* (adj.): worthy of love, pleasant — 6 *simpleton* (n.): a weak-minded trusting person, G. einfältige Person — 6 *unspotted* (p.p.): not stained — 7 *shrewd* (adj.): clever — 8 *Krafft-Ebing:* Baron Richard von Krafft-Ebing, 1840—1902, a famous psychiatrist, whose *Psychopatia Sexualis* was translated into 7 languages — 9 *Vienna:* the capital of Austria — 9 *incest* (n.): a sexual relationship between close relatives in a family — 9 *sodomy* (n.): anal sex between males or other unnatural sexual practises — 9 *bestiality* (n.): sexual relationships between a human being and an animal — 10 *sadism* (n.): fondness for cruelty to other persons often in order to achieve sexual pleasure — 10 *masochism* (n.): the wish to be hurt so as to get sexual pleasure — 11 *hayloft* (n.): the upper storey in a barn used for storing hay — 11 **rigid** (adj.): stiff, firm — 11 **piety** (n.): the showing and feeling of deep respect for God — 11 *profess* (v.): to make plain declaration of one's religious faith — 12 *varied* (adj.): characterized by variety — 13 *sophisticated* (adj.): world-wise — 14 *roughness* (n.): the quality of being rough — 16 *Thames river:* the Thames river in western Ontario — 20 *Anglican* (adj.): referring to the Church of England — 20 *supremacy* (n.): highest position, highest in degree — 21 *Presbyterian* (adj.): referring to a Protestant church governed by a body of people all of equal rank — 21 **solvent** (adj.): having enough money, not in debt — 22 *Methodist* (adj.): referring to a Christian group which follows the teaching of John Wesley, 1703—1791 — 22 *fervent* (adj.): strong — 22 *Baptist* (adj.): referring to a Protestant church in which only adult people are baptized — 24 **lawyer** (n.): a person who advises people about laws and represents them in court — 25 *magistrate* (n.): judge in the lowest court of law —

still existed at that time. We had two doctors: Dr. McCausland who was reputed to be clever, and Dr. Staunton, who was Percy's father and who was also clever, but in the realm of real estate—he was a great holder of mortgages and owned several farms. We had a dentist, a wretch without manual skill, whose wife underfed him, and who had positively the dirtiest professional premises I have ever seen; and a veterinarian who drank but could rise to an occasion. We had a canning factory, which operated noisily and feverishly when there was anything to can; also a sawmill and a few shops.

The village was dominated by a family called Athelstan, who had done well out of lumber early in the nineteenth century; they owned Deptford's only three-storey house, which stood by itself on the way to the cemetery; most of our houses were of wood, and some of them stood on piles, for the Thames had a trick of flooding. One of the remaining Athelstans lived across the street from us, a poor demented old woman who used from time to time to escape from her nurse-housekeeper and rush into the road, where she threw herself down, raising a cloud of dust like a hen having a dirt-bath, shouting loudly, "Christian men, come and help me!" It usually took the housekeeper and at least one other person to pacify her; my mother often assisted in this way, but I could not do so for the old lady disliked me—I seemed to remind her of some false friend in the past. But I was interested in her madness and longed to talk with her, so I always rushed to rescue when she made one of her breaks for liberty.

My family enjoyed a position of modest privilege, for my father was the owner and editor of the local weekly paper, *The Deptford Banner.* It was not a very prosperous enterprise, but with the job-printing plant it sustained us and we never wanted for anything. My father, as I learned later, never did a gross business of $ 5000 in any year that he owned it. He was not only publisher and editor, but chief mechanic and printer as well, helped by a melancholy youth called Jumper Saul and a girl called Nell Bullock. It was a good little paper, respected and hated as a proper local newspaper should be; the editorial comment, which my father composed directly on the typesetting

---

27 *was reputed to:* had the reputation of — 27 *Percy:* Dunstan Ramsay's friend — 28 *realm* (n.): a world, an area — 28 *real estate* (n.): land, houses etc. — 28 *mortgage* (n.): G. Hypothek — 29 *wretch* (n.): a poor or unhappy person — 29 **manual** (adj.): of or using the hands — 30 *positively* (adv.): really — 31 *premises* (n.): a house or building — 31 *veterinarian* (n.): an animal doctor — 31 *rise to an occasion:* to show that one can deal with a difficult matter — 32 *feverishly* (adv.): very fast and in a state of excitement — 33 *can* (v.): to put into a tin — 33 *sawmill* (n.): a factory where wood is cut into boards — 34 **dominate** (v.): to have controlling influence or power over — 35 **lumber** (n.): building wood — 36 *cemetery* (n.) /'semətrɪ/: an area for the burial of dead people — 37 *pile* (n.): a heavy wooden or other post hammered into the ground — 38 *trick* (n.): a strange or typical habit — 39 *demented* (adj.): mad — 43 *pacify* (v.): to make calm, quiet and satisfied — 46 *rescue* (n.): the act of saving — 47 *break* (n.): an escape — 49 *Banner* (n.): flag — 50 *enterprise* (n.): a business firm — 50 *job-printing plant:* a printing firm which accepts private orders 52 *a gross business of:* a total profit of — 52 *publisher* (n.): a person whose business it is to have some written work printed. G. Verleger — 56 *editorial comment:* the leading article in a newspaper —

machine, was read carefully every week. So we were, in a sense, the literary leaders of the community, and my father had a seat on the Library Board along with the magistrate.

Our household, then, was representative of the better sort of life in the village, and we thought well of ourselves. Some of this good opinion arose from being Scots; my father had come from Dumfries as a young man, but my mother's family had been three generations in Canada without having become a whit less Scots than when her grandparents left Inverness. The Scots, I believed until I was aged at least twenty-five, were the salt of the earth, for although this was never said in our household it was one of those accepted truths which do not need to be laboured. By far the majority of Deptford people had come to Western Ontario from the south of England, so we were not surprised that they looked to us, the Ramsays, for common sense, prudence, and right opinions on virtually everything.

Cleanliness, for example. My mother was clean—oh, but she was clean! Our privy set the sanitary tone of the village. We depended on wells in Deptford, and water for all purposes was heated in a tank called a "cistern" on the side of the kitchen range. Every house had a privy, and these ranked from dilapidated, noisome shacks to quite smart edifices, of which our own was clearly among the best. There has been much hilarity about privies in the years since they became rarities, but they were not funny buildings, and if they were not to become disgraceful they needed a lot of care.

As well as this temple of hygiene we had a "chemical closet" in the house, for use when someone was unwell; it was so capricious and smelly, however, that it merely added a new misery to illness and was rarely set going.

That is all that seems necessary to say about Deptford at present; any necessary additional matter will present itself as part of my narrative. We were serious people, missing nothing in our community and feeling ourselves in no way inferior to larger places. We did, however, look with pitying amusement on Bowles Corners, four miles distant and with a population of one hundred and fifty. To live in Bowles Corners, we felt, was to be rustic beyond redemption.

---

58 *Library Board:* a public committee which is responsible for the library in a town – 62 *Dumfries:* a town in Scotland – 64 *whit* (n.): a small amount – 64 *Inverness:* a town in Scotland – 67 *labour* (v.): to develop in too great detail – 70 *prudence* (n.): the state of being sensible and wise – 70 *virtually* (adv.): practically – 72 *privy* (n.) /ˈprɪvɪ/: outdoor toilet, esp. without a water supply – 72 *sanitary* (adj.): concerning health, here: esp. the treatment of human waste – 74 *rank* (v.): to be in a certain class – 75 *dilapidated* (adj.): broken and old, falling to pieces – 75 *noisome* (adj.): very unpleasant – 75 **shack** (n.): hut – 75 *smart* (adj.): elegant – 75 *edifice* (n.): building – 76 *hilarity* (n.): laughter – 77 *rarity* (n.): something uncommon – 78 *disgraceful* (adj.): shameful – 80 *capricious* (adj.): likely to change suddenly – 80 *smelly* (adj.): unpleasant-smelling – 87 *rustic* (adj.): referring to negative qualities that the countryside has – 88 *redemption* (n.): rescue

5: ALICE MUNRO: An Ounce of Cure

Alice Munro was born in Wingham, Ont. in 1931 and started writing at an early age. After two years at the University of Western Ontario she got married and moved to Vancouver, later to Victoria, B. C. In 1968 her first collection of short stories, containing *An Ounce of Cure*, was published under the title *Dance of the Happy Shades.* A novel, *Lives of Girls and Women* (1971), and four further collections of short stories followed.

Alice Munro often chooses a feminine perspective in her stories, mostly that of a young adolescent girl who feels artistic aspirations rising in her, who faces private and public expectations that she fails to meet, or who has problems with the other sex. The setting of many of these stories lies in Western Ontario where Alice Munro now lives in the town of Clinton.

An Ounce of Cure is taken from: *Dance of the Happy Shades*, Toronto, McGraw-Hill Ryerson Ltd., 1968, pp.75–88.

My parents didn't drink. They weren't rabid about it, and in fact I remember that when I signed the pledge in grade seven, with the rest of that superbly if impermanently indoctrinated class, my mother said, "It's just nonsense and fanaticism, children of that age." My father would drink a beer on a hot day, but my mother did not join him, and–whether accidentally or symbolically –this drink was always consumed *outside* the house. Most of the people we knew were the same way, in the small town where we lived. I ought not to say that it was this which got me into difficulties, because the difficulties I got into were a faithful expression of my own incommodious nature–the same nature that caused my mother to look at me, on any occasion which traditionally calls for feelings of pride and maternal accomplishment (my departure for my first formal dance, I mean, or my hellbent preparations for a descent on college), with an expression of brooding and fascinated despair, as if she could not possibly expect, did not ask, that it should go with me as it did with other girls; the dreamed-of spoils of daughters–orchids, nice boys, diamond rings–would be borne home in due course by the daughters of her friends, but not by me; all she could do was hope for a lesser rather than a greater disaster– an elopement, say, with a boy who could never earn his living, rather than an abduction into the White Slave trade.

---

ounce (n.): 28,35 grams – *B. C.:* British Columbia, Canada's westernmost province – **feminine** (adj.): female – **adolescent** (adj.): young teenager of about 13–16 – *aspiration* (n.): a strong desire to do something great or important – **setting** (n.): the time and place of the action of a book, film etc. – 1 *rabid* (adj.) /'ræbɪd/: not very enthusiastic, not fanatical – 2 *pledge* (n.): a solemn promise – 2 *grade* (n.): any particular year of a school course – 2 **superb** (adj.): wonderful – 3 *impermanently* (adv.): which will change or be lost – 3 *indoctrinate* (v.): to put rigid ideas into someone's mind – 9 *incommodious* (adj.): not convenient – 11 **maternal** (adj.): motherly – 11 *accomplishment* (n.): something completely and successfully done – 12 *departure* (n.): the action of leaving – 12 *hellbent* (adj.): determined to act and careless of danger – 13 *brood* (v.): to think sadly about something – 13 **fascinate** (v.): to attract beyond one's will – 15 *spoils* (n.): rewards gained by conquest – 15 *orchids* (n.): G. Orchideen – 16 *in due course:* in or at the proper time – 18 *elopement* (n.): running away secretely with a lover (to marry) – 18 *living* (n.): wages, income – 19 *abduction* (n.): taking a person away unlawfully –

But ignorance, my mother said, ignorance, or innocence if you like, is not always such a fine thing as people think and I am not sure it may not be dangerous for a girl like you; then she emphasized her point, as she had a habit of doing, with some quotation which had an innocent pomposity and odour of mothballs. I didn't even wince at it, knowing full well how it must have worked wonders with Mr. Berryman.

The evening I baby-sat for the Berrymans must have been in April. I had been in love all year, or at least since the first week in September, when a boy named Martin Collingwood had given me a surprised, appreciative, and rather ominously complacent smile in the school assembly. I never knew what surprised him; I was not looking like anybody but me; I had an old blouse on and my home-permanent had turned out badly. A few weeks after that he took me out for the first time, and kissed me on the dark side of the porch—also, I ought to say, on the mouth; I am sure it was the first time anybody had ever kissed me effectively, and I know that I did not wash my face that night or the next morning, in order to keep the imprint of those kisses intact. (I showed the most painful banality in the conduct of this whole affair, as you will see.) Two months, and a few amatory stages later, he dropped me. He had fallen for the girl who played opposite him in the Christmas production of *Pride and Prejudice.* [...]

That night [the first night of the play] was the beginning of months of real, if more or less self-inflicted, misery for me. Why is it a temptation to refer to this sort of thing lightly, with irony, with amazement even, at finding oneself involved with such preposterous emotions in the unaccountable past? That is what we are apt to do, speaking of love; with adolescent love, of course, it's practically obligatory; you would think we sat around, dull afternoons, amusing ourselves with these tidbit recollections of pain. But it really doesn't make me feel very gay—worse still, it doesn't really surprise me—to remember all the stupid, sad, half-ashamed things I did, that people in love always do. I hung around the places where he might be seen, and then pretended not to see him; I made absurdly roundabout approaches, in conversa-

---

20 *innocence* (n.): guiltlessness – 22 **emphasize** (v.): to place special force on – 23 **quotation** (n.): the act of repeating the words of another person – 23 *pomposity* (n.): the quality of being foolishly solemn – 24 *mothball* (n.): a small ball used for keeping away insects which eat wool – 24 *wince* (v.): to shrink or start back (mentally) – 28 *appreciative* (adj.): /ə'priʃətɪv/: admiring – 29 *ominously* (adv.): referring to a sign that something bad is going to happen in the future G.: verhängnisvoll – 29 *complacent* (adj.): pleased, self-satisfied – 31 *home-permanent* (n.) G.: selbstgemachte Dauerwelle – 33 *porch* (n.): veranda(h) – 35 *imprint* (n.): a mark left on something – 36 *intact* (adj.): whole – 36 *banality* (n.): something that is uninteresting because it is very common – 37 *amatory* (adj.): concerning sexual love – 38 *fall for* (v.): to fall in love with – 39 *Pride and Prejudice:* the title of a novel by Jane Austen (1775–1817) – 41 *inflict* (v.): to cause – 41 **temptation** (n.): attraction to do something unwise – 42 **irony** (n.): use of words which are opposite to one's meaning – 42 *amazement* (n.): a great surprise – 43 *preposterous* (adj.): absurd – 43 *unaccountable* (adj.): not easily explained – 44 *apt to do:* likely to do – 45 *obligatory* (adj.) /əb'lɪgətrɪ/: necessary – 46 *tidbit* (adj.): choice, or very specially chosen – 46 *recollection* (n.): memory – 50 *absurdly* (adv.) /əb'sɜdlɪ/: against reason, foolish – 50 *roundabout* (adj.): indirect – 50 *approach* (n.): the act of coming near or nearer to –

tion, to the bitter pleasure of casually mentioning his name. I day-dreamed endlessly; in fact if you want to put it mathematically, I spent perhaps ten times as many hours thinking about Martin Collingwood–yes, pining and weeping for him–as I ever spent with him; the idea of him dominated my mind relentlessly and, after a while, against my will. For if at first I had dramatized my feelings, the time came when I would have been glad to escape them; my well-worn daydreams had become depressing and not even temporarily consoling. As I worked my math problems I would torture myself, quite mechanically and helplessly, with an exact recollection of Martin kissing my throat. I had an exact recollection of *everything*. One night I had an impulse to swallow all the aspirins in the bathroom cabinet, but stopped after I had taken six. [...]

The night I went to the Berrymans' was a Saturday night. I baby-sat for them quite often on Saturday nights because they liked to drive over to Baileyville, a much bigger, livelier town about twenty miles away, and perhaps have supper and go to a show. [...]

When the Berrymans and their friends had gone I went into the living room and read a magazine. I was mortally depressed. The big softly lit room, with its green and leaf-brown colours, made an uncluttered setting for the development of the emotions, such as you would get on a stage. At home the life of the emotions went on all right, but it always seemed to get buried under the piles of mending to be done, the ironing, the children's jigsaw puzzles, and rock collections. It was the sort of house where people were always colliding with one another on the stairs and listening to hockey games and Superman on the radio.

I got up and found the Berrymans' "Danse Macabre" and put it on the record player and turned out the living-room lights. The curtains were only partly drawn. A street light shone obliquely on the windowpane, making a rectangle of thin dusty gold, in which the shadows of bare branches moved, caught in the huge sweet winds of spring. It was a mild black night when the last snow was melting. A year ago all this–the music, the wind and darkness, the shadows of the branches–would have given me tremendous happiness; when they did not do so now, but only called up tediously familiar, somehow humiliatingly personal thoughts, I gave up my soul for dead and walked into the kitchen and decided to get drunk. [...]

Gravely, with a glance at my set face in the black window above the sink,

---

51 *casually* (adv.): by chance – 53 *pine* (v.): to have an unfulfillable desire – 54 **dominate** (v.): to have controlling influence over – 55 *relentlessly* (adv.): without pity – 56 *dramatize* (v.): to make s.th. exciting – 57 **depressing** (adj.): sad – 58 **console** (v.): to comfort, cheer, relieve – 58 *math* (n.): mathematics – 61 *aspirins* (n.): a medicine that lessens pain and fever – 61 *cabinet* (n.): a piece of furniture for storing small objects – 69 *uncluttered* (adj.): tidy, orderly – 72 *jigsaw puzzles* /dʒɪgsɔ pʌzlz/ G. Puzzlespiele – 74 *collide* (v.): to strike or dash against each other – 78 *obliquely* (adv.): indirectly – 78 *windowpane* (n.): the glass in a window – 79 *rectangle* (n.): a figure with 4 right angles, G.: Rechteck – 83 *tedious* (adj.): long and tiring, uninteresting – 84 *humiliate* (v.): to cause to feel humble – 84 *give up for dead:* to consider s.th. absolutely lost –

I poured a little whisky from each of the bottles (I think now there were two brands of rye and an expensive Scotch) until I had my glass full. For I had never in my life seen anyone pour a drink and I had no idea that people frequently diluted their liquor with water, soda, et cetera, and I had seen the glasses the Berrymans' guests were holding when I came through the living room were nearly full.

I drank it off as quickly as possible. I set the glass down and stood looking at my face in the window, half expecting to see it altered. My throat was burning, but I felt nothing else. It was very disappointing, when I had worked myself up to it. But I was not going to let it go at that. I poured another full glass, then filled each of the bottles with water to approximately the level I had seen when I came in. I drank the second glass only a little more slowly than the first. I put the empty glass down on the counter with care, perhaps feeling in my head a rustle of things to come, and went and sat down on a chair in the living room. I reached up and turned on a floor lamp beside the chair, and the room jumped on me. [...]

From this point on I have no continuous picture of what happened; my memories of the next hour or two are split into vivid and improbable segments, with nothing but murk and uncertainty between. I do remember lying on the bathroom floor looking sideways at the little six-sided white tiles, which lay together in such an admirable and logical pattern, seeing them with the brief broken gratitude and sanity of one who has just been torn into pieces with vomiting. Then I remember sitting on the stool in front of the hall phone, asking weakly for Joyce's number. Joyce was not home. I was told by her mother (a rattlebrained woman, who didn't seem to notice a thing the matter–for which I felt weakly, mechanically grateful) that she was at Kay Stringer's house. I didn't know Kay's number so I just asked the operator; I felt I couldn't rise looking down at the telephone book. [...]

I got Joyce on the phone. She was very keyed-up, as she always was with boys around, and she hardly seemed to hear what I was saying. [...]

"I'm *sick*," I said, trying to speak distinctly; it came out an inhuman croak. "I'm *drunk*, Joyce!" Then I fell off the stool and the receiver dropped out of my hand and banged for a while dismally against the wall.

---

88 *brand* (n.): the name of the company that manufactures a certain product – 88 *rye* (n.): G.: Roggen, a kind of whisky, typical of Canada – 90 *dilute* (v.): /daɪ'ljuːt/: to make a liquid weaker or thinner – 90 *soda* (n.): water filled under pressure with gas – 95 *work oneself up to:* here: to overcome doubts and fears and finish the drink – 97 *approximate* (adj.): nearly correct but not exact – 100 *rustle* (n.): the sound of paper, dry leaves etc. – 104 **vivid** (adj.): that produces sharp clear pictures in the mind – 104 *segment* (n.): a part of something that has been cut or divided – 105 *murk* (n.): darkness – 107 *tile* (n.): G. Kachel – 107 **admirable** (adj.): excellent, causing admiration – 107 *logical* (adj.): according to the rules of reason – 108 *sanity* (n.): the quality of being healthy in mind or body – 109 **vomit** (v.): to throw up the contents of the stomach through the mouth – 109 *stool* (n.): a seat without back or arm rest – 111 *rattlebrained* (adj.): foolish and always talking – 112 *a thing the matter:* anything wrong – 114 *operator* (n.): a person who connects phone calls – 115 *keyed-up* (v.): to be excited or nervous – 117 *croak* (n.): a rough sound as produced by a frog – 119 *bang* (v.): to beat with a loud noise – 119 *dismally* (adv.): sadly –

I had not told Joyce where I was, so after thinking about it for a moment she phoned my mother, and using the elaborate and unnecessary subterfuge that young girls delight in, she found out. She and Kay and the boys—there were three of them—told some story about where they were going to Kay's mother, and got into the car and drove out. They found me still lying on the broadloom carpet in the hall; I had been sick again, and this time I had not made it to the bathroom.

It turned out that Kay Stringer, who arrived on this scene only by accident, was exactly the person I needed. She loved a crisis, particularly one like this, which had a shady and scandalous aspect and which must be kept secret from the adult world. She became excited, aggressive, efficient; that energy which was termed wildness was simply the overflow of a great female instinct to manage, comfort, and control. I could hear her voice coming at me from all directions, telling me not to worry, telling Joyce to find the biggest coffeepot they had and make it full of coffee (*strong* coffee, she said), telling the boys to pick me up and carry me to the sofa. Later, in the fog beyond my reach, she was calling for a scrub-brush. [...]

Kay brought me a huge breakfast mug full of coffee.

"I don't know if I can," I said. "Thanks."

"Sit up," she said briskly, as if dealing with drunks was an everyday business for her so I had no need to feel myself important. (I met, and recognized, that tone of voice years later, in the maternity ward.) "Now drink," she said. I drank, and at the same time realized that I was wearing only my slip. Joyce and Kay had taken off my blouse and skirt. They had brushed off the skirt and washed out the blouse, since it was nylon; it was hanging in the bathroom. I pulled the throw up under my arms and Kay laughed. She got everybody coffee. Joyce brought in the coffeepot and on Kay's instructions she kept filling my cup whenever I drank from it. Somebody said to me with interest. "You must have really wanted to tie one on."

"No," I said rather sulkily, obediently drinking my coffee. "I only had two drinks."

Kay laughed, "Well it certainly gets to you, I'll say that. What time do you expect *they'll* get back?" she said.

"Late, after one I think."

"You should be all right by that time. Have some more coffee."

Kay and one of the boys began dancing to the radio. Kay danced very sexily, but her face had the gently superior and indulgent, rather cold look it

---

121 *subterfuge* (n.) /'sʌbtəfjudʒ/: trick — 125 *broadloom carpet:* carpet, especially in one singular colour — 129 *shady* (adj.): very doubtful — 129 *scandalous* (adj.): offensive to feelings of what is right or proper — 130 **adult** (adj.): referring to a fully grown person — 130 *efficient* (adj.): working well and without waste — 131 *term* (v.): to call — 136 *scrub-brush* (n.): a stiff brush for heavy cleaning — 137 *mug* (n): a round drinking vessel with a flat bottom and a handle — 139 *briskly* (adv.): quickly and actively — 141 *maternity ward:* a division of a hospital in which women give birth to children — 145 *throw* (n.): a piece of fancy needlework to cover s.th. — 148 *tie one on* (v.): to get drunk — 149 *sulkily* (adv.): showing negative feelings against others —

had when she was lifting me up to drink the coffee. The boy was whispering to her and she was smiling, shaking her head. Joyce said that she was hungry, and she went out to the kitchen to see what there was—potato chips or crackers, or something like that, that you could eat without making too noticeable a dint. Bill Kline came over and sat on the sofa beside me and patted my legs through the crocheted throw. He didn't say anything to me, just patted my legs and looked at me with what seemed to me a very stupid, half-sick, absurd, and alarming expression. I felt very uncomfortable; I wondered how it had ever got around that Bill Kline was so good looking, with an expression like that. I moved my legs nervously and he gave me a look of contempt, not ceasing to pat me. Then I scrambled off the sofa, pulling the throw around me, with the idea of going to the bathroom to see if my blouse was dry. I lurched a little when I started to walk, and for some reason—probably to show Bill Kline that he had not panicked me—I immediately exaggerated this, and calling out, "Watch me walk a straight line!" I lurched and stumbled, to the accompaniment of everyones's laughter, towards the hall. I was standing in the archway between the hall and the living room when the knob of the front door turned with a small matter-of-fact click and everything became silent behind me except the radio of course; and the crocheted throw inspired by some delicate malice of its own slithered down around my feet, and there—oh, delicious moment in a well-organized farce—there stood the Berrymans, Mr. and Mrs., with expressions on their faces as appropriate to the occasion as any old-fashioned director of farces could wish. They must have been preparing those expressions, of course; they could not have produced them in the first moment of shock; with the noise we were making, they had no doubt heard us as soon as they got out of the car; for the same reason, we had not heard them. I don't think I ever knew what brought them home so early—a headache, an argument—and I was not really in a position to ask.

Mr. Berryman drove me home. I don't remember how I got into that car, or how I found my clothes and put them on, or what kind of a good night, if any, I said to Mrs. Berryman. I don't remember what happened to my friends, though I imagine they gathered up their coats and fled, covering up the ignominy of their departure with a mechanical roar of defiance. [...]

---

156 *indulgent* (adj.): forgiving – 161 *dint* (n.): the trace of something missing – 162 *pat* (v.): to touch or strike gently and repeatedly – 127 *scramble* (v.): to move quickly, not gracefully – 169 *lurch* (v.): to move with irregular sudden movements – 170 *panic* (v.): to cause somebody to feel fear – 171 **exaggerate** (v.): /ɪg'zædʒəreɪt/: to make something seem larger, better, worse than in reality – 172 *accompaniment* (n.) /'əkʌmpnɪmənt/: s.th. which is often found with s.th. else – 173 *archway* (n) /'ɑtʃweɪ/: an entrance through a curved top – 174 *knob* (n.): a round handle or control button – 174 *matter-of-fact:* realistic, not fanciful – 175 *click* (n.): a slight short sound – 176 *crocheted throw* (n.): /'krəuʃeɪd/: G. Häkeldecke – 176 *slither* (v.): to move in a slipping way – 178 *farce* (n.): a silly and empty show, a silly play – 179 **appropriate** (adj.): suitable – 190 *ignominy* (n.) /'ɪgnəmɪnɪ/: shame or dishonour – 190 *roar* (n.): a deep loud sound – 190 *defiance* (n.): in disregard, state of showing no fear or respect –

Mr. Berryman said to me, "Well I guess you know your behaviour tonight is a pretty serious thing." He made it sound as if I might be charged with criminal negligence or something worse. "It would be very wrong of me to overlook it," he said. I suppose that besides being angry and disgusted with *me*, he was worried about taking me home in this condition to my strait-laced parents, who could always say I got the liquor in his house. Plenty of Temperance people would think that enough to hold him responsible, and the town was full of Temperance people. Good relations with the town were very important to him from a business point of view.

"I have an idea it wasn't the first time," he said. "If it was the first time, would a girl be smart enough to fill three bottles up with water? No. Well, in this case, she *was* smart enough, but not smart enough to know I could spot it. What do you say to that?" I opened my mouth to answer, and although I was feeling quite sober the only sound that came out was a loud, desolate-sounding giggle. He stopped in front of our house. "Light's on," he said. "Now go in and tell your parents the straight truth. And if you don't, remember I will." He did not mention paying me for my baby-sitting services of the evening and the subject did not occur to me either.

I went into the house and tried to go straight upstairs but my mother called to me. She came into the front hall, where I had not turned on the light, and she must have smelled me at once for she ran forward with a cry of pure amazement, as if she had seen somebody falling, and caught me by the shoulders as I did indeed fall down against the banister, overwhelmed by my fantastic lucklessness, and I told her everything from the start, not omitting even the name of Martin Collingwood and my flirtation with the aspirin bottle, which was a mistake.

On Monday morning my mother took the bus over to Baileyville and found the liquor store and bought a bottle of Scotch whiskey. Then she had to wait for a bus back, and she met some people she knew and she was not quite able to hide the bottle in her bag; she was furious with herself for not bringing a proper shopping bag. As soon as she got back she walked out to the Berrymans'; she had not even had lunch. Mr. Berryman had not gone back to the factory. My mother went in and had a talk with both of them and made an excellent impression and then Mr. Berryman drove her home. She talked to them in the forthright and unemotional way she had, which was always agreeably surprising to people prepared to deal with a mother, and she told them that although I seemed to do well enough at school I was extremely backward—or perhaps eccentric—in my emotional development. I imagine that this analysis of my behaviour was especially effective with Mrs.

---

192 *charge* (v.): to accuse – 194 *disgusted* (adj.): showing a strong feeling or dislike – 195 *strait-laced* (adj.): having firm ideas about morals – 197 *Temperance people:* people who strictly avoid alcohol – 201 *smart* (adj.): clever – 204 **desolate** (adj.): sad, empty – 212 *amazement* (n.): great surprise – 213 *banister* (n.): G.: Treppengeländer – 215 *flirtation* (n.): a passing interest in s. th. – 225 *forthright* (adj.): direct – 225 *unemotional* (adj.): without (strong) feelings – 228 *eccentric* (adj.): peculiar, rather strange – 229 *analysis* (n.): an examination of something –

Berryman, a great reader of Child Guidance books. Relations between them warmed to the point where my mother brought up a specific instance of my difficulties, and disarmingly related the whole story of Martin Collingwood.

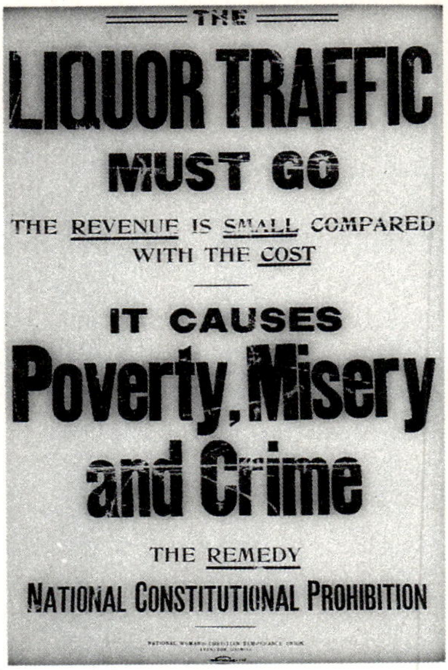

Within a few days it was all over town and the school that I had tried to commit suicide over Martin Collingwood. But it was already all over school and the town that the Berrymans had come home on Saturday night to find me drunk, staggering, wearing nothing but my slip, in a room with three boys, one of whom was Bill Kline. [...]

If you think that news of the Berrymans' adventure would put me in demand for whatever gambols and orgies were going on in and around that town, you could not be more mistaken. The extraordinary publicity which attended my first debauch may have made me seem marked for a special kind of ill luck, like the girl whose illegitimate baby turns out to be triplets: nobody wants to have anything to do with her. At any rate I had at the same time one of the most silent telephones and positively the most sinful reputation in the whole High School. I had to put up with this until the next fall, when a fat blonde girl in grade ten ran away with a married man and was picked up two months later, living in sin—though not with the same man—in the city of Sault Ste. Marie. Then everybody forgot about me.

But there was a positive, a splendidly unexpected, result of this affair; I got completely over Martin Collingwood. It was not only that he at once said, publicly, that he had always thought I was a nut; where he was concerned I had no pride, and my tender fancy could have found a way around that, a month, a week, before. What was it that brought me back into the world again? It was the terrible and fascinating reality of my disaster; it was *the way things happened.* Not that I enjoyed it; I was a self-conscious girl and I

---

230 *Child Guidance books:* books which give advice on the education of children – 232 *disarmingly* (adv.): acting so as to leave someone helpless – 234 **commit suicide:** to kill oneself – 239 *gambol* (n.) an activity done in play, esp. jumping about – 239 *orgy* (n.) /ˈɔdʒɪ/: a wild party – 241 *debauch* (n.) /dɪˈbɔtʃ/: going beyond certain limits of behaviour esp. in relation to sex and alcohol – 242 **illegitimate** (adj.) /ɪlɪˈdʒɪtɪmət/: born to a mother who is not married – 243 *triplets* (n.): 3 children born of the same mother at the same time – 245 *put up with* (v.): to suffer without complaining – 248 *Sault Ste. Marie* /ˈsu sent məˈri/: an industrial city in Ontario between Lakes Huron und Superior – 251 *nut* (n.): sl. a person who seems unbalanced in mind – 255 **self-conscious** (adj.): nervous and uncomfortable about oneself –

suffered a good deal from all this exposure. But the development of events on that Saturday night—that fascinated me; I felt that I had had a glimpse of the shameless, marvellous, shattering absurdity with which the plots of life, though not of fiction, are improvised. I could not take my eyes off it.

And of course Martin Collingwood wrote his Senior Matric that June and went away to the city to take a course at a school for Morticians, as I think it is called, and when he came back he went into his uncle's undertaking business. We lived in the same town and we would hear most things that happened to each other but I do not think we met face to face or saw one another, except at a distance, for years. I went to a shower for the girl he married, then everybody went to everybody else's showers. No, I do not think I really saw him again until I came home after I had been married several years, to attend a relative's funeral. Then I saw him; not quite Mr. Darcy but still very nice-looking in those black clothes. And I saw him looking over at me with an expression as close to a reminiscent smile as the occasion would permit, and I knew that he had been surprised by a memory either of my devotion or of my little buried catastrophe. I gave him a gentle uncomprehending look in return. I am a grown-up woman now; let him unbury his own catastrophes.

---

256 *exposure* (n.): the state of being left without protection — 258 *shattering* (adj.): having a strong effect on the feelings of s. o. — 258 *absurdity* (n.): s.th. that goes against reason or common sense — 258 **plot** (n.): a secret plan — 259 *improvise* (v.): to do something one has not prepared — 260 *Senior Matric* — final school exams — 261 *mortician* (n.) /mɔ'tɪʃn/: AE a person who makes all the arrangements for funerals — 262 *undertaking* (n.): referring to the arrangements for funerals — 265 *shower* (n.): a celebration at which gifts are presented — 270 *reminiscent* (adj.): that reminds one of — 272 *uncomprehending* (adj.): showing no understanding —

6: JAMES REANY: First Letter

James Reany, a major Canadian poet, dramatist and writer of children's books, was born near Stratford, Ont. in 1926. He studied English at University College, Toronto, took an M.A. and a doctorate there and later became a professor of English at the University of Manitoba. In 1960 he moved to the University of Western Ontario. He published his first book of poems "The Red Heart" in 1949, followed by three others. Reany is also widely known as a dramatist.

From: *Poems. James Reany*, ed. Germaine Warkenthin, Toronto, New Press, 1972, pp. 211–212.

---

dramatist (n.) /'dræmətɪst/: a writer of serious plays — *M. A.*: the "Master of Arts" degree, following the "Bachelor of Arts" —

FIRST LETTER

To the Avon River above Stratford, Canada

What did the Indians call you?
For you do not flow
With English accents.
I hardly know
What I should call you
    Because before
I drank coffee or tea
    I drank you
    With my cupped hands
And you did not taste English to me
    And you do not sound
    Like Avon
    Or swans & bards
But rather the sad wild fowl
    In prints down
    By Audubon
And like dear bad poets
    Who wrote
    Early in Canada
And never were of note
You are the first river
    I crossed
And like the first whirlwind
    The first rainbow
    First snow, first
    Falling star I saw,
You, for other rivers are my law.
    These other rivers:
    The Red & the Thames
    Are never so sweet
To skate upon, swim in
    Or for baptism of sin.
    Silver and light
The sentence of your voice,
    With a soprano
Continuous cry you shall
    Always flow
    Through my heart.
The rain and the snow of my mind
Shall supply the spring of that river
    Forever.
Though not your name
Your coat of arms I know
    And motto:
A shield of reeds and cresses
    Sedges, crayfishes
The hermaphroditic leech
Minnows, muskrats and farmers' geese
And printed above this shield
One of my earliest wishes
"To flow like you."

---

15 *bard* (n.): poet, singer – 16 *wild fowl* (n.): wild birds – 18 *Audubon:* John James Audubon (1785–1851) a famous American painter, esp. of birds – 22 *be of note* (v.): to be of fame or importance – 25 *whirlwind* (n.): air moving rapidly in a circle – 31 *Red:* the Red River, which rises in the USA and empties into Lake Winnipeg – 31 *the Thames:* the river which runs through London/Ont. – 32 *baptism* (n.): a Christian religious ceremony in which a person is touched or covered with water to make him pure – 45 *coat of arms* (n.): G.: Wappen – 47 *reed* (n.): G. Schilfrohr – 47 *cress* (n.): G. Kresse – 48 *sedge* (n.): G. Riedgras – 48 *crayfishes* (n.): G. Flußkrebs – 49 *hermaphroditic* (adj.): having the appearance of both sexes – 49 *leech* (n.): G. Blutegel – 50 *minnow* (n.): small freshwater fish. G. Elritze – 50 *muskrat* (n.): North American water rat, whose fur is valuable. G.: Bisamratte

V The Prairies

West of the Shield which insulates them so densely from Central Canada, the three prairie provinces really form a single region, since, whatever the slight difference in their topographies and the somewhat larger differences in their political histories, they are united geographically in the great plains that sweep virtually without interruption from Lake of the Woods to the foothills of the Rockies. In cultural traditions they have great similarities, since, despite the original ambition of Ontario to annex the plains by populating them, they were in fact mainly settled by European strains, Germanic and Slavic, quite distinct from the so-called founding peoples the French and the Anglo-Celts. The prairie provinces are also distinguished from the rest of Canada and drawn towards each other by the fact that generation after generation they have bred the great protest movements in Canada, from the Métis rebellions of 1870 and 1885, down through the women's liberation movement early in the twentieth century, the Winnipeg General Strike, the emergence of the Progressive Party and the CCF, to the strength in the Prairies even in our own day of essentially regional parties like the NDP and Social Credit. Politically, indeed, at least throughout the present century, the Prairies have remained quite different from the rest of Canada, except British Columbia, in their largely rural radicalism. Out of this situation has emerged a unique literary culture shaped alike by the extremities of climate and of passion. Only the land is ever level between the Shield and the Rockies.

George Woodcock: *The Meeting of Time and Space*, pp. 13–14.

---

1 *Shield* (n.): The Canadian Shield forms an incomplete ring around Hudson Bay and covers about half the total area of Canada. It is largely unsuitable for agriculture – 1 *densely* (adv.): impenetrably – 3 *topography* (n.): the character of a particular place in detail – 5 *virtually* (adv.): practically – 5 *Lake of the Woods:* a lake on the border between Ontario and Manitoba – 6 *Rockies* (n.): the Rocky Mountains – 6 **similarity** (n.): the quality of being alike – 7 *annex* (v.): to join or add to a greater thing – 8 *strain* (n.): a breed or type – 13 *Métis* (n.): people of mixed French and Indian origin – 14 *the Winnipeg General Strike:* it took place in 1919 – 15 *emergence* (n.): the act of coming or appearing from somewhere – 15 *Progressive Party:* it was formed by Ontario and prairie farmers after the First World War to fight for free trade, nationalization and direct democracy – 15 *CCF:* Cooperative Commonwealth Federation. A political party founded in Calgary in 1932 to fight the effects of the Great Depression. It proposed the nationalization of key industries and the establishment of the welfare state. In 1961 it became the New Democratic Party (NDP) – 16 *NDP:* the New Democratic Party – 17 *Social Credit:* the Social Credit Party, founded in Alberta in 1932 by William Aberhart. Its original idea was to provide the people with a certain amount of free purchasing power in order to bring up the economy again – 19 **rural** (adj.): of the country – 20 **unique** (adj.): being the only one of its type – 20 *extremity* (n.): the utmost point, the limit

Manitoba

Alberta

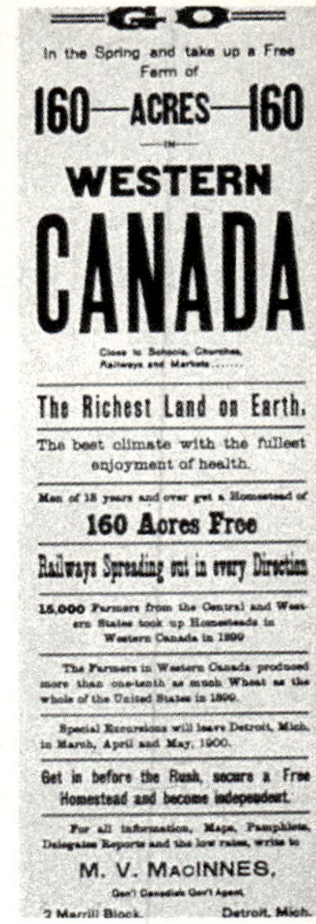

Saskatchewan

Canadian prairie fiction is about a basically European society spreading itself across a very un-European landscape. It is rooted in that first settlement process in which the pioneer faced two main obstacles: the new land and the old culture. The land was a challenge not only physically but psychologically; like all unsettled territory it had no human associations, no ghosts, none of the significance imagination gives to the expressionless face of the earth after men have lived and died there. The prairie, in effect, lacked the fictions which make a place entirely real.

Dick Harrison: *Unnamed Country. The Struggle for a Canadian Prairie Fiction.* Edmonton/Alta., The University of Alberta Press, 1977, p. IX.
Dick Harrison is a professor of English at the University of Alberta in Edmonton.

---

1 **fiction** (n.): novels and stories – 1 *basically* (adv.): in reality – 2 **landscape** (n.): open country – 3 **pioneer** (n.): one of the first settlers in a new land – 3 *obstacle* (n.): s.th. that stands in the way – 5 *association* (n.): connection – 6 **significance** (n.): meaning – 6 *expressionless* (adj.): without expression – 7 *in effect* (n.): here: it is more or less true to say

1: The Alberta Homestead

From: *The Waterloo Folks Songs of Canada*,
ed. Edith Fulton Fowke and Richard Johnston,
Waterloo/Ont., Waterloo Music Comp. Ltd., 1967 pp. 122–113.

THE ALBERTA HOMESTEAD

3. We travelled through Battle Lake Valley,
Through muskeg, mud, and mire,
Till we came where they were surveying
A road for the C.P.R.

4. I built a little log cabin
With a roof of natural clay.
Dear friends, I'm sorry to tell you,
But I'm bound for the U.S.A.

5. Of money I haven't one dollar,
And the grubstake she's run mighty low.
Just as soon as the frog pond froze over,
It's back to the U.S. I'll go.

6. Farewell to the poor homesteader,
Farewell to the land so free,
Farewell to sunny Alberta—
She's too damn cold for me.

2: W. O. MITCHELL: Gopher Hunting*

William Ormond Mitchell was born in Weyburn, Sask. in 1914 and grew up there as well as in St. Petersburg, Florida. After graduating from the University of Alberta he taught at various country schools in Alberta. During this period he started writing fiction, plays and magazine articles, finally becoming a full-time writer. In 1947 he published his most famous novel *Who Has Seen the Wind.* Besides being a novelist and a playwright Mitchell is also known as a teacher of creative writing and a popular radio and television personality. He won the Stephen Leacock Medal for Humour for his radio series *Jake and the Kid* and he was honoured by becoming a member of the Order of Canada.

In *Who Has Seen the Wind* Mitchell narrates formative events in the life of the young Brian O'Connal, who is growing up in a small town in Saskatchewan. Between the ages of four and twelve Brian experiences a number of confrontations, on the prairie, in his family and his town, which make him come to terms with his environment and help him to grasp "the ultimate meaning of the cycle of life". The wide prairie in particular plays an important part on Brian's way to maturity. In chapter 14 Mitchell describes a gopher-hunting expedition by Brian and his friends which ends in a bitter fight between the cruel Art and the Young Ben, who represents unhampered vitality and respect for the sacredness of life. The novel also contains biting criticism of the narrowness and bigotry of small-town society.

The text is taken from:
William Ormond Mitchell: *Who Has Seen the Wind*, Toronto, Macmillan of Canada, repr. 1979, pp. 122–129.

Painting by William Kurelek

Sask.: Saskatchewan /səs'kætʃwən/: the central Canadian prairie province – **graduate** (v.): to take one's final exams at a university – **fiction** (n.): novels, short stories – **playwright** (n.): an author of plays – *creative writing:* the art of writing literature – *Stephen Leacock* (1869–1944): a famous Canadian humorist writer – *Order of Canada:* the most important Canadian award, which has 3 classes of membership – **narrate** (v.): to tell – **formative** (adj.): forming a person's character – *come to terms* (v.): to accept – **environment** (n.) /ɪn'vaɪərnmənt/: surroundings – **grasp** (v.): to understand – **ultimate** (adj.): final – **cycle** (n.): a number of events happening in a regularly repeated order – **maturity** (n.): the state of being fully grown – *gopher* (n.) /'goufə/: G. Erdhörnchen – *unhampered* (adj.): free and easy – **vitality** (n.): power to live, energy – *biting* (adj.): sharp – *bigotry* (n.) /bɪgətrɪ/: intolerance –

Throughout the summer Brian found himself with a heightened eagerness to discover again the strange elation he had experienced early in the spring. He found that many simple and unrelated things could cause the same feeling to lift up and up whithin him till he was sure that he could not contain it. The wind could do this to him, when it washed through poplar leaves, when it set telephone wires humming and twanging down an empty prairie road, when it ruffled the feathers on one of Sherry's roosters standing forlorn in a bare yard, when it carried to him the Indian smell of a burning straw stack. Once the feeling had been caused by the sound of Gaffer Thomas's bucksaw wheehawing impatiently on the other side of the O'Connal back fence; another time, by a crow calling; still another, by the warm smell of bread baking. A tiny garden toad became suddenly magic for him one summer day—the smell of leaf mold, and clover, and wolf willow. Always, he noted, the feeling was most exquisite upon the prairie or when the wind blew.

There had been the day, well on in summer, that he and Forbsie Hoffman, now called "Fat" by one of the mutations common to boyhood, and Art Sherry had gone out drowning gophers. Bobbie had tagged along with them.

Out Sixth Street toward the spreading prairie they walked, Brian and Fat carrying between them Art's mother's washtub. Each carried in addition a red lard pail; Bobbie's bumped awkwardly against his fat legs as he alternately trotted and walked to keep up with the older boys. Once upon the prairie they turned east toward Haggerty's Coulee, where they had heard there were many gophers. While Fat's dog and Jappy ran ahead, the boys wandered in leisurely fashion, their conversation rambling as it usually did, until it arrived at the question of what a gopher did when he was being drowned out.

"Sometimes," Fat said, "you get three washtubs down their hole, and the water stays there quite a while, and you think he ain't ever comin' up, and then all of a sudden she goes down."

"She goes down." Bobbie always echoed the conversation of the other boys, who paid little attention to him.

---

1 *heighten* (v.): to increase — 2 *elation* (n.): the state of being filled with pride and joy — 4 *contain* (v.): to hold back — 5 *poplar* (n.): G. Pappel — 6 *hum* (v.): to make a sound like a continuous "m" — 6 *twang* (v.): to make a quick ringing sound by freeing a very tight string — 7 *ruffle* (v.): to move the smooth surface of s. th. — 7 *rooster* (n.): cock — 7 *forlorn* (adj.): left alone — 8 *Indian* (n./adj.): referring to the "Indian" or late summer — 9 *stack* (n.): a large pile — 10 *bucksaw* (n.): a framed saw operated by hand, G. Steifsäge — 10 *wheehawing* (v.): making the sound of a handsaw — 33 *crow* (n.): G. Krähe — 12 *toad* (n.): G. Kröte — 13 *leaf mold* (n.): good soft soil of leaves — 13 *clover* (n.): G. Klee — 13 *wolf willow* (n.): several kinds of bushes on the prairie — 14 *exquisite* (adj.): very great — 17 *mutation* (n.): change — 18 *tag* (v.): to follow closely — 20 *washtub* (n.): a container for the washing — 21 *lard pail* (n.): a round open vessel with handles which holds pig fat — 21 *bump* (v.): to strike or knock with force — 21 *awkwardly* (adv.): inconveniently — 21 *alternately* (adv.) /ɔl'tɜnətlɪ/: first one then the other — 23 *Coulee* (n.) /'kulɪ/: a deep gully, usually dry in summer — 25 *leisurely* (adv.): moving without haste — 25 *ramble* (v.): to talk in a disordered and wandering way

"They back into the hole an' plug her up," Art explained, his face, as always, grimacing behind the thick spectacles that rode his nose. "When he unplugs, then the water comes down."

"The water comes down."

"You take the end of the washtub now," Brian said to Art.

"Not yet. I'll carry after Haggerty's Coulee."

"You never carry," Brian accused him.

"He never carries." Bobbie echoed his brother's speech most often. [...]

"Look!" Fat cried and pointed to the dogs in scurrying chase over the prairie ahead. "They found one!"

"I don't see any!"

"Where?" yelled Art.

"A girl gopher," said Bobbie mildly. "I knew–"

"There it is!" Brian caught a glimpse of a brown back rolling in frantic gallop, saw the flirt of a tail as the gopher, inches from Jappy's eager nose, was swallowed down a hole. "He's down the hole!"

Both dogs were at the opening. Jappy ecstatically threw the dirt behind him–stopped to insert his nose right to the eyes–took it out–began to dig again. Fat's dog circled anxiously.

"You an' Fat fill the tub!" directed Art. "I'll watch."

"I'll watch too," said Bobbie as Brian and Fat ran off toward the river, the tub between them, the lard pails swinging in their free hands.

They brought back two tubs of water, tipped them carefully down the hole, after each one, watched eagerly for the gopher to come out. Jappy sat with his ears cocked, his head solicitously on one side; he made anxious sounds in the back of his throat.

"Maybe he's got him a back door," suggested Fat after the second tub. "Maybe he's went out the back door–"

"The dogs would of seen him go," said Art. "He hasn't got any back door –more water is what he–look! She's going down now!" One great bubble burst itself on the surface of the water filling the hole; it was followed by many little ones wobbling to the top. "He's took his ass outa the hole, an' he's comin' up now!" shouted Ike with excitement. "Git ready!"

The gopher's flat head broke the surface of the water; just out of reach in the throat of his burrow, he crouched with his head barely above water, his

– 32 *plug* (v.): to block or close up – 33 *grimacing* (v.): to make an unnatural twisting of the face – 40 *scurry* (v.): to move in haste – 45 *frantic* (adj.): wildly anxious – 46 *flirt* (n.): a sudden movement – 46 *inch* (n.): 2,54 cm – 48 *ecstatically* (adv.): showing very strong feeling – 49 *insert* (v.): to put something inside – 54 *tip* (v.): to cause to upset or fall over – 56 *cock* (v.): to stand up – 56 *solicitous* (adj.): carefully interested – 61 *bubble* (n.): a hollow ball of water containing air or gas – 63 *wobble* (v.): to move unsteadily – 63 *ass* (n.): bottom, the lower part of the human back – 66 *burrow* (n.): a hole in the ground made by an animal – 66 *crouch* (v.): to lower the body –

almond eyes looking up at the boys and the dogs. Out of the corner of his eye, Brian could see Jappy's tapered body quivering.

"More water!" shrieked Art. "All he wants is more water! Halfa lard pail an' he'll come all the way out!" Ike rushed to the tub himself, tilted it over the lard pail, ran back, and soused the contents down on the waiting gopher. It came out in a lunging rush, its fawn hair dark with water, plastered wet against its skin. The dogs darted for it. Jappy got it by the scruff of the neck, shook his head, and threw it over his back. The gopher hurtled through the air to land near Art; it lay still upon the prairie. Art ran to it. He picked up the wet, tan body. It began to kick. "He's still alive!"

"He'll bite," said Fat fearfully. "They kin bite!"

"No, he wont't. I got him round the belly. He isn't biting anybody. All he kin do is squeak."

It was squeaking now; the thin and frantic sound threaded from Art's closed hand. Brian looked away. He saw with a start that the Young Ben was standing there; he had come upon them without a sound, and was staring at them with his pale, gray eyes under hair the color of the prairie itself. He was barefooted, and as he turned toward Art, Brian saw the beginning of the crease of his bare bottom through the tear hanging open in the seat of his faded overall pants held round his middle by several frayed strands of binder twine.

"I'm gonna take the tail offa him," said Art, with the gopher still struggling and squeaking in his hand.

"I knew a girl gopher once," said Bobbie.

Art saw the Young Ben then. "I'm gonna rip the tail off of him," he said again.

"She cut off her sister's finger an' it grew back on."

"Their tails grow back on if you let 'em go." Art was speaking to the Young Ben.

"An' she cut off her head an't it grew back on an' she cut off her legs an't they grew back on," chanted Bobbie.

---

67 *almond* (n.) /'ɑlmənd/ AE /'ælmənd/: G. Mandel – 68 *tapered* (adj.) /'teɪpəd/: gradually decreased in thickness – 68 *quiver* (v.): to tremble a little – 71 *souse* (v.) /saus/: to pour water – 72 *lunge* (v.) /lʌndʒ/: to make a sudden forceful forward movement – 72 *fawn* (adj.): a light yellowish-brown colour – 72 *plaster* (v.): to spread – 73 *dart* (v.): to move suddenly and quickly – 73 *scruff* (n.): the loose skin covering the back of the neck – 74 *hurtle* (v.): to move with great speed – 76 *tan* (adj.): yellowish-brown – 78 *belly* (n.): G. Bauch – 79 *squeak* (v.): to make a short very high but not loud sound – 80 *frantic* (adj.): wildly anxious – 81 *start* (n.): a sudden quick movement – 85 *crease* (n.): a line made by folding, crushing or pressing – 85 *tear* (n.): a torn place in cloth, paper etc. – 86 *overall* (n.): loose trousers fastened over the shoulders by means of straps – 86 **pants** (n.): trousers – 86 *fray* (v.): (of clothes): to become thin or worn so that loose threads develop – 86 *strand* (n.): a piece of string – 86 *binder twine* (n.): a string for binding corn when it is cut –

Brian stared at the high and circling cheekbones under the tanned skin, at the freckles under the gray eyes. He looks like a coyote, thought Brian, like a watching coyote. He realized with a start that an excitement, akin to the feeling that had moved him so often, was beginning to tremble within him. His knees felt weak with it; the Young Ben could cause it too. The Young Ben was part of it. He's something I *know*, thought Brian.

Art had taken the gopher by the tip of its tail and was holding it head down by his thumb and forefinger. He raised his arm above his head and began to swing the gopher in a large circle. "Hold yer dogs back!" he cried. He snapped his arm. The tail remained in his hand.

"They all grow back on," said Bobbie sadly as the gopher thudded to the prairie sod.

Now to one side, now to the other, the gopher ran in squeaking, erratic course, both dogs after it. The Young Ben leaped. He passed the dogs, threw himself full length upon the tailless gopher. He lay there with the squeaking under him. While the boys watched open-mouthed, he reached under himself. With one mercyful squeeze he choked the life from the animal. As he stood up he dropped it to the ground. He began to walk toward Art.

Fierce exultation gripped Brian as he realized what was about to happen. Face twitching nervously, Art backed away. He knew that something was wrong. Just as he had thrown himself upon the gopher, the Young Ben leaped at Art, who fell backward under his attacker's weight. The Young Ben fought as the boys had never seen anyone fight before. He was a clawing, wild thing on top of Art. He gouged Art's eyes, from which the glasses had fallen; blood sprang in long tracks as he drew his crooked fingers again and again and again down Art's face. He pounded him about the head, the throat, the ribs. He stood up and kicked Art rolling helpless on the prairie. When he stopped, one felt that he had done so simply because he was exhausted. He looked at the terror on Fat's face, at Bobbie sobbing, then for long and level moments at Brian. [...]

And Brian, quite without any desire to alleviate Art's suffering, shaken by his discovery that the Young Ben was linked in some indefinable way with the magic that visited him often now, was filled with a sense of the justness, the rightness, the completeness of what Young Ben had done—what he himself would like to have done.

---

98 *tan* (v.): to become brown, esp. by sunlight – 99 *freckles* (n.): G. Sommersprossen – 99 *coyote* (n.) /kɔiəutɪ/: a type of small wolf – 100 *akin* to (adj.) /ə'kɪn/: similar to – 108 *thud* (v.): to cause a dull sound by striking s. th. soft – 109 *sod* (n.): earth with grass and roots growing in it – 110 *erratic* (adj.): not regular in movement – 114 *merciful* (adj.): showing mercy – 114 *squeeze* (n.): an act of pressing in from around – 116 **exultation** (n.): the feeling and expressions of delight – 117 *twitch* (v.): to move suddenly and quickly without control – 120 *claw* (v.): to tear as if with claws – 121 *gouge* (v.): /gaʊdʒ/: to press with force, esp. with the thumbs – 122 *crooked* (adj.): not straight – 123 *pound* (v.): to strike again and again – 128 *alleviate* (v.): to make less – 129 *indefinable* (adj.): which cannot be described – 130 *justness* (n.): the quality of being just –

Art had to be led home like a blind boy; he was unable to see a foot in front of himself without his thick glasses.

Brian thought often of the prairie incident, always with the same thrill of excitement. He would remember the feeling of revulsion that had gripped him when Art had jerked the tail from the gopher. He would wander out to Haggerty's Coulee, hoping that he would run across the Young Ben, his whole being tingling with expectation. He would return disconsolately home.

On one such occasion he was accompanied by Bobbie and Jappy. As the boys walked, the dog ran ahead of them, to come back and jump up on their legs, then run out again. Suddenly he stopped at a wild rose bush ahead, his nose to the ground, tenseness in every line of his lean and quivering body. Brian and Bobbie went up to see what he had found.

The tailless gopher lay upon an ant pile, strangely still with the black bits of ants active over it. A cloud of flies lifted from it, dispersed, then came together again as at a command. Brian stared down at the two rodent teeth, the blood that had run down the nose and crusted there; he saw a short stump of tail skeleton with a ragged tab of skin that had stayed with the body when Art had ripped away the tail. It was difficult to believe that this thing had once been a gopher that ran and squeaked over the prairie. It was difficult to believe that this was anything but dirt.

Bobbie began to cry. He turned away from the still body over the coning ant hill. He pulled on Brian's arm. The feeling was in Brian now, fierce—uncontrollably so, with wild and unbidden power, with a new, frightening quality.

"I don't like it!" Bobbie cried. "I want to go home—I want to go home—I want to go home!"

Prairie's awful, thought Brian, and in his mind there loomed vaguely fearful images of a still and brooding spirit, a quiescent power unsmiling from everlasting to everlasting to which the coming and passing of the prairie's creatures was but incidental. He looked out over the spreading land under intensely blue sky. The Young Ben was part of all this.

"I want to go home, Brian!"

Brian put his arm protectively around his brother's shoulder, and the two began to walk back across the prairie to the town.

---

136 *revulsion* (n.): a feeling of being shocked – 139 *tingle* (v.): to feel a slight sensation – 139 *disconsolately* (adv.): hopelessly sad – 143 *tenseness* (n.): nervous anxiety – 143 *lean* (adj.): very thin – 143 *quiver* (v.): to tremble – 145 *ant pile* (n.): G. Ameisenhaufen – 146 *disperse* (v.): to scatter in different directions – 147 *rodent teeth:* G. Nagezähne – 148 *crust* (v.): to become a hard outer covering – 149 *stump* (n.): the remaining part of a limb which has been cut off – 149 *skeleton* (n.): G. Skelett – 149 *ragged* (adj.): torn – 149 *tab* (n.): a small piece – 153 *coning* here: G. kegelförmig – 159 *loom* (v.): to appear great and very worrying in the mind – 159 **vaguely** (adv.): not clear in shape or form – 160 *brood* (v.): to think angrily or sadly – 160 *quiescent* (adj.): still, at rest – 162 *incidental* (adj.): unimportant – 165 **protectively** (adv.): having or showing a wish to protect

"Thunderstorm on the prairie", painting by William Kurelek

3: SINCLAIR ROSS: A Field of Wheat

Sinclair Ross (1908–) was born in Saskatchewan where he grew up on farms and went to school. In 1924 he joined the Royal Bank of Canada. His first and most important novel *As For Me And My House* was published in New York in 1941. Three more novels and two collections of short stories, *The Lamp at Noon and Other Stories* (1968) and *The Race and Other Stories* (1982) followed later. Ross retired from the Royal Bank in 1968 and now lives in Vancouver. In his fiction Ross often presents the problems of prairie farmers and small-town people during the years of the Depression.

Sinclair Ross' 'A Field of Wheat' is taken from: *The Lamp at Noon and Other Stories*, Toronto, McCelland and Stewart, repr. 1983, pp.73–82.

As For Me: as regards myself – **fiction**: novels and stories – *Depression* (n.): the period of worldwide economic decline which began in 1929 –

It was the best crop of wheat that John had ever grown; sturdy, higher than the knee, the heads long and filling well; a still, heat-hushed mile of it, undulating into a shimmer of summercolts and crushed horizon blue. Martha finished pulling the little patch of mustard that John had told her about at noon, stood a minute with her shoulders strained back to ease the muscles that were sore from bending, then bunched up her apron filled with the yellow-blossomed weeds and started towards the road. She walked carefully, placing her feet edgeways between the rows of wheat to avoid trampling and crushing the stalks. The road was only a few rods distant, but several times she stopped before reaching it, holding her apron with one hand and with the other stroking the blades of grain that pressed close against her skirts, luxuriant and tall. Once she looked back, her eyes shaded, across the wheat to the dark fallow land beside it. John was there; she could see the long, slow-settling plume of dust thrown up by the horses and the harrow-cart. He was a fool for work, John. This year he was farming the whole section of land without help, managing with two outfits of horses, one for the morning and one for the afternoon; six, and sometimes even seven hours a shift.

It was John who gave such allure to the wheat. She thought of him hunched black and sweaty on the harrow-cart, twelve hours a day, smothering in dust, shoulders sagged wearily beneath the glare of sun. Her fingers touched the stalks of grain again and tightened on a supple blade until they made it squeak like a mouse. A crop like this was coming to him. He had had his share of failures and set-backs, if ever a man had, twenty times over.

Martha was thirty-seven. She had clinched with the body and substance of life; had loved, borne children—a boy had died—and yet the quickest aches of life, travail, heartbrokenness, they had never wrung as the wheat wrung. For the wheat allowed no respite. Wasting and unending it was struggle, struggle against wind and insects, drought and weeds. Not an heroic struggle to give a man courage and resolve, but a frantic, unavailing one. They were only poor, taunted, driven things; it was the wheat that was invincible. They only

---

1 *sturdy* (adj.): strong and firm – 2 *hush* (v.): to cause to be silent or calm – 2 *undulate* (v.): to move like waves rising and falling – 3 *colt* (n.) /kəult/: a young male horse – 4 *mustard* (n.): G. Senf – 9 *stalk* (n.): the main upright part of a plant – 9 *rod* (n.): a measure of length (5,03 m) – 11 *blade* (n.): a long flat leaf – 11 *luxuriant* (adj.): growing well – 13 *fallow land:* land ploughed but left unplanted to improve its quality – 14 *plume* (n). /plum/: something that rises into the air like a feather – 14 *harrow-cart* (n.): G. Egge – 16 *outfit* (n.): a team – 18 *allure* (n.): attraction – 18 *hunch* (v.): to pull the body into a rounded shape – 19 *smother* (v.): to die from lack of air – 20 *sag* (v.): to bend downward – 20 *glare* (n.): a hard, unpleasant light – 21 **tighten** (v.): to become tight or tighter – 21 *supple* (adj.): bending or moving easily – 21 *squeak* (v.): to make a short, very high but not loud sound – 23 *set-back* (n.): a defeat – 24 *clinch* (v.) here: to fight – 26 *travail* (n. arch.): the pains of giving birth to a child – 26 *wring* (v.): to press hard – 27 *respite* (n.): pause or rest – 28 *drought* (n.) /draut/: a long period of dry weather – 29 *resolve* (n.): resolution – 29 *frantic* (adj.): marked by hurried and disordered activity – 29 *unavailing* (adj.): not having any effect – 30 *taunt* (v.): here: to torture – 30 *invincible* (adj.): too strong to be conquered –

dreaded, built bright futures; waited for the first glint of green, watched timorous and eager while it thickened, merged, and at last leaned bravely to a ripple in the wind; then followed every slip of cloud into the horizon, turned to the wheat and away again. And it died tantalizingly sometimes, slowly: there would be a cool day, a pittance of rain.

Or perhaps it lived, perhaps the rain came, June, July, even into August, hope climbing, wish-patterns painted on the future. And then one day a clench and tremble to John's hand; his voice faltering, dull. Grasshoppers perhaps, sawflies or rust; no matter, they would grovel for a while, stand back helpless, then go on again. Go on in bitterness and cowardice, because there was nothing else but going-on.

She had loved John, for these sixteen years had stood close watching while he died—slowly, tantalizingly, as the parched wheat died. He had grown unkempt, ugly, morose. His voice was gruff, contentious, never broke into the deep, strong laughter that used to make her feel she was living at the heart of things. John was gone, love was gone; there was only wheat.

She plucked a blade; her eyes travelled hungrily up and down the field. Serene now, all its sting and torment sheathed. Beautiful, more beautiful than Annabelle's poppies, than her sunsets. Theirs—all of it. Three hundred acres ready to give perhaps a little of what it had taken from her—John, his love, his lips unclenched.

Three hundred acres. Bushels, thousands of bushels, she wouldn't even try to think how many. And prices up this year. It would make him young again, lift his head, give him spirit. Maybe he would shave twice a week as he used to when they were first married, buy new clothes, believe in himself again.

She walked down the road towards the house, her steps quickening to the pace of her thoughts until the sweat clung to her face like little beads of oil. It was the children now, Joe and Annabelle: this winter perhaps they could send them to school in town and let them take music lessons. Annabelle, anyway. At a pinch Joe could wait a while; he was only eight. It wouldn't take Annabelle long to pick up her notes; already she played hymn tunes by ear on

---

31 *glint* (n.): a light colour – 32 *timorous* (adj.): fearful, nervous – 32 *merge* (v.): to combine – 33 *ripple* (n.): a gentle waving movement – 34 *tantalizing* (adj.): causing anger by raising hopes that cannot be satisfied. G.: aufreizend – 35 *pittance* (n.): a very small amount – 37 *clench* (n.): the act of closing tightly – 38 *falter* (v.): to speak in a weak or broken manner – 38 *grasshopper* (n.): G. Heuschrecke – 39 *sawfly* (n.): G. Blattwespe – 39 *rust* (n.): a disease of plants, G. Rost, Brand – 39 *grovel* (v.) /'grovəl/: to move in fear of something powerful – 40 **cowardice** (n.): lack of courage – 43 *parch* (v.): to become hot and dry – 43 *unkempt* (adj.): having untidy clothes and hair – 44 *morose* (adj.): not cheerful – 44 *gruff* (adj.): deep and rough – 44 *contentious* (adj.): tending to argue – 48 *serene* (adj.) completely calm and peaceful – 48 *sting* (n.): a sharp pain – 48 **torment** (n.): very great pain or suffering in mind or body – 48 *sheath* (v.): to enclose in a protective outer cover, G. umhüllen, ummanteln – 49 *poppy* (n.): G. Mohn – 51 *unclench* (v.): to open something that is tightly closed – 52 *acre* (n.): 0,4 ha. G. Morgen – 52 *bushel* (n.): 35,24 litres, G. Scheffel – 57 *bead* (n.): a small drop – 60 *at a pinch:* if necessary – 61 *hymn* (n.): a religious song –

the organ. She was bright, a real little lady for manners; among town people she would learn a lot. The farm was no place to bring her up. Running wild and barefoot, what would she be like in a few years? Who would ever want to marry her but some stupid country lout?

John had never been to school himself; he knew what it meant to go through life with nothing but his muscles to depend upon; and that was it, dread that Annabelle and Joe would be handicapped as he was, that was what had darkened him, made him harsh and dour. That was why he breasted the sun and dust a frantic, dogged fool, to spare them, to help them to a life that offered more than sweat and debts. Martha knew. He was a slow, inarticulate man, but she knew. Sometimes it even vexed her, brought a wrinkle of jealousy, his anxiety about the children, his sense of responsibility where they were concerned. He never seemed to feel that he owed her anything, never worried about her future. She could sweat, grow flatfooted and shapeless, but that never bothered him.

Her thoughts were on their old, trudging way, the way they always went; but then she halted suddenly, and with her eyes across the wheat again found freshening promise in its quiet expanse. The children must come first, but she and John—mightn't there be a little of life left for them too? A man was young at thirty-nine. And if she didn't have to work so hard, if she could get some new clothes, maybe some of the creams and things that other women had ...

As she passed through the gate, Annabelle raced across the yard to meet her. "Do you know what Joe's done? He's taken off all his clothes and he's in the trough with Nipper!" She was a lanky girl, sunburned, barefoot, her face oval and regular, but spoiled by an expression that strained her mouth and brows into a reproachful primness. It was Martha who had taught her the expression, dinning manners and politeness into her, trying to make her better than the other little girls who went to the country school. She went on, her eyes wide and aghast, "And when I told him to come out he stood right up, all bare, and I had to come away."

"Well, you tell him he'd better be out before I get there."

"But how can I tell him? He's all bare."

---

65 *lout* (n.): a rough, awkward man with bad manners – 68 *handicapped* (p.p.): here: (educationally) to be prevented from acting and living in the way ordinary people do – 69 *dour* (adj.): hard and cold, unfriendly – 69 *breast* (v.): to stand up fearlessly against – 70 *dogged* (adj.) /'dogɪd/: showing a character which refuses to give up in the face of difficulty – 71 *inarticulate* (adj.): not able to express o.s. well – 72 *vex* (v.): to cause s.o. to feel angry – 72 *wrinkle* (n.): suggestion, hint – 72 *jealousy* (n.) /'dʒeləsɪ/: G. Eifersucht – 76 *bother* (v.): to annoy, to trouble – 77 *trudge* (v.): to walk slowly and with effort – 79 *expanse* (n.): a wide space – 84 *trough* (n.) /trof/: G. Trog – 86 *lanky* (adj.): very thin and tall – 88 *reproachful* (adj.): expressing blame or contempt – 88 *primness* (n.): stiffness – 89 *din* (v.): to repeat something over and over again – 89 **politeness** (n.): consideration for others – 91 *aghast* (adj.): filled with surprise and wonder –

Then Joe ran up, nothing on but little cotton knee-pants, strings of green scum from the water-trough still sticking to his face and arms. "She's been peekin'." He pointed at Annabelle. "Nipper and me just got into the trough to get cooled off, and she wouldn't mind her own business."

"Don't you tell lies about me." Annabelle pounced on him and slapped his bare back. "You're just a dirty little pig anyway, and the horses don't want to drink after you've been in the trough."

Joe squealed, and excited by the scuffle Nipper yelped and spattered Martha with a spray of water from his coat and tail. She reached out to cuff him, missed, and then to satisfy the itch in her fingers seized Joe and boxed his ears. "You put your shirt on and then go and pick peas for supper. Hurry now, both of you, and only the fat ones, mind. No, not you, Annabelle." There was something about Annabelle's face, burned and countrified, that changed Martha's mind. "You shell the peas when he gets them. You're in the sun too much as it is."

"But I've got a poppy out and if he goes to the garden by himself he'll pick it–just for spite." Annabelle spun round, and leaving the perplexity in her voice behind her, bolted for the garden. The next minute, before Martha had even reached the house, she was back again triumphant, a big fringed pink and purple poppy in her hand. Sitting down on the doorstep to admire the gaudy petals, she complained to herself, "They go so fast–the first little winds blows them all away." On her face, lengthening it, was bitten deeply the enigma of the flowers and the naked seed-pods. Why did the beauty flash and the bony stalks remain?

Martha had clothes to iron, and biscuits to bake for supper; Annabelle and Joe quarelled about the peas until she shelled them herself. It was hot–heat so intense and breathless that it weighed like a solid. An ominous darkness came with it, gradual and unnoticed. All at once she turned away from the stove and stood strained, inert. The silence seemed to gather itself, hold its breath. She tried to speak to Nipper and the children, all three sprawled in a heap alongside the house, but the hush over everything was like a raised finger, forbidding her.

---

95 *knee-pants* (n.): G. halblange (Unter)hosen – 96 *scum* (n.): dirt on the surface of still water – 97 *peek* (v., infml.): to look quickly, esp. when one should not – 99 *pounce* (v.): to seize eagerly – 99 *slap* (v.): to strike quickly with the flat part of the hand – 102 *squeal* (v.): to make a long very high sound, like that of pigs – 102 *scuffle* (n.): fight – 102 *yelp* (v.): to make a short sharp high cry, as of a dog – 102 *spatter* (v.): to cover with water – 103 *spray* (n.): water in very small drops – 103 *cuff* (v.): to strike lightly with the open hand – 104 *itch* (n.): a restless desire – 109 *shell* (v.): to remove from a natural covering – 111 *spite* (n.): the desire to annoy another person – 111 *perplexity* (n.): the state of being confused and troubled – 112 *bolt* (v.): to run away suddenly – 113 *fringed* (p.p.): surrounded by – 113 *pink* (adj.): pale red – 115 *gaudy* (adj.): too bright in colour – 115 *petal* (n.): the leaf of a flower – 117 *enigma* (n.): s. th. mysterious and very hard to understand – 117 *seed-pod* (n.): seed vessel – 117 *flash* (v.): to exist for a moment – 121 *solid* (n.): object – 121 *ominous* (adj.): threatening – 123 *inert* (adj.): lacking the power to move – 124 *sprawl* (v.): to stretch out awkwardly – 125 *hush* (n.): silence –

A long immobile minute; suddenly a bewildering awareness that the light was choked; and then, muffled, still distant, but charged with resolution, climaxing the stillness, a slow, long brooding heave of thunder.

Martha darted to the door, stumbled down the step and around the corner of the house. To the west there was no sky, only a gulf of blackness, so black that the landscape seemed slipping down the neck of a funnel. Above, almost overhead, a heavy, hard-lined bank of cloud swept its way across the sunwhite blue in august, impassive fury.

"Annabelle!" She wanted to scream a warning, but it was a bare whisper. In front of her the blackness split—an abrupt, unforked gash of light as if angry hands had snatched to seal the rent.

"Annabelle! Quick—inside—!" Deep in the funnel shaggy thunder rolled, emerged and shook itself, then with hurtling strides leaped up to drum and burst itself on the advancing peak of cloud.

"Joe, come back here!" He was off in pursuit of Nipper, who had broken away from Annabelle when she tried to pull him into the house. "Before I warm you!"

Her voice broke. She stared into the blackness. There it was—the hail again—the same white twisting little cloud against the black one—just as she had seen it four years ago.

She craned her neck, looking to see whether John was coming. The wheat, the acres and acres of it, green and tall, if only he had put some insurance on it. Damned mule—just work and work. No head himself and too stubborn to listen to anyone else.

There was a swift gust of wind, thunder in a splintering avalanche, the ragged hail-cloud low and close. She wheeled, with a push sent Annabelle toppling into the house, and then ran to the stable to throw open the big doors. John would turn the horses loose—surely he would. She put a brace against one of the doors, and bashed the end into the ground with her foot. Surely—but he was a fool—such a fool at times. It would be just like him to risk a runaway for the sake of getting to the end of the field.

---

127 *immobile* (adj.): unmoving – 128 *muffle* (v.): to make a sound less easily heard – 129 *climax* (v.): to raise s.th. to its highest point – 129 *brood* (v.): to spread over – 129 *heave* (n.): swell, increase – 132 *funnel* (n.): G. Trichter – 134 *august* (adj.): noble and grand – 134 *impassive* (adj.): that cannot be injured – 136 *unforked* (adj.): undivided – 136 *gash* (n.): a long deep cut – 137 *rent* (n.): opening – 138 *shaggy* (adj.): rough, uneven – 139 *hurtle* (v.): to move with great speed – 139 *stride* (n.): a long step – 144 *hail* (n.): G. Hagel – 147 *crane* (v.): to stretch out in order to get a better view – 149 *mule* (n.): lit. G. Maultier, here: stures Arbeitstier – 151 *gust of wind:* a sudden strong rush of air, G. Bö – 151 *splinter* (v.): to break into small pieces – 151 *avalanche* (n.) /'ævəlɑnʃ/: G. Lawine – 152 *ragged* (adj.): /'rægɪd/: with uneven edges or surfaces – 153 *topple* (v.): to cause to become unsteady and fall down – 154 *brace* (n.): s.th. used for supporting, G. Stütze – 155 *bash* (v.): to hit hard – 157 *to risk a runaway:* to risk losing a horse –

The first big drops of rain were spitting at her before she reached the house. Quietly, breathing hard, she closed the door, numb for a minute, afraid to think or move. At the other side of the kitchen Annabelle was tussling with Joe, trying to make him go down cellar with her. Frightened a littly by her mother's excitement, but not really able to grasp the imminence of danger, she was set on exploiting the event; and to be compelled to seize her little brother and carry him down cellar struck her imagination as a superb way of crystallizing for all time the dreadfulness of the storm and her own dramatic part in it. But Martha shouted at her hoarsely, "Go and get pillows. Here, Joe, quick, up on the table." She snatched him off his feet and set him on the table beside the window. "Be ready now when the hail starts, to hold the pillow tight against the glass. You, Annabelle, stay upstairs at the west window in my room."

The horses were coming, all six at a break-neck gallop, terrified by the thunder and the whip stripes John had given them when he turned them loose. They swept past the house, shaking the earth, their harness jangling tinny against the brattle of thunder, and collided headlong at the stable door.

John, too; through Joe's legs Martha caught sight of his long, scarecrow shape stooped low before the rain. Distractedly, without purpose, she ran upstairs two steps at a time to Annabelle. "Don't be scared, here comes your father!" Her own voice shook, craven. "Why don't you rest your arms? It hasn't started yet."

As she spoke there was a sharp, crunching blow on the roof, its sound abruptly dead, sickening, like a weapon that has sunk deep into flesh. Wildly she shook her hands, motioning Annabelle back to the window, and started for the stairs. Again the blow came; then swiftly a stuttered dozen of them.

She reached the kitchen just as John burst in. With their eyes screwed up against the pommelling roar of the hail they stared at each other. They were defeaned, pinioned, crushed. His face was a livid blank, one cheek smeared with blood where a jagged stone had struck him. Taut with fear, her throat

---

158 *spit* (v.): lit. to force liquid from the mouth, here to hit – 159 *numb* (adj.): unable to feel anything – 160 *tussle* (v.): to struggle roughly – 162 *imminence* (n.): the nearness of something – 163 *set on* (p.p.): determined to – 163 **exploit** (v.): to use unfairly for one's own profit – 164 **superb** (adj.): perfect – 165 *crystallize* (v.): to take on a definite form – 166 *hoarsely* (adv.): in a rough voice – 171 *break-neck* (adj.): very fast – 171 **terrify** (v.): to fill with fear – 172 *whip stripes* (n. pl.): marks of the whip – 173 *harness* (n.): G. Pferdegeschirr – 173 *jangle* (v.): to make a dull bell-like sound – 173 *tinny* (adj.): having a thin metallic sound – 174 *brattle* (n.): any rattling sound – 174 *collide* (v.): to strike together violently – 174 *headlong* (adv.): in foolish haste – 175 *scarecrow* (n.): G. Vogelscheuche – 176 *stoop* (v.): to bend forwards and down – 176 *distracted* (adj.): unable to think clearly – 178 *craven* (adj.): completely lacking courage – 180 *crunch* (v.): to make a crushing noise – 181 **abruptly** (adv.): suddenly – 182 *motion* (v.): to direct – 183 *stuttered* (p.p.): here: with pauses in between – 185 *pommel* (v.): to beat – 186 *deafen* (v.): to make someone unable to hear – 186 *pinion* (v.): to tie up – 186 *livid* (adj.): very pale – 186 *blank* (n.): an empty space – 186 *smear* (v.): to spread across a surface – 187 *jagged* (adj.): with a rough edge – 187 *taut* (adj.) /tɔːt/: showing signs of worry or anxiety –

aching, she turned away and looked through Joe's legs again. It was like a furious fountain, the stones bouncing high and clashing with those behind them. They had buried the earth, blotted out the horizon; there was nothing but their crazy spew of whiteness. She cowered away, put her hands to her ears.

Then the window broke, and Joe and the pillow tumbled off the table before the howling inrush of the storm. The stones clattered on the floor and bounded up to the cealing, lit on the stove and threw out sizzling steam. The wind whisked pots and kettles off their hooks, tugged at and whirled the sodden curtains, crashed down a shelf of lamps and crockery. John pushed Martha and Joe into the next room and shut the door. There they found Annabelle huddled at the foot of the stairs, round-eyed, biting her nails in terror. The window she had been holding was broken too; and she had run away without closing the bedroom door, leaving a wild tide of wind upstairs to rage unchecked. It was rocking the whole house, straining at the walls. Martha ran up to close the door, and came down whimpering.

There was hail heaped on the bed, the pictures were blown off the walls and broken, the floor was swimming; the water would soak through and spoil all the ceilings.

John's face quietened her. They all crowded together, silent, averting their eyes from one another. Martha wanted to cry again, but dared not. Joe, awed to calmness, kept looking furtively at the trickle of blood on his father's face. Annabelle's eyes went wide and glassy as suddenly she began to wonder about Nipper. In the excitement and terror of the storm they had all forgotten him.

When at last they could go outside they stumbled over his body on the step. He had run away from Joe before the storm started, crawled back to the house when he saw John go in, and crouching down against the door had been beaten lifeless. Martha held back the children, while John picked up the mangled heap and hurried away with it to the stable.

Neither Joe nor Annabelle cried. It was too annihilating, too much like a blow. They clung tightly to Martha's skirts, staring across the flayed yard and

---

189 *bounce* (v.): to spring up again from the ground – 190 *blot out* (v.): to darken – 191 *spew* (n.) /spju/: s.th. that is cast forth violently, lit. the contents of the mouth – 191 *cower* (v.): to bend low and draw back – 194 *inrush* (n.): a strong draught – 194 *clatter* (v.): to move with rapid short knocking sounds – 195 *bound* (v.): to jump – 195 *lit* (past tense of alight): to come down from and settle – 195 *sizzle* (v.): to make a hissing sound – 196 *whisk* (v.): to wipe – 196 *tug* (v.): to pull hard – 197 *sodden* (adj.): heavy with wetness – 197 *crockery* (n.): cups, pots etc. made from baked earth – 199 *huddled* (p.p.): pressed tightly together – 201 *tide* (n.): current – 202 *rock* (v.): to move backwards and forwards – 203 *whimper* (v.): to make small weak cries – 205 *soak* (v.): (of water etc.) to enter through the material of a surface – 207 *quieten* (v.): to cause to become quiet – 207 *crowd* (v.): to press tightly together – 207 *avert* (v.): to turn away – 208 *awed to calmness:* filled with awe so that he was calm – 209 *furtively* (adv.): secretly, not directly – 209 *trickle* (n.): a small thin flow – 214 *crouch* (v.): to lower the body close to the ground – 216 *mangle* (v.): to tear or cut to pieces – 217 *annihilate* (v.): to destroy completely – 218 *flay* (v.): lit. to skin, here to damage severely –

garden. The sun came out, sharp and brilliant on the drifts of hail. There was an icy wind that made them shiver in their thin cotton clothes. "No, it's too cold on your feet." Martha motioned them back to the step as she started towards the gate to join John. "I want to go with your father to look at the wheat. There's nothing anyway to see."

Nothing but the glitter of sun on hailstones. Nothing but their wheat crushed into little rags of muddy slime. Here and there an isolated straw standing bolt upright in headless defiance. Martha and John walked to the far end of the field. There was no sound but their shoes slipping and rattling on the pebbles of ice. Both of them wanted to speak, to break the atmosphere of calamity that hung over them, but the words they could find were too small for the sparkling serenity of wasted field. Even as waste it was indomitable. It tethered them to itself, so that they could not feel or comprehend. It had come and gone, that was all; before its tremendousness and havoc they were prostrate. They had not yet risen to cry out or protest.

It was when they were nearly back to the house that Martha started to whimper. "I can't go on any longer; I can't, John. There's no use, we've tried." With one hand she clutched him and with the other held her apron to her mouth. "It's driving me out of my mind. I'm so tired—heart-sick of it all. Can't you see?"

He laid his big hands on her shoulders. They looked at each other for a few seconds, then she dropped her head weakly against his greasy smock. Presently he roused her. "Here come Joe and Annabelle!" The pressure of his hands tightened. His bristly cheek touched her hair and forehead. "Straighten up, quick, before they see you!"

It was more of him than she had had for years. "Yes, John, I know—I'm all right now." There was a wistful little pull in her voice as if she would have had him hold her there, but hurriedly instead she began to dry her eyes with her apron. "And tell Joe you'll get him another dog."

Then he left her and she went back to the house. Mounting within her was a resolve, a bravery. It was the warming sunlight, the strength and nearness of John, a feeling of mattering, belonging. Swung far upwards by the rush and swell of recaptured life, she was suddenly as far above the desolation of the

---

220 *shiver* (v.): to shake, to tremble – 225 *rag* (n.): a small piece – 225 *muddy* (adj.): dirty – 225 *slime* (n.): watery mud – 225 *isolated* (adj.): standing out on its own – 226 *bolt upright:* straight and stiffly – 228 *pebble* (n.): a small roundish stone – 229 *calamity* (n.): a serious misfortune – 230 *serenity* (n.): complete calmness and peacefulness – 230 *indomitable* (adj.): not easily conquered – 231 *tether* (v.): to bind, to tie – 231 *comprehend* (v.): to understand – 232 *havoc* (n.): widespread damage – 233 *prostrate* (adj.): powerless – 235 *whimper* (v.): to make small weak cries – 236 *clutch* (v.): to hold tightly – 240 *greasy* (adj.): covered with soft fat – 240 *smock* (n.): a loose coatlike garment – 242 *bristly* (adj.): full of short coarse hair – 245 *wistful* (adj.): showing a wish which may not be satisfied – 249 *bravery* (n.): courage – 250 *of mattering:* of being important – 251 *recapture* (v.): to get into one's power again – 251 *desolation* (n.): destruction –

storm as a little while ago she had been abject before it. But in the house she was alone; there was no sunlight, only a cold wind through the broken window; and she crumpled again.

She tried to face the kitchen, to get the floor dried and the broken lamps swept up. But it was not the kitchen; it was tomorrow, next week, next year. The going on, the waste of life, the hopelessness.

Her hands fought the broom a moment, twisting the handle as if trying to unscrew the rusted cap of a jar; then abruptly she let it fall and strode outside. All very fine for John: he'd talk about education for Joe and Annabelle, and she could worry where the clothes were to come from so that they could go clean and decent even to the country school. It made no difference that she had wanted to take out hail insurance. He was the one that looked after things. She was just his wife; it wasn't for her to open her mouth. He'd pat her shoulder and let her come back to this. They'd be brave, go on again, forget about the crop. Go on, go on—next year and the next—go on till they were both ready for the scrap-heap. But she'd had enough. This time he'd go on alone.

Not that she meant it. Not that she failed to understand what John was going through. It was just rebellion. Rebellion because their wheat was beaten to the ground, because there was this brutal, callous finish to everything she had planned, because she had will and needs and flesh, because she was alive. Rebellion, not John at all—but how rebel against a summer storm, how find the throat of a cloud?

So at a jerky little run she set off for the stable, for John. Just that she might release and spend herself, no matter against whom or what, unloose the fury that clawed within her, strike back a blow for the one that had flattened her.

The stable was quiet, only the push of hay as the horses nosed through the mangers, the lazy rub of their flanks and hips against the stall partitions; and before its quietness her anger subsided, took time for breath. She advanced slowly, almost on tiptoe, peering past the horses' rumps for a glimpse of John. To the last stall, back again. And then there was a sound different from the stable sounds. She paused.

She had not seen him the first time she passed because he was pressed against one of the horses, his head pushed into the big deep hollow of its neck and shoulder, one hand hooked by the fingers in the mane, his own shoulders

---

252 *abject* (adj.): showing lack of self-respect – 254 *crumple* (v.): to lose strength – 264 *pat* (v.): to strike gently with a flat hand – 267 *scrap-heap* (n.): the place where unwanted things go – 271 *callous* (adj.): /'kæləs/: hard, unkind – 275 *jerky* (adj.): making short quick movements – 277 *claw* (v.): to hear, to pull – 279 *nose* (v.): to push with the nose – 280 *manger* (n.) /meɪndʒə/: G. Futterkrippe – 280 *flank* (n.): the side of an animal – 280 *hip* (n.): G. Hüfte – 280 *partition* (n.): a thin wall for subdividing a room – 281 *subside* (v.): to cease – 282 *on tiptoe:* on one's toes – 282 *peer* (v.): to look very carefully – 282 *rump* (n.): G. Rumpf – 287 *hook* (v.) /huk/: to fasten as if with a hook – 287 *mane* (n.): the long hair on a horse's neck –

drawn up and shaking. She stared, thrust out her head incredulously, moved her lips, but stood silent. John sobbing there, against the horse. It was the strangest, most frightening moment of her life. He had always been so strong and grim; had just kept on as if he couldn't feel, as if there was a bull's hide over him, and now he was beaten.

She crept away. It would be unbearable to watch his humiliation if he looked up and saw her. Joe was wandering about the yard, thinking about Nipper and disconsolately sucking hailstones, but she fled past him, head down, stricken with guilty shame as if it were she who had been caught broken and afraid. He had always been so strong, a brute at times in his strength, and now–

Now–why now that it had come to this, he might never be able to get a grip of himself again. He might not want to keep on working, not if he were really beaten. If he lost heart, if he didn't care about Joe and Annabelle any more. Weeds and pests, drought and hail–it took so much fight for a man to hold his own against them all, just to hold his own, let alone make headway.

"Look at the sky!" It was Annabelle again, breathless and ecstatic. "The far one–look how it's opened like a fan!"

Withdrawn now in the eastern sky the storm clouds towered, gold-capped and flushed in the late sunlight, high still pyramids of snowiness and shadow. And one that Anabelle pointed to, apart, the farthest away of them all, this one in bronzed slow splendour spread up mountains high to a vast, plateau-like summit.

Martha hurried inside. She started the fire again, then nailed a blanket over the broken window and lit the big brass parlour lamp–the only one the storm had spared. Her hands were quick and tense. John would need a good supper tonight. The biscuits were water-soaked, but she still had the peas. He liked peas. Lucky that they had picked them when they did. This winter they wouldn't have so much as an onion or potato.

---

288 *incredulously* (adv.): not believing – 291 *grim* (adj.): hard – 291 *hide* (n.): skin – 293 *humiliation* (n.): the act of lowering the pride or dignity of s. o. – 295 *disconsolately* (adv.): sadly – 295 *suck* (v.): to draw into the mouth – 297 *brute* (n.): an animal-like person – 302 *pest* (n.): G. Schädling – 303 *make headway:* to make progress – 304 *ecstatic* (adj.): with a strong feeling – 305 *fan* (n.): an instrument waved by hand to make cool air – 307 *flush* (v.): to become red – 307 *snowiness* (n.): the condition of being white like snow – 309 *bronzed* (p.p.): like the colour of bronze – 309 *plateau* (n.) /'plætəu/: level land, much higher than the land around it – 310 *summit* (n.): the highest part 313 *tense* (adj.): showing nervous anxiety

5: GEORGE BOWERING: prairie music

George Bowering (born 1935) was raised in the Okanagan Valley of British Columbia. During his studies at the University of British Columbia he became influenced by the American poets Robert Duncan, Robert Creely and Charles Olson. In 1961 he cofounded the little magazine *TISH*. He now teaches at Simon Fraser University in Vancouver. After his first poetry collection *Sticks and Stones* (1963) George Bowering has published 40 books of poetry and prose fiction. He came into closer contact with the Canadian prairies when he taught at the University of Calgary/Alberta.

George Bowering: "prairie music" is taken from *Rocky Mountain Foot*, Toronto, McClelland and Stewart, 1968, p. 88.

Okanagan Valley: a sunny and dry valley in south-central British Columbia, which is known for its fruit and wine – *cofound* (v.): to found s.th. together with other people – *Simon Fraser University:* a private university in Vancouver – *prose fiction:* novels and stories – 1 *bugle* (n.) /'bjugl/: horn – 3 *phantom* (n.): s.th. that exists only in one's imagination – 7 *Winnipeg:* the capital of Manitoba – 16 *expanse* (n.): a wide space – 16 *headlights* (n.pl.): the main front lights of a car

prairie music

Some bugle blow
over these cold bare fields

phantom sound to meet
prairie night, this I

know has to be prairie sound
the music I heard that night

on Winnipeg highway
miles from the nearest light

the stars, a bugle blow
away. The loneliest place

Kanada, a place for Kanada
the great prairie, formerly

a colour picture in a
book about the country

lonely place, the black
expanse, waiting for headlights

the sound of an engine
the soundlessness of the night

where no bugle played
in that cold.

VI British Columbia

British Columbia, the "sea of mountains" parted by the Continental Divide from the rest of Canada, with its people living on small pieces of level land in the valleys that filter down to the steep fjord-bitten and forested coastline, with its mild winters and moist summers, has likewise its special historical pattern complementing a unique geographical conformation. The memory of the great native culture of the Coast Indians still broods over it and inspires much of its painting and poetry. White settlement began with sea traders and overland-travelling agents of the Northwest Company, and its towns started as fur trading posts before the coming of the gold miners, and afterwards the CPR, turned them from tiny clusters of log buildings into mining or farming or communications centres or seaports. Even then much of the population came by sea from Europe or by coastal shipping or overland from California and the Oregon territory, bringing with it not only the San Francisco architecture which survives to this day in the wharfside streets of Victoria, but also the ruthless exploitative attitudes of lumber and mining barons and the labor radicalism of the IWW. An extraordinary combination of forest and dryland, of moun-

---

2 *Continental Divide:* the line that separates the rivers that flow to opposite sides of the North American continent – 6 *filter* (v.): here: to stretch down – 7 *fjord-bitten:* G. von Fjorden zerfurcht – 7 *forested* (adj.): covered with forests – 9 *likewise* (adv.): in the same way – 10 *complement* (v.): to make s.th. complete – 11 **unique** (adj.): the only one of its type – 11 *conformation* (n.): shape – 12 *brood over* (v.): to hang closely over – 14 *Northwest Company:* 1779–1821. A mainly fur-trading company in Canada, later taken over by the Hudson's Bay Company – 15 *CPR:* the Canadian Pacific Railway – 11 *cluster* (n.) a number of things of the same kind, here: group – 11 *log* (n.): a thick piece of wood from a tree – 18 *Oregon territory:* it was disputed between Britain and the USA and even jointly 20 *wharf* (n.) /wɔf/: a place where ships can be tied up to unload goods – 20 *Victoria:* the capital of British Columbia, situated on Vancouver Island – 20 *ruthless* (adj.): very cruel, without pity – 21 *exploitative* (adj.): using a person unfairly for one's own profit – 21 *baron:* here: wealthybusinessman – 22 *IWW:* Industrial Workers of the World. A radical labour union, which was founded in the USA in 1905 –

Scenes from British Columbia

tain and island and ocean, played its part in differentiating the literature of the Coast, while the mild climate and the relaxed and almost luxuriant way of living was attractive to writers and painters alike, so that British Columbia, and especially Vancouver and Victoria, had not only produced its own native artists in considerable number, but has attracted many more from outside, from Ethel Wilson and Roderick Haig-Brown and Malcolm Lowry down to, in our generation, David Watmough, P.K. Page and Jane Rule. More than most other parts of Canada it is, for its writers, an adoptive *patria chica.*

George Woodcock: *The Meeting of Time and Space*, p. 14.

---

23 *differentiate* (v.): to distinguish – 24 *relaxed* (p.p.): made less severe – 24 *luxuriant* (adj.): having or showing the comforts of wealth – 26 *Vancouver:* the largest city in B.C. and the third largest in Canada – 28 *Roderick Haig-Brown*, 1908–1976: an author of stories about wildlife, novels and children's books. A keen conservationist. – 28 *Ethel Wilson*, 1888–1980: a writer of short stories and novels – 28 *Malcolm Lowry*, 1909–1957: a famous novelist (*Under the Volcano*) – 29 *David Watmough*, 1926–: a novelist, literary journalist, commentator and author of plays, who lives in Vancouver – 29 *P. K. Page*, 1916–: Patricia Kathleen Page is a writer, painter and poet who lives in B. C. – 29 *Jane Rule*, 1931–: a writer of novels, short stories and essays – 30 *adoptive* (adj. fml.): adopted – 30 *patria chica:* fashionable home country

Vancouver

1: ERIC NICOL: First Province on the Left

Eric Nicol is one of Canada's best known humorists. Born in Kingston, Ont. in 1919 he moved with his parents to Vancouver when he was six. After his studies at the University of British Columbia and the Sorbonne in Paris he began writing for radio, television and the stage. Three of his many books of humour have won him the Leacock Medal for Humour.

From: *The West Coast Experience*, ed. Jack Hodgins, Macmillan of Canada, Toronto, 1976, pp. 9–13.

Although Vancouver, British Columbia, is more than sixty years old and its population is nudging the half-million mark, many strangers, including some Eastern Canadians, still don't know exactly where it is. Responsible for this geographical vagueness are several false impressions: for instance, the common belief that British Columbia is a steaming colony in the heart of the South American jungle. Something about the name, British Columbia, apparently suggests a tattered Union Jack fluttering over a few square miles of monkeys and malaria. [...]

Leacock: Stephen Leacock (1869–1944), a famous Canadian humorist writer – *medal* (n.): an award – 2 *nudge* (v.) lit.: to move by gently, here: to pass. Today Vancouver has a population of about 1,200,000 – 4 **vagueness** (n.): lack of clarity – 6 *jungle* (n.): a tropical forest too thick to walk through easily – 7 *tattered* (pp.): torn – 7 *Union Jack:* the British flag – 8 *malaria* (n.): a disease of hot countries –

Another popular misconception about Vancouver's location is that it is on Vancouver Island. In Toronto, Montreal, and throughout the United States there are small but well-organized groups who insist that the logical place for Vancouver is on Vancouver Island and who are liable to turn ugly if you try to prove otherwise. Actually, of course, they are confusing Vancouver with Victoria, the capital of the Province, thereby annoying the citizens of Victoria, who resent being associated with the continent of North America.

Victoria, it may be noted incidentally, has gained considerable celebrity as "a little bit of Old England". When a British colonel anywhere in the world is wounded or feels death at hand, unerring instinct leads him eventually to the windswept waste of whitening flannel that is Victoria, and there, after snorting defiance through the local press, he passes on.

Thirdly, there are a few persons who fail to distinguish Vancouver, B.C., from Vancouver, Washington, which sits just below the border and refuses to go away. And lastly, some people haven't the faintest idea where Vancouver may be, other than perhaps a forest-bound clearing periodically traversed by Indians and Nelson Eddy singing excerpts from "Rose Marie".

The truth is, of course, that Vancouver lies on the mainland, at the foot of the snow-tipped coastal range, between Burrard Inlet and the mighty Fraser River. You can't miss it, the first Province on the left.

In 1946 Vancouver celebrated her Diamond Jubilee, enjoying a bumper crop of American tourists, a hardy staple which comes up every year. Many Vancouver residents insisted that the house they were renting was obviously more than sixty years old, failing to realize that, although the city wasn't incorporated until 1886, there was a shack town here for some time before that, known variously as Hastings, Gastown, and Granville. Vancouver was so tough in those days she *had* to keep changing her name. [...]

---

9 *misconception* (n.): an example of understanding wrongly – 9 **location** (n.): place, position – 10 *Vancouver Island:* a large island off the City of Vancouver, with Victoria, the capital of B.C., on it – 12 *liable* (adj.): likely to – 15 *resent* (v.): to feel angry or bitter – 16 *incidentally* (adv.): by the way – 16 *celebrity* (n.): fame – 17 *colonel* (n.) /'kɜnl/: G. Oberst – 18 *unerring* (adj.): without making a mistake – 18 *eventually* (adv.): finally – 19 *waste* (n.): a wide empty stretch of land. here: referring to a sportsground as for cricket or bowls – 19 *whitening flannel:* here: referring to clothes worn for playing Cricket or Bowls – 19 *snort* (v.): lit. to utter loud sounds through the nose, here: to voice one's opinion loudly – 20 *pass on* (v.): to die – 24 *forest-bound:* surrounded by forests – 24 **periodically** (adv.): from time to time – 24 *traverse* (v.) /'trævɜs/: to cross – 25 *Nelson Eddy* (1901–1967) a popular American singer and actor of the thirties – 25 *excerpt* (n.): here: a piece from a musical work – 25 *Rose Marie:* a pop song of the thirties and the title of a popular film starring Nelson Eddy – 27 *snow-tipped:* with snow-covered mountain tops – 27 *coastal range:* the chain of mountains along the coast – 27 *Burrard Inlet:* a bay which stretches east from the Pacific on the north side of Vancouver's inner city – 27 *Fraser River:* it rises in the western slopes of the Rocky Mountains, passes through a famous canyon and after a total length of 1368 km empties into the Pacific at Vancouver. – 29 *Diamond Jubilee:* the 60th return of its foundation – 29 *bumper crop:* a large number – 30 *hardy staple:* a strong financial basis on which to live – 31 **resident** (n.): inhabitant – 33 *incorporate* (v.): to become organized as a legal body, here: to become a city officially – 33 *shack* (n.): a small roughly built house – 34 *tough* (adj.): rough, violent –

The original settlers around Vancouver were, of course, the coastal Indians, who were great canoe-makers and who thought nothing of paddling hundreds of miles to visit another tribe and spend an enjoyable afternoon slaughtering the men and carrying off the women. The fierce Haidas of the Queen Charlottes, for instance, were accustomed to paddle south to California for their scalps, probably because the heads were larger down there. The Indians were interrupted in these cheerful pursuits by the arrival of the Spanish explorers, who sailed in and planted the flag of Spain, only to have the English come right along behind and dig it up. For, just as the Spanish were leaving, Captain George Vancouver rowed in triumphantly. (There is no historical corroboration of the story that, as he passed the Spaniards' ships, Captain Vancouver yelled: "How many miles do you get to the galleon?")

Anyhow, Captain Vancouver, as the sharp students in the front row have already guessed, was the man after whom Vancouver was named. Yet, at the time, Vancouver thought he was barquing up the wrong inlet until he saw the Indians' welcoming committee standing on the shore. Approaching the Indians in his yawl, Vancouver hailed them:

"I am Captain Vancouver. I come in my yawl."

"How yawl," drawled the Indians, who belonged to the southern tribes, "Have you any cheap beads or worthless bits of glass you'd care to trade for these priceless furs?"

"Now that you mention it," chuckled Vancouver, "I have."

Thus the morning was filled with gay chatter and one-sided trading until the Indians suddenly realized that they were late for a massacre and politely excused themselves. Captain Vancouver, well satisfied with the site of the city that was to be named after him, sailed away in his gallant little H.M.S. *Discovery*, the prow of which was already dinted from repeated attempts to find the Northwest Passage.

Some years later the Hudson's Bay Company opened a trading post near Vancouver, and soon the traders were busy breaking glass up into worthless

---

37 *canoe* (n.) /kə'nu/: a paddle boat — 38 *slaughter* (v.): to kill — 39 *Haidas:* an Indian tribe that lives along the coast of the Queen Charlotte Islands in B.C. and in Alaska — 40 *Queen Charlottes:* a group of about 150 islands off the north coast of B.C. — 41 *scalp* (n.) /skælp/: the skin of the human head — 43 **explorer** (n.): a person who travels into a place for the purpose of discovery — 45 **triumphantly** (adv.) victoriously — 46 *corroboration* (n.): proof — 47 **yell** (v.): to cry out loud — 47 *galleon* (n.): a type of Spanish ship. Here it should actually read: gallon, G. Gallone (4,541. UK, 3,781. US), a play with words — 50 *barquing:* directing a small sailing ship — 52 *yawl* (n.) /jɔl/: a small boat carried on a ship — 52 *hail* (v.): to greet — 54 *How yawl:* how do you do — 54 *drawl* (v.): to speak slowly — 55 *bead* (n.): a small ball of glass — 56 *priceless* (adj.): of very great value — 57 *chuckle* (v.): to laugh quietly — 58 *chatter* (n.): rapid informal conversation — 60 **site** (n.): a piece of ground for building on — 61 *gallant* (adj.): splendid, beautiful — 61 *H.M.S.:* Her Majesty's Ship — 62 *prow* (n.): the front part of a ship — 63 *dint* (v.): to make a hollow place on the surface — 63 *Northwest Passage:* the water route through the Arctic north of the Canadian mainland, first traversed by Roald Amundsen 1903–1906 — 64 *Hudson's Bay Company:* an English trading company founded in 1670. It explored vast areas in western Canada and set up many trading posts. In 1867 the lands of the company became part of the Canadian Confederation. —

bits and destringing cheap beads. Most of the early trading was done at Victoria, which was a lot quieter than Vancouver, where people like Alex Mackenzie and Simon Fraser kept bursting out of the bush every few years expecting to be congratulated and put up for the night.

The next big moment in Vancouver's life was the Gold Rush. We may as well face it—a good many of Vancouver's early lovers were interested in her for her money. This was the period of building and lawlessness, when men worked the mines and women worked the miners. Bands of ruffians roamed the streets, until one day Queen Victoria made the whole place into a crown colony, giving Vancouver a respectability from which the city has never recovered.

Shortly afterward the gleaming rails of the Canadian Pacific Railway came down the Fraser Valley, to stop short at Port Moody, about fifteen miles east of Vancouver. The C.P.R. had it on good authority that Port Moody was where the ocean began, and saw no point in taking its locomotives any farther (they would get soaking wet for one thing). While Port Moody was still thumbing its nose at Vancouver (they never had got along very well), a champion, Van Horne, arose to persuade the company to extend the line to Vancouver, the City with a Future. Impressed with the personality of this virile town, which had just burned itself down (Port Moody had never burned *itself* down—a pretty stuffy place), the C.P.R. extended its line. It was a gay and stirring sight as the first transcontinental train puffed into the station, covered with people and freight rates.

The rest of the story is one of phenomenal growth, of Vancouver's rise to the position of third largest city in Canada. The largest and second largest are two places called Montreal and Toronto, situated inland. There is a legend that when the good people of Toronto die they go to Vancouver. "Retiring to the west coast," they call it, to this spawn of mountain and sea, home of the world's heaviest dew—our Vancouver.

---

66 *destring* (v.): to remove from a string – 67 *Alex Mackenzie:* Sir Alexander Mackenzie, 1764–1820, a furtrader and explorer who first reached the Pacific overland in Canada – 68 *Simon Fraser*, 1776–1862: a famous fur-trader and explorer. The Fraser River was named after him. – 69 *congratulate* (v.): to speak to a person with praise and admiration – 69 **put up** (v.): to provide food an lodging – 70 *Gold Rush:* G. Goldrausch – 73 *ruffian* (n.): a brutal person – 73 *roam* (v.): to wander around – 75 *respectability* (n.): the state of having a certain character and standard – 78 *Fraser Valley:* the valley of the Fraser River with its famous canyon – 78 *Port Moody:* a city of about 15,000 inhabitants, 20 km east of Vancouver, which can be reached by ocean-going vessels – 79 *C.P.R.:* the Canadian Pacific Railway – 81 *soaking wet:* completely wet – 82 *thumb* (v.): here: to put – 82 *champion* (n.): a person who fights for s.th. – 83 *Van Horne, Sir William Cornelius* (1843–1915): General Manager, later President of the Canadian Pacific Railway – 84 **virile** (adj.) /'vɪraɪl/: full of active strength – 88 *freight rate* (n.): the costs of carrying goods – 89 *phenomenal* (adj.) /fɪ'nomɪnl/: very unusual – 91 **legend** (n.): an old story – 93 *spawn* (n.): here: product

2: ETHEL WILSON: The Fishing Lodge at Three Loon Lake*

Ethel Wilson (1888–1980) was born in South Africa as the daughter of a Methodist missionary. At the age of two she was taken to England and in 1898 came to Canada where she lived with her grandmother in Vancouver. After attending boarding schools and a teacher training college she taught at various local schools until 1920. In the late twenties Ethel Wilson began writing short stories. Her first novel *Hetty Dorval* was published in 1947. *Swamp Angel* (1954), her greatest success as a novelist, tells the story of a woman, Maggie Lloyd, escaping her meaningless marriage and starting a new life on a remote lake in northern British Columbia. It is interwoven with the memories of Nell Severance, a former circus-performer.

In chapter 14 Ethel Wilson describes the location of Three Loon Lake in the mountains near Kamloops and the life that Haldar Gunnarsen and his wife are leading in their fishing lodge before Maggie arrives there in search of peace, harmony and personal fulfillment.

The text is taken from: Ethel Wilson, *Swamp Angel,* Toronto, McClelland and Stewart, repr. 1982, pp. 67–73.

As you drive up the winding ascent into the hills behind Kamloops, past the Iron Mask mine, and on, the driver does not look down, but the passenger looks down, and still farther down, towards the beautiful confluence of the North Thompson and South Thompson Rivers which are fluid monuments

---

Methodist (adj.): referring to a Christian group which follows the teaching of John Wesley – *missionary* (n.): person sent to a foreign country to spread his religion there – **remote** (adj.): distant – *interweave* (v.): to weave with s.th. else – *circus-performer* (n.): an artiste, G. Artist – **location** (n.): place – *Loon* (n.): G. Haubentaucher – *Kamloops:* a city in southern B.C., 420 km northeast of Vancouver – **lodge** (n.): a house for hunters, fishermen, sportsmen – **fulfillment** (n.): satisfaction –

1 *ascent* (n.): /ə'sent/ the act of climbing or travelling up – 3 *confluence* (n.): the flowing together of two or more streams – 4 *North Thompson:* it rises in the Rocky Mountains and flows south as the North Thompson River. – 4 *South Thompson:* it flows out of Shuswap Lake. Both rivers join at Kamloops and the Thompson River then empties into the Fraser River at Lytton B.C. – 4 *fluid* (adj.): having the quality of flowing – 5 **explorer** (n.): a person who travels into a place for the purpose of discovery. Here: referring to David Thompson (1770–1857) –

to the great explorer's name. At Kamloops the rivers join and become the Thompson River which flows westward between the sagebrush hills, spreads into a wide lake, narrows, and races on. The first Fort Kamloops was built at the vantage ground of the junction of the rivers. Kamloops is the Meeting of the Waters.

About twenty-five miles from the town of Kamloops, following a progressively bad road into the hills, is Three Loon Lake. Between Kamloops and Three Loon Lake—which is one of several scattered lakes among the hills—folds of the high land rising and falling away disclose occasional ranch buildings. Some cattle graze, and some sheep, domestically incongruous in these hills. For the last five miles, as the road becomes a rocky trail, taxing the driver, there is no habitation. Yet, by the standards of that country, Three Loon Lake is not far from town.

For the last five miles, you drive among trees. The higher sage hills are, by some authority of nature, clothed with spruce and aspen and lodge-pole pines. You cannot see a gleam, even, of the water of the lake until you are nearing the lodge. But, as soon as you hear the occasional wild and lonely cry of the loon clattering through trees, you know that you are near some water.

These lakes lie like giant dew-ponds in depressions at the summits of the hills. The ground rises slightly round them, and, if the hill is high enough, the lake is always rimmed with pine forest, very dark and close. In certain parts of the lake shore there is tulé grass growing out into the water, thick at the shore, thin and sparse as it stretches into the lake. Where the tulé grass—which is a tall reed-like grass—is sparse, its angled reflections fall into the water and form engaging patterns. Where the tulé grass is dense, Canada geese may make their nests and lie there with their young, but, more often, smaller water birds nest there and the geese go farther north. Fish feed in the tulé and are fairly safe. Perhaps they become bold, and some acquired knowledge tells them that the fisherman cannot cast into the dense part of the tulé grass. But he casts into the edge of the grass, where a dimple reports that a fish is feeding. The lake gets its name, of course, from the loons who own the lake and have always owned it. There is a mother, large and handsome, and her two lordly children who swim one on each side of her. When they are big enough, she

---

6 *sagebrush* (n.): G. nordamerikanischer Beifuß (Steppengewächs) – 8 *vantage* (n.): a good position from which to see s.th. – 8 *junction* (n.): a place of joining, meeting or uniting – 10 *progressively* (adv.): s.th. that becomes increasingly worse – 13 *disclose* (v.): to make known – 13 *ranch* (n.): a very large farm where sheep, cattle or horses are produced – 14 *graze* (v.): to feed on grass – 14 *domestically incongruous:* out of place – 15 *tax* (v.): to make heavy demands on – 16 *habitation* (n.): a house to live in – 19 *spruce* (n.): G. Rottanne – 19 *aspen* (n.): G. Espe – 19 *lodge-pole pines:* pines that can be used as supports in building a small wooden house – 22 *clatter* (v.): to move with short knocking sounds – 23 **giant** (adj.): very big – 23 *depression* (n.): a part of a surface lower than the other parts – 23 **summit** (n.): top – 25 *rimmed with* (p.p.): surrounded by – 26 *tulé* (n.): a large kind of grass, G. große Binse – 27 *sparse* (adj.): scattered – 28 *reed* (n.): G. Reet – 28 *angled* (adj.): not upright or straight, G. winklig – 29 *engaging patterns:* attractive patterns – 34 *dimple* (n.): G. leichte Kräuselung des Wassers –

leaves them sometimes and flies high, circling higher, and is joined by another loon from somewhere else. He may be her consort; or perhaps another mother loon has come to her lake. They fly together, and then the visiting loon returns home. The mother swims with her two big babies and sometimes she utters her loud and vacuous clattering cry. Is it a laugh? Is it a cry? It is melancholy, particularly at nightfall. It belongs completely to the lake and is part of these regions. It epitomizes that place. All the creatures on the lake hear it. What does it mean? The shores echo the cry back across the lake, and the loon cries again and the echoes clatter again and then silence closes over as always.

Sometimes the fish osprey cruises above. He has a nest at the top of a high tree at the far end of the lake. He cruises and cruises. Then suddenly he drops. He hits the water hard in flying spray. He rises and shakes himself like a dog and the spray flies in a fountain on the still lake.

He rises into the sky. In his talons he carries a fish that looks silver in the sunlight. It is a rainbow trout. He does not carry the fish at right angles to his body. His talons hold the trout parallel under his body, and so he rises unimpeded and rapidly and moves off towards his home, looking like a bird with one slim shining pontoon suspended underneath him. Sometimes the loon seems to warn the creatures of the lake that the osprey is coming, for he is a great hunter. He has to be. Sometimes he comes in silence.

When the naked lake is placid beneath the sky, the Kamloops—or rainbow-trout leap and leap. That does not mean that they will take the fly. It may mean that they are lousy, or perhaps they leap for joy. It must be great fun, leaping straight up from water into air, propelled by those small strong smooth muscles—two, three feet or more above the lake—and falling again. In the evening, when the sky and the water are shot with tender colours which grow more violent in lake and sky, this leaping is beautiful to see, here, there, there, near at hand, and diminished across the water. You hear the delayed plop of the leaping fish. Little fountains are everywhere on the lake. One at a time—no—two, three, four. It exasperates, at last, because the leaping fish has no intention of taking the fly. It is when he weaves—bold, timid, swift, secret, hidden—through the opaque waters, or when he is feeding at the edge of the weeds or in some fine undisclosed rich place that he will, perhaps, try the fly, either from hunger, curiosity, or some other fishy attribute of which we

---

39 *consort* (n.): partner – 42 *vacuous* (adj.): without purpose or meaning – 43 *melancholy* (n.): sadness – 44 *epitomize* (v.): to summarize – 48 *fish osprey* (n.): G. Fischadler – 49 *cruise* (v.) /kruz/: to fly in an unhurried way, searching for s.th. – 50 *in flying spray:* with water splashing about – 52 *talon* (n.): a sharp powerful nail on the foot – 53 *rainbow trout:* G. Regenbogenforelle – 55 *unimpeded* (adj.): not stopped in progress – 56 *pontoon* (n.): G. Ponton – 56 *suspend* (v.): to hang from above – 56 *underneath* (prep.): under s.th. – 59 *placid* (adj.): quiet – 61 *lousy* (adj.): parasitic, G. von Parasiten befallen – 62 *propel* (v.): to drive forward – 67 *plop* (n.): a sound made when s.th. drops smoothly into the water – 68 *exasperate* (v.): to annoy or make angry – 69 **timid** (adj.): fearful – 70 *opaque* (adj.) /ɔu'pəɪk/: not allowing light to pass through – 71 *undisclosed* (p.p.): unknown –

know nothing. At Three Loon Lake the water is nearly always very cold, and the fish are lively, striking and running, like whiplashes; the fisherman must play strongly and delicately, for the fish is never his until it lies in his net, impotent.

On the edge of Three Loon Lake a man called Haldar Gunnarsen had cleared land and built, in the Scandinavian fashion and also in the fashion of the western interior country, a rather large log cabin with eating-place, kitchen, a small bedroom for his wife and himself, a cubbyhole for his son, and a store room. There was, of course, a stove in the kitchen, and there was also an iron stove of the kind called an air-tight heater in the eating-room which was a living-room for guests if they had any. He added a plank verandah to the front of the lodge and an extension of the cedar shake roof, supported by lodge poles over the verandah. There were two privies at the back. Then he built five very small log cabins among the trees, each with a stove. He would build a smoke-house when he could afford it. He had, at first, another returned man to help him for a while, and two neighbours who lived some miles away and had a buzz-saw helping him too. He used his gratuity money after the war. The wood cost him nothing, except some labour and some planking for the floors. He had to buy nails, stoves, windows, and cement for chimneys and chinking. How he grudged the money for beds and blankets and tin washbasins and many more things which, to his surprise, he found to be necessary—and boats, of course.

His wife was nearly as much interested as he was, but not quite. She was city bred. Looking forward, she was able to see a row of nice cabins, a better car to make deliveries easier, an improved road, and kitchen help, money in the bank and retirement. She was not quite sure that she wanted her little boy Alan to grow tied up, as it were, to the country but she knew that you can't have everything the way you want it, and if Alan grew up to be as good a man as his father Haldar, her heart and her head told her that she should be satisfied; yet she was not. However, at first her mind jumped the next few years, and saw the Lodge at Three Loon Lake as well known, filled, and famous to the far parts of the continent. Americans from California, New York, Honolulu come for the fishing to remote points of British Columbia, so she was right to be hopeful. Canadians come from all over the west.

She did not like living outside a city. She would, of course, rather have

---

74 *whiplash* (n.): the crack of a whip – 78 *clear* (v.): to remove unwanted objects from s. th. – 79 **log cabin** (n.): a small hut made of thick pieces of wood from a tree – 80 *cubbyhole* (n.): a small enclosed space – 83 *plank* (n.): a long heavy piece of board – 84 *cedar shake* (n.): G. Zedernschindel – 85 *lodge pole* (n.): a strong wooden support – 85 *privy* (n.): an outdoor toilet without running water – 87 *smoke-house* (n.): a place in which meats or fish are smoked so that they can be eaten – 87 *returned man:* a man who has returned from the war – 89 *buzz-saw* (n.): G. Kreissäge – 89 *gratuity money* (n.): a gift of money given to a person when he leaves the armed forces – 92 *chink* (v.): to close spaces by filling with a substance – 92 *grudge* (v.): to allow unwillingly – 98 *retirement* (n.): to stop working at one's job because of age –

lived in Kamloops which, though nominally a city, does not look like one. The little boy was very happy about the whole affair.

There was, in Kamloops, this man called Henry Corder who knew Haldar Gunnarsen very well. Henry Corder knew every fishing place in the region, and the owners, and the fishing, and the kind of place that would suit the enquiring visitor. He could sum you up as he sat at his bench, and knew how much roughing-it you could take or whether you wanted tablecloths and indoor plumbing. He also knew the kind of fishing you would get at these places and whether, at that very moment, the fishing was good there. He was honest. He did this for love, although some benefits accrued, because he had the gift and the passion. Everyone deferred to Henry Corder. He liked Haldar Gunnarsen very much and encouraged him in his venture. He could not see why Haldar's lodge at Three Loon should not, in a few years, have as fine and justified a reputation as any lodge in the district.

It was therefore a keen disappointment to Henry Corder and to many other people when, the summer after a promising but incomplete first season, Haldar Gunnarsen's car slid in the gumbo off the trail in one of the bad spots about six miles from his lodge, and he was pinned beneath the car. Some fishermen driving in that evening found him. Haldar was alive but his hip was broken and he had other injuries of various kinds. The car was salvaged. That was in the middle of the first full season. Mrs Gunnarsen and the child Allan closed up the lodge and came down to Kamloops. After eight months in hospital, Haldar began to move about a bit. While he had lain in hospital, and, partly in order to divert his mind from severe physical pain, he had planned his next season, and the next season after that. He was undefeatable (he thought), and as time went on he communicated with a man whom he knew, and liked moderately well, who might find it worth his while to see him through the next season, and then, of course, Haldar would be all right. He did not wish to do this, as he had a fiercely possessive feeling for Three Loon Lake, and did not really want this man to have any part in it. But the poor, who also meet with misfortune, cannot always choose. So, as Haldar did not at any time consider pulling out of Three Loon Lake, he had to compromise. Things were made still more difficult for him as his hip did not knit well. He suffered, daily and nightly a good deal of pain, but, as he was a philosopher, he disdained the pain and attempted to ignore it. He refused to recognize the fact that he would not be of much use at the lodge.

---

108 *nominally* (adv.): by name – 113 *sum up* (v.): to consider and judge quickly – 114 *roughing it:* living in a simple and not very comfortable way – 114 *indoor plumbing:* here: running water, bathroom, flushtoilet etc. – 117 *accrue* (v.): to become bigger or more by addition – 118 *defer* (v.): to yield to, esp. in opinion – 119 **venture** (n.): a course of action in business whose result is uncertain – 124 *in the gumbo:* in sticky wet soil – 126 *hip* (n.): G. Hüfte – 127 *salvage* (v.): to save – 131 *divert* (v.): to turn from – 132 *undefeatable* (adj.): not to be defeated – 133 **communicate** (v.): to exchange opinions – 134 *to see him through:* to help him through – 136 *possessive* (adj.): unwilling to share one's own things with other people – 139 *compromise* (v.): to follow a middle course, to give in – 140 *knit* (v.): to unite closely – 142 *disdain* (v.): to regard with contempt –

His wife conceived a strong dislike for Three Loon Lake, and wished Haldar to sell it. This she urged him to do as soon as she thought he was well enough to be faced with her strong feelings on the subject. A difference of opinion grew to a bickering and then the subject was closed. Haldar persisted in regarding his crippled condition as a temporary affair and irrelevant, and the lodge at the lake as being intrinsically established and permanent. His judgment had become impaired to the extent that he thought that his wife was unreasonable, and he did not see, or know, that below her argument was a growing fear and dislike of the future with a crippled man and a child at Three Loon Lake. She also developed a jealousy against the lake as against a person. He did not even know that he would be a care to her. He regarded himself as a strong man, but temporarily a little lame. There were several reasons that bound Haldar Gunnarsen to Three Loon Lake and it was remarkable that these binding attachments had grown so fast, but land can do that. The land was his, and had at once assumed the character of having been intrinsically his, always, waiting only, ever since lake and shore were made, for Haldar. The place was his future, and he had never had a future, only an imperative present. The character of the place was so much the character of Haldar that he conceived of it as being almost sentient, waiting for him, and that it would wait for his son. This waiting feeling was intensified by the nights and the days that he spent in the hospital when, tirelessly, he roamed Three Loon Lake, and knew that it was his, water and shore. None of these reasons, or passions, bound Mrs Gunnarsen to Three Loon Lake. She blamed the place for her husband's disability and accumulated within herself other reasons why she did not wish to see it again. By May, however, the Gunnarsens and a man called Chuffey, together with further supplies for which Haldar had to raise a loan, were at the lake again. They began once more and a few fishermen came, recommended by Henry Corder. The lodge was not well run, and the cabins were not very clean. Mrs Gunnarsen was not efficient and had too much to do. Chuffey was lazy, talkative, irresponsible about money, and had a large appetite. Haldar Gunnarsen, in his effort not to show that he suffered pain, was morose, and he worked far too hard, moving slowly in a manner that was painful to witness. Their little boy became bad-tempered because people had no time for him, but he carried the firewood to the cabins and saw that the boats were really tied up, and he helped to hang out the washing, a job which he despised.

---

147 *bickering* (n.): a quarrel, esp. about small matters – 149 *intrinsically* (adv.): being part of the nature of s.th. – 150 *impair* (v.): to weaken – 153 *jealousy* (n.): /'dʒeləsɪ/: G. Eifersucht – 154 *a care:* G. ein Pflegefall – 157 *attachment* (n.): fondness – 161 *imperative* (adj.): urgent – 163 *sentient* (adj.): having feelings and consciousness – 164 *roam* (v.): to wander about – 167 *disability* (n.): the state of being unable to use one's body properly – 167 *accumulate* (v.): to collect – 172 *efficient* (adj.): working well and without waste – 173 *talkative* (adj.): liking to talk a lot – 173 *irresponsible* (adj.): showing lack of ability to behave carefully – 175 *morose* (adj.): not cheerful, looking as if angry – 176 **bad-tempered** (adj.): angry

3: EARLE BIRNEY: Pacific Door

Early Birney was born in Calgary, Alta., in 1904 but later moved with his parents to British Columbia. In 1922 he enrolled at the University of British Columbia as a chemistry student, but soon became interested in English literature. After receiving his Ph.D. from the University of Toronto he taught there, became literary editor of the *Canadian Forum* and began writing poetry. His first collection, *David*, was published in 1942. From 1948 to 1965 he was professor of medieval literature at the University of British Columbia. Besides a wealth of poetry, which ranks him among the best known Canadian poets, Birney has published a novel and a collection of stories and sketches.

From: *Selected Poems 1940–1966*, Toronto, McClelland and Stewart Ltd., 1966, p. 142.

PACIFIC DOOR

Through or over the deathless feud
of the cobra sea and the mongoose wind
you must fare to reach us
Through hiss and throttle come
by a limbo of motion humbled
under cliffs of cloud
and over the shark's blue home
Across the undulations of this slate
long pain and sweating courage chalked
such names as glimmer yet
Drake's crewmen scribbled here their paradise
and dying Bering lost in fog
turned north to mark us off from Asia still

Alta: Alberta. Canada's most western prairie province – *enrol* at (v.): here: to become a student at – *Ph.D.:* Doctor of Philosophy – *editor* (n.): a person who is responsible for the organisation and opinions of a newspaper or magazine – *Canadian Forum:* Canada's oldest continually published political magazine, founded in 1920 – *medieval* (adj.): /ˈmedɪˈiːvl/: referring to the Middle Ages – 1 *feud* (n.) /fjud/: enmity, lasting quarrel – 2 *cobra* (n.): a poisonous snake – 2 *mongoose* (n.): an animal that is good at killing rats and snakes. G. Mungo – 3 *fare* (v.): poet. to travel – 4 *hiss* (n.): a sound like a continuous "s"– 4 *throttle* (n.): G. Drosselventil – 5 *limbo* (n.): an obstacle like the rope in a West Indian Dance under which a dancer has to pass – 7 *shark* (n.): G. Hai – 8 *undulation* (n.): the rising and falling of the waves – 8 *slate* (n.): G. Schiefertafel – 10 *glimmer* (v.): to give a very faint, unsteady light – 11 *Drake:* Sir Francis Drake (1540–1596), a great seaman and adventurer – 11 *scribble* (v.): to write carelessly or in a hurry – 12 *Bering, Vitus Jonassen* (1680–1741): a famous explorer who proved that Asia and America were not joined –

Captain Vancouver's ships at Salmon Cove, a sketch by T. Heddington

Here cool Cook traced in sudden blood his final bay
and scurvied traders trailed the wakes of yesterday
until the otter rocks were bare
and all the tribal feathers plucked
Here Spaniards and Vancouver's boatmen scrawled
the problem that is ours and yours
that there is no clear Strait of Anian
to lead us easy back to Europe
that men are isled in ocean or in ice
and only joined by long endeavour to be joined
Come then on the waves of desire that well forever
and think no more than you must
of the simple unhuman truth of this emptiness
that down deep below the lowest pulsing of primal cell
tar-dark and still
lie the bleak and forever capacious tombs of the sea

Dollarton 1947

---

14 *Cook, James* (1728–1779): the famous seaman and explorer of the Pacific Ocean and the shores of North America – 15 *scurvied:* G. von Skorbut befallen – 15 *wake* (n.): G. Kielwasser, Spur – 16 *otter* (n.): G. Otter – 18 *Vancouver, George* (1757–1798): a naval officer who explored the west coast of North America – 18 *scrawl* (v.): to write in an irregular, awkward way – 20 *Strait of Anian:* part of the legendary North-West Passage linking the Atlantic and Pacific Oceans – 22 *isled:* to be left on an island – 24 *well* (v.): to rise – 27 *pulse* (v.): to beat steadily as the heart does – 27 *primal* (adj.): original – 28 *tar* (n.): G. Teer – 29 *bleak* (adj.): cold and cheerless – 29 *capacious* (adj.): able to hold a lot –

4: EMILY CARR: Wild Geese

Emily Carr (1871–1945) is best known as a painter. After studying in San Francisco, in England and Paris she won international recognition. In 1898 she started making trips to distant Indian villages on the west coast of British Columbia gathering new impressions for her paintings. Later she also turned to other remote regions of B.C. After 1926 she took creative writing courses and in 1940 some of her stories were broadcast. Her first book *Klee Wyck*, a series of short stories, was published in 1941, followed by *The Book of Small* and *The House of All Sorts*. Her autobiography *Growing Pains* appeared posthumously in 1946.

From: Emily Carr: *Growing Pains*, Toronto, Oxford University Press, 1946, pp. 378–381.

Use your own dictionary for unknown words.

SPRING was young, I over seventy. With Spring all about me I sat sketching in the clearing that was now given over to second growth—baby pines, spruce, hemlock, cedar and creeping vines, fireweed, bracken.

The clearing was off the Happy Valley Road at Metchosen, not far from Victoria. Seventy years had maimed me, loggers had maimed the clearing. I could no longer scramble over great logs nor break my way through networks of brambles, creep under bushes and drown myself crown-high in lush, young growth. I had to be taken out, set down and called for, which was a nuisance, but I got immense delight in just being there, in the quiet wood, nobody for company but Spring.

Though everything was so still, you were aware of tremendous forces of growth pounding through the clearing, aware of sap gushing in every leaf, of push, push, push, the bursting of buds, the creeping of vines. Everything expanding every minute but doing it so subtly you did not actually see anything happen.

In spite of the doctor I went into the woods to paint a few times more. The longing was too terrific to subdue and I felt better. I did not go in my old van (it was deteriorating with unuse so I had sold it). I rented a cabin and took a maid along to cook and carry for me.

The maid was too busy attending to her own work to bother about me; she carried my things out into the woods and came back for them and me later. I was very happy but the last expedition I over-did and came smash.

---

creative writing: the art of writing literature – *autobiography* (n.): a book written by oneself about one's own life – *posthumously* (adv.): here: after her death

For a year painting lay dormant but I did some writing. One day a friend took my sister driving. On the way they planted me in a thick lonely place just off the high road while they took a long ride. It was here that I painted *The Clearing* and here the wild geese flew over.

Hark! Hark! High up in the blue, above the clearing, wild geese migrating. Honk, honk, ya honk! A triangle of noisy black dots.

Every Canadian thrills at the sound—the downpour of cackling honks broken, irregular, scattering with the sharp monotony of hailstones while the geese sail smooth and high, untroubled by fear of men, for migrating geese fly far, far above man's highest shooting.

On the ground the wild goose is a shy, quiet fellow. In the sky he is noisy and bold.

I lifted my face to watch the honking triangle pass across the sky. The day was clear, not dazzle-bright. I could look into the face of the sky without blinking. There was just one cloud. The geese caught up with the cloud. The leader dove into it, his flock followed. For a few seconds the cloud nestled the geese to her breast, emptying the sky, muffling the honkings, but the company pierced through the cloud. The leader and those few birds that fly in close formation behind him appeared, then the two long wavering side lines of singly-spaced birds emerged, to continue their way sailing, sailing into the north, one glad rush of going, one flock unswervingly following one leader. At that height each bird appeared no bigger than a small black bead, evenly strung one goose behind the other, a live necklace flung across the throat of heaven.

The racket passed over the clearing, the sky was again still, my eyes came back to the greying stumps amongst which I sat. Young growth had already hidden some. Even the echoes had forgotten how they had shrieked sympathy when the axes bit into the great original forest giants, forgotten the awful crash, the groan, the tremble of the ground as each tree fell.

Today the clearing was not sun-dazzled, rather it was illumined with Spring, every leaf was as yet only half unfurled and held light and spilled some.

Today at seventy I marvelled more at the migration of the geese than I had at the age of seven when, standing in our cow-pasture holding Father's hand and looking up into the sky, I heard Father tell the story of birdmigration and only half believed. Today a new wondering came to me as I watched the flight. What of the old or the maimed goose who could not rise and go with the flock? Of course there *was* the old, the maimed goose. What of him when the flock, young and vigorous, rose leaving him grounded? Did despair tear his heart? No, old goose would fill the bitter moment, pouring out proud, exultant honks that would weave among the clatter of the migrating flock. When the flock were away, animal-wise he would nibble here and nibble there, quietly accepting.

Old age has me grounded too. Am I accepting? God give me the brave unquestioning trust of the wild goose! No, being humans, we need more trust, our hopes are stronger than creatures' hopes. Walt Whitman's words come ringing,—*We but level this lift to pass and continue beyond.*

VII The North

Finally, there is the North, the great sweep of territory mainly above the sixtieth parallel, which forms the southern boundary of the Yukon and Northwest Territories, but also, because of the southeasterly pull of the dividing line between tundra and northern forest, embraces the northern parts of Manitoba and Ontario around Hudson's Bay, the Ungava peninsula of Quebec, and the north of the Labrador coast which forms part of the province of Newfoundland.

The North has had its own great native culture, that of the Inuit, which flowered after contact with white culture into a splendid tradition of sculptural art, but which also developed an oral poetry that, like the superb hunting techniques of the northern people, was beautifully attuned to the nature of the region.

George Woodcock: *The Meeting of Time and Space*, pp. 14–15.

---

1 *sweep* (n.): a long curved area of country – 2 **parallel** (n.): any number of lines on a map drawn parallel to the Equator – 5 *peninsula* (n.) /pə'nınsjulə/: a piece of land almost completely surrounded by water but joined to a larger mass of land – *Inuit:* a name applied by Eskimos to themselves – 9 *sculptural* (adj.): concerning the art of shaping solid figures out of stone, wood, etc.– 10 **oral** (adj.): spoken – 10 *superb* (adj.) /su'pɜb/: perfect in form, quality; wonderful – 11 *attune to* (v.): to bring into harmony, accord with

A dog team in the Arctic

The dangers of the Arctic: *HMS Investigator* caught in the ice, 1845

1: ROBERT W. SERVICE: The Land God Forgot

Robert W. Service was born in England in 1874 and educated in Glasgow. Search for adventure brought him across the Atlantic and the whole Canadian continent: in 1896 he settled on a farm in B.C., but later he resumed his restless life by travelling up and down the Pacific Coast. He reached the Yukon as a bank clerk and lived in Whitehorse and Dawson from 1904 to 1912. There he saw the end of the great Gold Rush, on the occasion of which he published his first collection of Yukon poems in Toronto, *Songs of a Sourdough* (1907). It was followed by other books of poems, e.g., *Rhymes of a Red-Cross Man* (1916), which was one of the most popular books of the First World War. During that time he got his nicknames "the Canadian Kipling" and "the Poet of the Yukon". After the war Service went to France, where he married and lived in Paris, Brittany, and on the Riviera for some time. During the Second World War he and his family lived quietly in Hollywood. His later works include *Rhymer of a Roughneck* (1950) and two autobiographical works: *Ploughman of the Moon* (1945) and *Harper of Heaven* (1948). Robert Service died in Brittany in 1958.

The text is taken from: *Collected Poems of Robert Service*, London, Ernest Benn, 1978, p. XVIII.

---

nickname (n.): a name used informally instead of one's own name – *Rudyard Kipling* (1865–1936): British author of short stories and novels (often with Indian background), esp. famous for his *Jungle Books* (1894–5) – *Brittany:* French Bretagne (the north-west part of France) – **autobiographical** (adj.): concerning the facts of one's own life –

The Land God Forgot

The lonely sunsets flare forlorn
   Down valleys dreadly desolate;
The lordly mountains soar in scorn
   As still as death, as stern as fate.

The lonely sunsets flame and die;
   The giant valleys gulp the night;
The monster mountains scrape the sky
   Where eager stars are diamond-bright.

So gaunt against the gibbous moon,
   Piercing the silence velvet-piled,
A lone wolf howls his ancient rune–
   The fell arch-spirit of the Wild.

O outcast land! O leper land!
   Let the lone wolf-cry all express
The hate insensate of thy hand,
   Thy heart's abysmal loneliness.

---

1 *flare* (v.): to burn with a bright flame but uncertainly or for a short time – 1 *forlorn* (adj.): lit. left alone, unhappy – 2 *dread* (adj.): causing great fear or anxiety – 2 **desolate** (adj.): sad and without people in it – 3 *soar* (v.): lit. to be very high – 3 *scorn* (n.): strong, angry feeling of contempt, disrespect – 5 *flame* (v.): to burn brightly – 6 **gulp** (v.): to swallow hastily – 7 *scrape* (v.): to rub roughly, scratch – 9 *gaunt* (adj.) /gɔːnt/: thin, as if ill or hungry – 9 *gibbous* (adj.): (of the moon) having the bright part filling more than half a circle – 11 *rune* (n.): characters of an alphabet used by ancient Germanic-speaking peoples, magic charm – 12 *fell* (adj.): lit. evil, dangerous, terrible – 12 *arch-*: (prefix) of the highest rank or class – 13 *outcast* (n. adj.): (s.o.) forced from his home or without friends – 13 *leper* (n.): s.o. who has the disease leprosy (G. Lepra) and who is avoided by healthy people – 15 *insensate* (adj.) /ɪnˈsenseɪt/: without the power to have feelings – 16 *abysmal* (adj.) not fml.: here: hopeless –

2: AL PURDY: Innuit

Alfred (Al) Purdy was born near Wooler, Ont., in 1918. He lost his father when he was 2 years old and was left in the care of his very religious mother. Part of his youth was spent under the influence of the Depression. He practiced a variety of odd jobs and served in the RCAF in the Second World War. Later he was a visiting professor at Simon Fraser University at Vancouver and teacher of creative writing at Banff School of Fine Arts (1971–73).

His book *Poems for all the Annettes*, which appeared in 1962, was an immediate success, to be followed by other collections (of plays, prose and poetry) like *Selected Poems* (1972) and *The Stone Bird* (1981), which Purdy considers his best book.

The poem is taken from: Al Purdy, *North of Summer: Poems from Baffin Island*, Toronto, McClelland and Stewart, 1967, p. 32.

INNUIT

An old man carving soapstone
at the co-op in Frobisher Bay
and in his faded eyes
it is possible to see them
shadowy figures
past the Dorset and pre-Dorset Cultures
5,000 years ago
if you look closely
But the race-soul has drawn back
drawn back
from settlements and landing fields
from white men
into secret vaults
and catacombs of marrow
bone rooms
that reveal nothing
The Innuit which is to say
THE PEOPLE

Depression: the period of reduced business activities and high unemployment (the 1930s in the USA and Canada) – *variety* (n.): different sorts – *RCAF:* Royal Canadian Air-Force – *In(n)uit:* the name applied by Eskimos to themselves – 1 *soapstone* (n.): a kind of soft stone which feels like soap – 2 *co-op* (n.): cooperative, any of a larger chain of shops – 2 *Frobisher Bay:* a Bay in the south-east of Baffin Island, named after Sir Martin Frobisher (1535?–94), English sailor and explorer – 5 *shadowy* (adj.): hard to see or know about, not distinct – 6 *Dorset Culture:* 500 BC–1500 AD, culture of the Dorset people, descendants from the Paleoeskimos of the Pre-Dorset Culture. They occupied the Labrador coast and the island of Newfoundland – 13 *vault* (n.): an underground room (e.g. beneath the floor of a church) in which things are stored – 14 *catacomb* (n.): an underground burial place, tunnel – 14 *marrow* (n.): the soft fat substance in the hollow centre of bones –

as the Greeks called all foreigners
barbaroi
something other than themselves
un-GREEK
so the Innuit
The People
these unknowable human beings
who have endured 5,000 years
on the edge of the world
a myth from long ago
that reaches into the past
but touches an old man still living
Looking into his eyes

it is possible to see the first hunters
(if you have your own vision)
after the last ice age
moving eastward from Siberia
without dogs or equipment
toward the new country
pausing on the sea-ice
for a moment of rest
then pushing on thru the white smother
—Flying generations

leap and converge on this face
an old man carving soapstone
with the race-soul of The People
THE PEOPLE
moving somewhere
behind his eyes

Pangnirtung *—1967*

---

20 *barbaroi:* s.o. who didn't speak Greek, later: any person without civilization – 25 *unknowable* (adj.): (s.th.) that can never be fully understood – 28 *myth* (n.): ancient story containing religious ideas which may explain life – 33 **vision** (n.): power of imagination – 39 *thru:* A.E. infml. through – 39 *smother* (n.): a thick and heavy mass – 41 *converge* (v.): to come together (towards a common point)

3: DUNCAN CAMPBELL SCOTT: The Forsaken

Duncan Campbell Scott was born in Ottawa in 1862 as the son of a Methodist missionary. He grew up in small towns in Ontario and Québec. After school, at the age of seventeen, the young Scott took a position in the Department of Indian Affairs in Ottawa and stayed there for 52 years. Travels as an official among the Indians offered him ample material for writing verse. He published *The Magic House and Other Poems*, his first collection of poetry, in 1893. It was followed by numerous others, e.g., *New World Lyrics and Ballads* (1905), containing "The Forsaken", a haunting ballad of Indian Life. Scott was an effective short-story writer, too, *In the Village of Viger* (1896) being his best-known collection. A volume of poems, essays and short stories, *The Circle of Affection*, appeared in 1947, the year D. C. Scott died.

The text is taken from: Duncan Campbell Scott, *Selected Poetry*, ed. Glenn Clever, Ottawa, The Tecumseh Press, 1974, pp. 37–39.

THE FORSAKEN

1

Once in the winter
Out on a lake
In the heart of the north-land,
Far from the Fort
And far from the hunters,
A Chippewa woman
With her sick baby,
Crouched in the last hours
Of a great storm.
Frozen and hungry,
She fished through the ice
With a line of the twisted
Bark of the cedar,
And a rabbit-bone hook
Polished and barbed;
Fished with the bare hook
All through the wild day,
Fished and caught nothing;
While the young chieftain
Tugged at her breasts,
Or slept in the lacings
Of the warm *tikanagan.*
All the lake-surface
Streamed with the hissing
Of millions of iceflakes
Hurled by the wind;
Behind her the round

---

missionary (n.): a person sent to a foreign country to teach and spread his religion there – *haunting* (adj.): s.th. which remains in the thoughts – *forsake* (v.): to desert, leave for ever – 4 **fort** (n.) /fɔt/: a strongly made building/place used for defence – 6 *Chippewa:* an Ojibwa Indian of a large tribe of North American Indians of the Algonquian family, from the Lake Superior region – 8 *crouch* (v.): to lower the body close to the ground by bending knees and back – 13 *cedar* (n.) /'sidə(r)/: an evergreen tree, G. Zeder – 15 *barbed* (adj.): with one or more sharp points – 20 *tug* (v.): to pull hard with force – 21 *lacing* (n.): lace, netlike cloth with ornaments made of fine thread – 22 *tikanagan* (n.): a moss-filled cradle board for carrying very small children in, G. wiegenförmiges Brettchen – 24 *hiss* (v.): to make a sound like a continuous "s" – 25 **flake** (n.): G. Flocke – 26 *hurl* (v.): to throw with force – 27 *round* (n.): a round form, a curved bend –

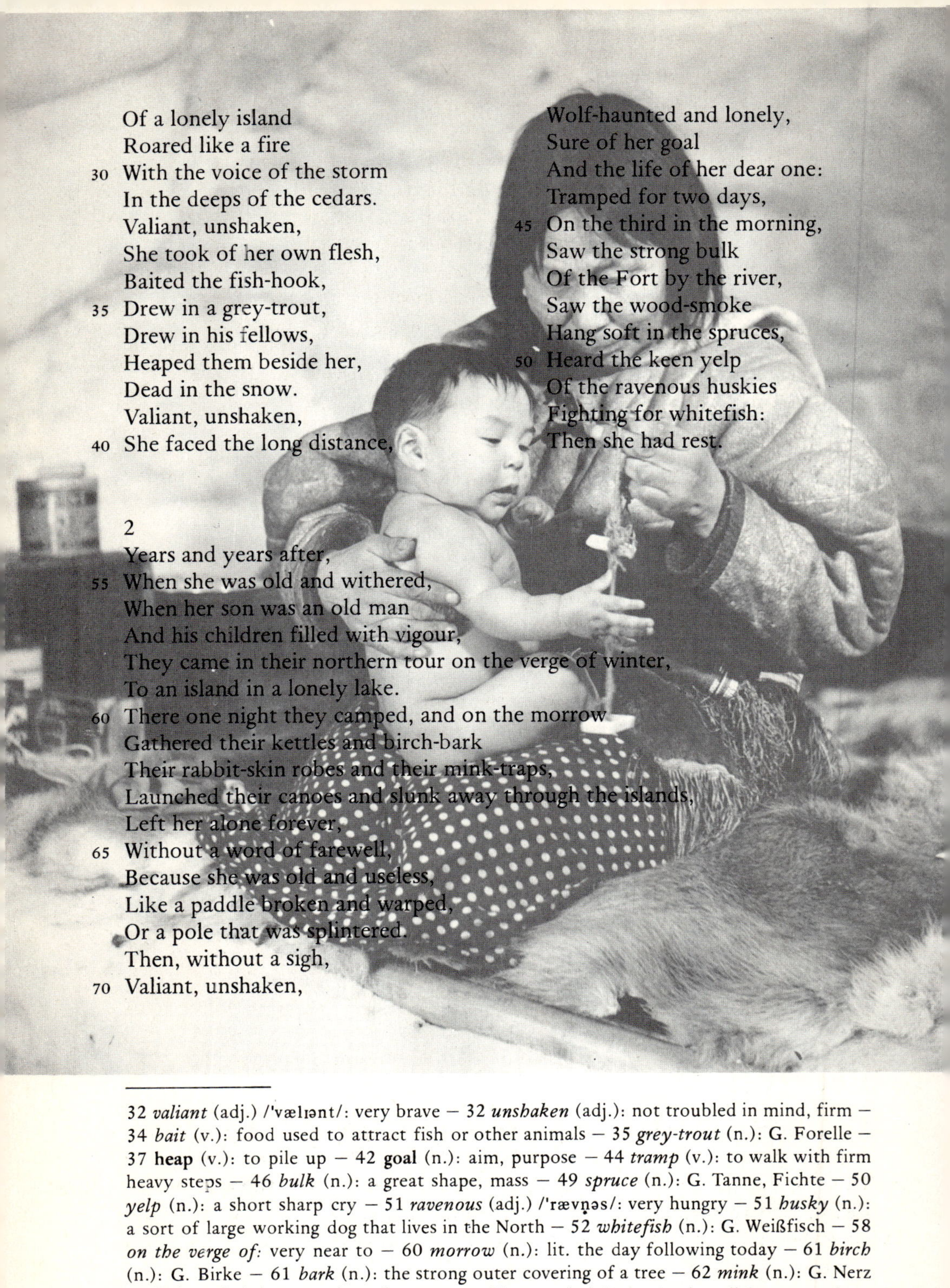

Of a lonely island
Roared like a fire
With the voice of the storm
In the deeps of the cedars.
Valiant, unshaken,
She took of her own flesh,
Baited the fish-hook,
Drew in a grey-trout,
Drew in his fellows,
Heaped them beside her,
Dead in the snow.
Valiant, unshaken,
She faced the long distance,
Wolf-haunted and lonely,
Sure of her goal
And the life of her dear one:
Tramped for two days,
On the third in the morning,
Saw the strong bulk
Of the Fort by the river,
Saw the wood-smoke
Hang soft in the spruces,
Heard the keen yelp
Of the ravenous huskies
Fighting for whitefish:
Then she had rest.

2

Years and years after,
When she was old and withered,
When her son was an old man
And his children filled with vigour,
They came in their northern tour on the verge of winter,
To an island in a lonely lake.
There one night they camped, and on the morrow
Gathered their kettles and birch-bark
Their rabbit-skin robes and their mink-traps,
Launched their canoes and slunk away through the islands,
Left her alone forever,
Without a word of farewell,
Because she was old and useless,
Like a paddle broken and warped,
Or a pole that was splintered.
Then, without a sigh,
Valiant, unshaken,

---

32 *valiant* (adj.) /'vælɪənt/: very brave – 32 *unshaken* (adj.): not troubled in mind, firm – 34 *bait* (v.): food used to attract fish or other animals – 35 *grey-trout* (n.): G. Forelle – 37 **heap** (v.): to pile up – 42 **goal** (n.): aim, purpose – 44 *tramp* (v.): to walk with firm heavy steps – 46 *bulk* (n.): a great shape, mass – 49 *spruce* (n.): G. Tanne, Fichte – 50 *yelp* (n.): a short sharp cry – 51 *ravenous* (adj.) /'rævn̩əs/: very hungry – 51 *husky* (n.): a sort of large working dog that lives in the North – 52 *whitefish* (n.): G. Weißfisch – 58 *on the verge of*: very near to – 60 *morrow* (n.): lit. the day following today – 61 *birch* (n.): G. Birke – 61 *bark* (n.): the strong outer covering of a tree – 62 *mink* (n.): G. Nerz – 63 *launch* (v.): to set into the water – 63 *canoe* (n.) /kə'nu/: a long light narrow boat moved by paddles – 63 *slink* (v.): slunk, slunk, to move quietly and secretly – 67 *warp* (v.): to turn or twist out of shape – 68 *splinter* (v.): to break into small needle-like pieces –

She smoothed her dark locks under her kerchief,
Composed her shawl in state,
Then folded her hands ridged with sinews and corded with veins,
Folded them across her breasts spent with the nourishing of children,
Gazed at the sky past the tops of the cedars,
Saw two spangled nights arise out of the twilight,
Saw two days go by filled with the tranquil sunshine,
Saw, without pain, or dread, or even a moment of longing:
Then on the third great night there came thronging and thronging
Millions of snowflakes out of a windless cloud;
They covered her close with a beautiful crystal shroud,
Covered her deep and silent.
But in the frost of the dawn,
Up from the life below,
Rose a column of breath
Through a tiny cleft in the snow,
Fragile, delicately drawn,
Wavering with its own weakness,
In the wilderness a sign of the spirit,
Persisting still in the sight of the sun
Till day was done.
Then all light was gathered up by the hand of God and hid in His breast,
Then there was born a silence deeper than silence,
Then she had rest.

---

71 *smooth* (v.): to make s.th. even – 71 *kerchief* (n.): a square piece of cloth worn to cover the head etc. – 72 *compose* (v.): to place in proper from – 72 *shawl* (n.) /ʃɔl/: a piece of soft cloth for wearing over head or shoulder – 72 *in state:* orderly, in its due place – 73 *ridge* (v.): G. zerfurchen – 73 *sinew* (n.): /ˈsɪnju/: G. Sehne – 73 *corded* (p.p.): looking as if formed with cords – 74 **nourish** (v.): to feed – 76 *spangled* (adj.): filled with stars – 76 *twilight* (n.): time when night is to become day or day night – 77 *tranquil* (adj.): calm, peaceful – 79 *throng* (v.): to gather in huge numbers – 81 *crystal* (n.): a transparent natural mineral that looks like pure ice – 81 *shroud* (n.): a cloth for covering a dead body (at burial) – 86 *cleft* (n.): a small opening, split – 87 *fragile* (adj.) /ˈfrædʒaɪl/: faint, easily broken, not likely to last – 87 *delicate* (adj.): finely made – 88 *waver* (v.): to flutter

Some say that we kill our old people. That is not true. Our old people have the strength and pride to kill themselves if they believe that their lives should come to an end. Sometimes they may command us to help them with their death, and so powerful is the word of a parent that his children may be forced to obey his wishes. That is our way, an ancient custom that we do not think is wrong.

From: James Houston, *The White Dawn: an Eskimo Saga*, Don Mills, Ont., Academic Press Canada, 1983, p. 222.

4: FARLEY MOWAT: Snow

Farley Mowat was born in Belleville, Ont., in 1921. His father, Angus Mowat, was a versatile man—he wrote novels, kept bees, sailed boats, etc.—whose restlessness made him move from place to place. In 1929 the family settled in Saskatoon, Sask., where Angus Mowat was in charge of the library. The prairie landscape had a lasting influence upon Farley, who had once wanted to become a biologist. The boy's adventures were later recounted in *The Dog Who Wouldn't Be* (1957). When World War II broke out, Mowat volunteered for military service; when the war was over, he became a student at the University of Toronto, but spent two years in the Arctic before completing his degree and becoming a freelance writer. *People of the Deer* (1952), *Never Cry Wolf* (1963) and *The Snow Walker* (1975) are the results of his visits to the Arctic.

Mowat's involvement with the North and also with the Atlantic Ocean is a recurring theme in all his widely-read books. His concern for endangered peoples and species, such as the Eskimos has won him an endless readership, not least among young people. Mowat now spends most of his time in Cape Breton, N.S.

The Snow Walker, from which the following text is taken, is a collection of stories about Canadian Innuit. It was published as a paperback by Seal Books, Toronto, 1977, and anthologized in *The World of Farley Mowat: A Selection from his Works*, ed. Peter Davison, Boston, Little, Brown and Company, 2nd printing, 1980, pp. 60–62.

---

versatile (adj.): having many different kinds of skill or ability – **restlessness** (n.): the state of being not quiet, always moving about – *in charge of*: responsible for – **landscape** (n.): open country – *recount* (v.): to tell a story – *volunteer* (v.): to offer to join the army of one's own free will – *Arctic:* the most northern part of the world – *freelance* (adj.): writing for a newspaper without being in its regular employment – *recur* (v.): to happen again and again – *endanger* (v.): to cause danger to, being in danger – *Innuit:* the name applied by Eskimos to themselves – *anthologize* (v.): to print in a collection of texts (often of the same kind, e.g. poems, or on the same subject) –

How do *we* envisage snow?

It is the fragility of Christmas dreams sintering through azure darkness to the accompaniment of the sound of sleigh bells.

It is the bleak reality of a stalled car and spinning wheels impinging on the neat time schedule of our self-importance.

It is the invitation that glows ephemeral on a woman's lashes on a winter night.

It is the resignation of suburban housewives as they skin wet snowsuits from runny-nosed progeny.

It is the sweet gloss of memory in the failing eyes of the old as they recall the white days of childhood.

It is the banality of a TV advertisement pimping Coca-Cola on a snowbank at Sun Valley.

It is the gentility of utter silence in the muffled heart of a snow-clad forest.

It is the brittle wind-rush of skis; and the bellicose chatter of snowmobiles.

Snow is these things to us, together with many related images; yet all deal only with obvious aspects of a multi-faceted, kaleidoscopic, and protean element.

Snow, which on our planet is a phoenix continually born again from its own dissolution, is also a galactic and immortal presence. In the nullity of outer space, clouds of snow crystals, immeasurably vast, drift with time, unchanged since long before our world was born, unchangeable when it will be gone. For all that the best brains of science and the sharpest of the

---

1 *envisage* (v.): to see in the mind – 2 *fragility* (n.): being easily broken or destroyed – 2 *sinter* (v.): G. (durch)sickern – 2 *azure* (adj.): /'æʒə(r)/: bright blue, as of the sky – 3 *accompaniment* (n.): s.th. found with s.th. else – 3 *sleigh* (n.): usu. wooden carriage made to slide along snow or over ice, drawn by a horse – 4 *bleak* (adj.): cold, hard, without comfort – 4 *stall* (v.): to stop moving for lack of power, etc. – 4 *impinge on* (v.): to have an effect on – 5 *neat* (adj.): well arranged, in good order – 5 *schedule* (n.): fixed plan, programme – 6 *ephemeral* (adj.) /ɪ'femərəl/: having a very short life – 6 *lash* (n.): eyelash, G. Wimper – 8 *suburban* (adj.): living in an outer area of a town – 9 *runny-nosed* (adj.): having watery noses – 9 *progeny* (n.) /'prodʒɪnɪ/: descendants, children – 10 *gloss* (n.): a superficial soft glowing or brightness – 10 *fail* (v.): to become weak – 10 **recall** (v.): to remember – 12 **advertisement** (n.): a notice of s.th. for sale – 12 *pimp* (v.): to sell (like a prostitute's agent) – 12 *snowbank* (n.): a mass of snow – 13 *Sun Valley:* a ski-resort in Idaho (USA) – 14 *gentility* (n.): the quality of being elegant, well-behaved, noble – 14 *muffle* (v.): to make a sound less easily heard – 14 *clad* (adj.): lit. clothed, covered – 15 *brittle* (adj.): making a short, harsh sound – 15 *rush* (n.): a sudden rapid hasty movement – 15 *bellicose* (adj.): warlike – 15 *chatter* (n.): a rapid knocking sound (e.g. made by machines) – 17 *multi-faceted* (adj.): having many sides to be considered – 17 *kaleidoscopic* (adj.): changing quickly and often – 17 *protean* (adj.) /'prəʊtɪən/: lit. continually changing, appearing in various forms – 19 *phoenix* (n.): a bird of ancient times believed to live very long which burnt itself to death and was reborn from the ashes – 20 *dissolution* (n.): (v. dissolve) death, fading away – 20 *galactic* (adj.): concerning the Milky Way (large group of stars in which our own sun and its planets lie) – 20 *nullity* (n.): nothingness – 21 *crystal* (n.): a mineral that looks like pure ice – 21 *immeasurable* (adj.): s.th. that cannot be measured

cyclopean eyes of astronomers can tell, the glittering crystals flecking the illimitable void are as one with those that settle on our hands and faces out of the still skies of a December night.

Snow is a single flake caught for an instant on a windowpane. But it is also a signboard in the solar system. When astronomers peer up at Mars they see the Red Planet as a monochromatic globe—except for its polar caps from which gleaming mantles spread toward the equatorial regions. As the antelope flashes its white rump on the dun prairies, so does Mars signal to worlds beyond it with the brilliance of our common sun reflected from its plains of snow.

And so does Earth.

When the first star voyager arcs into deep space, he will watch the greens and blues of our seas and lands dissolve and fade as the globe diminishes until the last thing to beacon the disappearing Earth will be the glare of our own polar heliographs. Snow will be the last of the elementals in his distant eye. Snow may provide the first shining glimpse of our world to inbound aliens ... if they have eyes with which to see.

— 24 *cyclops* (n.): (in old Greek stories) a one-eyed giant — 24 *astronomer* (n.): a person who studies the stars scientifically — 24 *fleck* (v.): to mark or cover with spots, drops, etc. — 25 *illimitable* (adj.): with no known limit — 25 *void* (n.): an empty space around our world — 27 **flake** (n.): G. Flocke — 27 *(window) pane* (n.): flat glass for use in a frame — 28 **solar** (adj.): concerning the sun — 28 *peer* (v.): to look very carefully or hard — 29 *monochromatic* (adj.): having only one colour — 29 **polar** (adj.): of the poles — 30 *mantle* (n.): cover (of netlike material) — 30 *equatorial* (adj.): concerning the Equator, a line drawn round the earth halfway between the North and South Poles — 31 *flash* (v.): to shine for a moment, move very fast — 31 *rump* (n.): part of an animal at the back above the legs — 31 *dun* (adj.): brownish-grey — 32 **brilliance** (n.): great brightness — 35 *arc* (v.): to follow a curved course — 36 *diminish* (v.): to become or seem smaller — 37 *beacon* (v.): to flash a signal to inform s.o. — 37 *glare* (n.): a hard, unpleasant effect given by a strong light — 38 *heliograph* (n.): an instrument which sends messages by directing flashes of sunlight with a mirror — 38 *elemental* (n.): element, form of nature; here also an elementary concern, a first principle — 39 *inbound* (adj.): AE coming home, to the Earth — 39 *alien* (n.): a foreigner belonging to another race, country, planet

The merry side of a Canadian winter

5: YVES THÉRIAULT: The White Wolf

Yves Thériault, who was born in Québec City in 1915, was partly of Indian descent. He was educated at Montreal until he was 15, when he started to work at all sorts of jobs (e.g. radio announcer and script writer). He travelled around the world and lived in Italy for some years. Formative years were those spent as cultural director for the Department of Indian and Northern Affairs in Ottawa. In 1968 he returned to a small farm in Québec, his health problems in those years being a severe drawback to his career. He nevertheless received a number of literary prizes prior to his death in 1983.

Y. Thériault can be said to be one of the most prolific and versatile of contemporary Québec writers; thus he is widely studied at high schools and universities not only in Québec. The themes treated in his stories and novels are primitivism, naturalism, exotism, basic human instincts and passion in conflict with the forces of tradition and repression. Eskimos, Indians, Jews and peasants, striving against all sorts of domination, people his books. Thériault often becomes a biting critic of French-Canadian society and human civilization in general. Among his most important novels are *La fille laide* (1950), *Aaron* (1954), *Agaguk* (1958), *Ashini* (1960), and *Tayaout, fils d'Agaguk* (1969), all of which have been translated into English and other languages.

The text is taken from: Yves Thériault, *Agaguk*, translated by Miriam Chapin, Toronto, McGraw-Hill Ryerson, 1983, pp. 134–138.

The novel *Agaguk* is set in the tundra wilderness of Canada's Eastern Arctic, the time being the end of the 1930s.

The young hunter, Agaguk, has taken the girl Iriook as his wife; together they leave their native tribe to start a new life—also of hardships—in the wilderness. They thus turn away from the tyrannical and primitive past of a static Eskimo existence to the compromise of a more modern way of life which accepts some of the new traditions brought about by the overwhelming white civilization. Agaguk's fight against the white wolf may symbolize the clash of the two opposing worlds.

Use your own dictionary for unknown words.

---

descent (n.) /dɪ'sent/: family origins – *script* (n.): the written form of a speech, play or broadcast to be spoken – *formative* (adj.) /'fɔmətiv/: having influence in forming or developing – *drawback* (n.): difficulty, s.th. that can cause trouble – *prior* (adj.): earlier, coming before – *profilic* (adj.): producing many works – *versatile* (adj.): having many different kinds of skill or ability – **contemporary** (adj.): modern – *exotism* (n.): strange and unusual things – *basic* (adj.): that on which everything else rests or is built – *repression* (n.): the state of being ruled, controlled by being held back from natural feelings – *domination* (n.): the act of having or exercising controlling influence or power (over) – **critic** (n.): a person skilled in expressing judgement about the good and bad qualities of s.o. or s.th., here: person blaming s.o. or s.th. – *Arctic* (n.): the most northern part of the world – **hardship** (n.): difficult conditions of life – *overwhelm* (v.): to defeat or make powerless by much greater force – *clash* (n.): fight, battle

An Innuit hunter

The summer would not last more than another few weeks. It had hardly arrived, and already it was giving way to the cold from the north. The short autumn was on its way. Then—the winter!

The midnight sun would give place to the dull, gray, rarely brilliant, always-cold, half darkness. Sometimes it would be as savage as a horde of starving meat-eaters. Already the light of days and nights was not as it had been. The band of gold on the horizon was losing its brightness and was nothing but a dull line, barely luminous. And, in the daytime, wind came cold, freezing puffs, small gusts that troubled the animals and yellowed the moss.

The ground no longer had the elasticity of the warm damp layers, and the chill of the surface would soon join with the ice below and be sealed to the permafrost through the long months to come. At night it was not so pleasant to lie out on the ground, to sleep there, wedded to the earth, sprawled in the moss.

The caribou became scarcer, and the minks' fur began to grow thick, to become more silky. The day before, Agaguk had seen a rabbit. Its sides were white; it was the moulting season and a sure sign of the approaching cold. The time of good living was ending. Coming over the horizon was the time of misery.

And so, in a cold wind, Agaguk wandered about. He had left the hut without following any particular trail, but going almost at random, making a wide circle. He relied on his eyesight, on the instinct he had of any living presence on the tundra. He could stop and without turning around, without making the slightest effort, feel far behind him the presence of the hut and of the two beings who lived in it. Even in darkness, when night, hard on the heels of the day, was falling over the plain, crushing it so as to leave but a tiny ribbon of light, something, some inner alertness, a new rhythm in his blood, a nothingness warned him of its presence.

This would be, on such a night, his best weapon. He would know the nearness of danger at the same moment as the wolf. As soon as the beast sensed him at a distance, he himself would perceive the beast's presence. It was simple; it proceeded from a physical faculty inherited from many generations. But Agaguk would not have been able to explain how the mechanism worked, nor where within him was located the sense that gave the alert. Many times before he had stopped on the tundra, conscious all at once of an animal's presence. He had no need to see it to feel the certitude that it was there, not far away.

And then followed the ambush, the waiting. The animal rose, and Agaguk ate a few days more, or clothed himself, or added to the bundle of raw skins to barter at the trading post.

He kept on walking.

How long, he could not have said. He knew only the direction, and he knew that because of the way he had taken on leaving the hut, he could not go back to Iriook and the child the way he had come, but rather he must bear to the left, toward the big star that was poised in the sky.

But there was no white wolf. In fact, no wolf at all.

If a pack had been howling earlier, and then yelping, it was quiet now. Doubtless the pack had tracked a caribou and brought it down. Now it was appeased, and only later it would begin the hunt again, silently, once the moon went down. But the white wolf? Did he howl with them? Did he hunt with the pack? If he was wandering alone on the tundra, where could he be found? White blot against the darkness? Silhouette perhaps? If he was lurking somewhere waiting, it would be easy. Agaguk would know his presence, would go right to him. He had cocked his gun, the knife with the fine blade hung on his leg. Another knife with a short, very thick blade was at his belt. With one weapon or the other, the white wolf would perish.

An hour went by, another. The moon went down and the tundra grew darker. Standing, motionless, Agaguk scrutinized the vast plain of death. There was not even the sound of an insect.

A tightening in his belly warned him. He felt an animal's presence not far away. He could not have said in what direction or at what distance, but some beast, a fairly big one, not a badger or a mink, was watching him.

Slowly he slid to the ground and squatted, his rifle ready close to his cheek. He must have time. It would be simple to check the direction and the length of the leap toward the animal, but he needed to be close to the ground, to let the wind come to his nostrils, to wait and listen.

A gust went by, rustling the moss, and all was calm again. His eyes at the level of the ground, Agaguk looked slowly around him. In the direction of the hut, at the place where the band of the horizon ended, he saw a shadow against the shadow. There was only a reflection of the light, hardly enough to outline a silhouette. He fixed his eye on the shadow that appeared to stick up over the plateau of moss. He saw the shadow was moving, as if it were crawling. Toward him.

He waited. Some minutes later, he was sure. The odour on the wind was that of a wolf, and the shadow was no longer dark, but gray. And only one animal was capable of creating this picture. The Great White Wolf? No other could make a pale spot on the darkness.

Agaguk, glued to the ground, completely motionless, with his gun ready, waited for the animal to come nearer. Soon the smell was so strong that it made him sick. Now there was not a spot, but the clearly visible form of a wolf crawling on its belly. The wolf also was stalking his prey, seeking to find the silhouette of Agaguk, who was now lying flat on the ground, blotted out in the darkness. Man against beast, two strategies confronting each other. If the wolf came close, Agaguk would fire and the bullet would kill the animal. And if he missed?

Within hailing distance, then the distance of a spear's throw, finally a hundred steps, fifty ... the wolf was almost within reach of his hand. Only he was coming straight toward Agaguk; he was a narrow target, hard to determine in the night. Agaguk kept his eye on his sights, the beast well in view against the midnight sun on the horizon. Ten steps. It was now or never. Everything depended on one move, on the rapid pressure on the trigger, the aim, the bullet. Less than a second, less still. His fate decided. The death of the wolf? The death of the man?

Agaguk pressed the trigger. The bullet burst from the barrel. But it did not kill the wolf, it only scratched him. He rolled over on the ground and picked himself up ten paces away. At once he was on his feet. Agaguk was standing too, his knife in his fist. The wolf jumped.

A phantom mass, a sort of meteor lanced from the air, landed on Agaguk. Man and beast struggled in the dark. The wolf's jaw was open, slobbering with rage, and with a devilish growling he bit at the man who was fighting furiously between his paws. A horrible wrestling match went on, a deadly gymnastic. At each bite the man's piercing cry rose in the night. The wolf hung on in fury, tearing the man's flesh with his claws, until Agaguk seized the right moment as the animal drew back to plunge again, and pulled back his arm to drive the knife home in the beast's hide. Then he dodged away, but leaped anew on the man, who stiffened against the pain. Great shreds of flesh hung from the animal's teeth. It was a terrible conflict, punctuated by shrieks and growls, where by turns first man and then beast was ahead. Suddenly the knife blade flashed. The fist fell like an arrow, once, then again and again.

Agaguk had the sweet taste of blood in his mouth, which restored his nerve and his grip. Now he was astride the wolf. It was writhing under him and howling. He struck with all his might, his vigor renewed, all pain assuaged. Then he stood up, wiped his forearm over his bloody face and took account of what force he had left. The white wolf, disembowelled, lay at his feet.

Agaguk took off the cord he used as a belt, tied one end around the wolf's hind feet, bent himself to the burden and dragged it over the tundra.

When he reached the hut, Iriook, unable to sleep, was standing there, trembling. Her voice was little more than a whisper, a faint moan.

"Agaguk?"

The man straightened up. "Tayaout?"

"He is safe. The wolf did not come here."

Agaguk pointed to the carcass. "I killed him."

Iriook was crying quietly. "I'm going to light the lamp," she said, "so I can dress your wounds."

From where she was, she saw Agaguk's blood make a black stain which was spreading on the moss. His parka was in ribbons. The wolf had torn great hunks of flesh from the back of his thighs to his shoulders. But there was worse still, and Iriook saw this when the lamplight in the hut fully disclosed her man. Then she began to weep in long sobs, as if she were mourning the dead, and she let herself slip to the ground.

"What's the matter?" asked Agaguk. "What is it?"

She could only raise her head and point with her finger to the man's face. He tried to understand her gesture, and put his hand to his face. In place of a nose there was only an immense hole.

In one mouthful the wolf had torn the nose and part of the cheeks from Agaguk's face. He leaned over as if he were going to touch Iriook gently on the shoulder, but instead of this caress she felt her husband's body fall senseless on the floor beside her. Overcome by weariness and pain, Agaguk fainted and lay unconscious.

Outside the wolf's hind foot was still trembling spasmodically, though the tongue was dangling from the jaws and the eyes were glassy. An owl, crying mournfully, flew overhead. On the horizon a pack commenced to howl. Tayaout woke up whining in the light within the hut.

"The chief is dead," murmured Iriook. Suddenly she felt proud. "The chief of all the wolves," she went on, "of all the wolves on earth and the back of the world, and it is my husband, Tayaout's father, who has killed him."

Active Vocabulary

The numbers refer to the respective chapters (I, II etc.), text and line (1/2 etc.). References with "int." are to the introduction of a text. "Qu." refers to the initial quotation at the beginning of each chapter. "Pref." refers to the Preface.

For example: **abridge** (v.) I, 1/int. 11 occurs in Chapter I, text 1, introduction line 11.

abridge (v.) I, 1/int. 11
abrupt (adj.) V, 3/181
achievement (n.) II, 5/30; III, 2/int. 8
additional (adj.) IV, 2/int. 11
admirable (adj.) IV, 5/107
adolescent (n.) IV, 5/int. 8
adult (adj.) IV, 5/130
ad(vertisement) (n.) VII, 4/12
ally (n.) IV, 1/23
ambiguity (n.) III, 5/96
ambiguous (adj.) III, 5/236
ancestor (n.) IV, 1/52
anthology (n.) II, 5/int. 6
appropriate (adj.) IV, 5/179
area (n.) II, 5/6; III, 6/41
aspect (n.) II, Qu. bio. 7
astonishing (adj.) III, 1/18
autobiographical (adj.) III, 3/int. 11; IV, 2/int. 9; VII, 1/int. 14
autonomy (n.) II, Qu. 14

bad-tempered (adj.) VI, 2/176
barren (adj.) II, 1/10
basically (adv.) I, 1/36
bilingual (adj.) III, 5/int. 1; III, 5/208
boom (n.) III, 3/90
brilliance (n.) VII, 4/32

cabin (n.) III, 6/30
civilian (n.) IV, 1/19
claim (n.) III, 5/191
commit suicide IV, 5/234
communicate (v.) VI, 2/133
compatriot (n.) III, 2/int. 18
concept (n.) II, 4/59
Confederation (n.) I, 5/35; II, 4/64
console (v.) IV, 5/58
contemporary (adj.) II, 5/71; VII, 5/int. 9
cowardice (n.) V, 3/40
craftsman (n.) IV, 1/31
creator (n.) II, 5/11; III, 1/19; III, 4/13
critic (n.) II, Qu. bio. 5; VII, 5/
cycle (n.) V, 2/int. 16
int. 15

decade (n.) I, 1/68
depict (v.) IV, 4/int. 2
depressing (adj.) IV, 5/57
descent (n.) VII, 5/int. 2
desolate (adj.) IV, 5/204; VII, 1/2
distinct(ive) (adj.) I, 1/19
dominate (v.) IV, 1/59; IV, 4/34; IV, 5/54
dramatist (n.) IV, 6/int. 1
drought (n.) V, 4/28

emerge (v.) II, Qu. 15
emigrate (v.) IV, 2/int. 1
emphasize (v.) II, 5/27; IV, 5/22
employee (n.) III, 3/7
employment (n.) IV, 2/33
environment (n.) V, 2/int. 15
epic (adj.) II, 5/64
ethnic (adj.) Pref. 8; II, Qu. 4; III, 4/44
exaggerate (v.) IV, 5/171
exploit (v.) V, 3/163
explorer (n.) I, 5/32; IV, 1/38; VI, 1/43; VI, 2/5
exultation (n.) V, 2/116

Acknowledgements

The texts reprinted in this volume have been taken from various sources. Where the law of copyright still applies, every effort has been made to inform the copyright owners. The following texts have been reprinted within the terms of § 46 URG.

I Introduction

Text 1: John Saywell, *Canada Past and Present*, Toronto, Clarke Irwin, rev. ed. 1984.

Text 4: *Ben Wick's Canada*, Toronto, McClelland and Stewart, 1976.

Text 5: *Canadian Myths and Legends*, ed. Michael O. Nowlen, Toronto, Macmillan of Canada, 1977. Copyright © 1976. Reprinted by permission of Macmillan of Canada, a Division of Canada Publishing Corporation.

Text 6: *The Maple Leaf Forever: An Anthology of Canadian Comic Poetry*, ed. Douglas Barbour and Stephen Scobie, Edmonton, Hurtig Publishers, 1981. Originally from *Variable Cloudiness*, Hounslow Press, 1977. Reprinted by permission of the author.

II Atlantic Provinces

Text 4: *Easterly: 60 Atlantic Writers*, ed. B. E. Hatt, Don Mills, Ontario, Academic Press Canada, 1983.

Text 5: see Text 4

III Québec

Text 2: Hugh MacLennan, *Two Solitudes*, Toronto, Laurentian Library 1, 1967. Reprinted by permission of Russell + Volkening, Inc., as agents for the author. Copyright © 1945, renewed 1973 by Hugh MacLennan.

Text 3: Mordecai Richler, *The Apprenticeship of Duddy Kravitz*, Markham, Ont., Penguin Books Canada Ltd.

Text 4: "Gaston Miron; Poetic Voice of Québec Nationalism" by Henry Giniger, April 2, 1978. Copyright © 1978 by The New York Times Company. Reprinted by permission.

Text 5: Hugh Hood, *Around the Mountain, Scenes from Montral Life*, Paperback, Richmond Hill, Ont. Irwin Publishing, 1976.

Text 6: Roch Carrier, *La Guerre, Yes sir!* (translated by Sheila Fischman), Toronto, House of Anansi Press, 1970.

IV Ontario

Text 1: William Kilbourne, "In the Beginning". In: *Ontario: A Bicentennial Tribute*, Toronto, Key Porter Books, 1983.

Text 3: Rick Salutin, *1837. William Lyon Mackensie and the Canadian Revolution*, Rick Salutin and Theatre Passe Muraille, Toronto, James Lorimer and Company, 1976.

Text 4: Robertson Davies, *Fifth Business*, New York, The Viking Press, 1970. Copyright © 1970 by Robertson Davies. Reprinted by permission of Viking Penguin, Inc.

Text 5: Alice Munro, "An Ounce of Cure" from *Dance of the Happy Shades*, Toronto, McGraw-Hill Ryerson Ltd., 1968.

Text 6: "First Letter" from *Selected Longer Poems* by James Reany, reprinted by permission of the author and Press Porcepic Ltd., Victoria and Toronto.

V The Prairies

Text 1: *The Waterloo Folk Songs of Canada*, ed. Edith Fulton Fowke and Richard Johnston, Waterloo, Ont., Waterloo Music Company Ltd., 1967.

Text 2: *Who Has Seen the Wind* © 1947 by W. O. Mitchell. Reprinted by permission of Macmillan of Canada, a Division of Canada Publishing Corporation, Toronto.

Text 3: Sinclair Ross "A Field of Wheat" from *The Lamp at Noon and Other Stories*, Toronto, McClelland and Stewart, repr. 1983.

Text 4: George Bowering, "prairie music" from *Rocky Montain Foot*, Toronto, McClelland and Stewart, 1968.

VI British Columbia

Text 1: Eric Nicol, "First Province on the Left" from *The West Coast Experience*, ed. Jack Hodgins, © 1976. Reprinted by permission of Macmillan of Canada, a Division of Canada Publishing Corporation, Toronto.

Text 2: Ethel Wilson, *Swamp Angel*, Toronto, McClelland and Stewart, 1982.

Text 3: Earle Birney, *Selected Poems 1940–1966*, Toronto, McClelland and Stewart Ltd., 1966.

Text 4: Emily Carr, *Growing Pains*, Richmond Hill, Ont., Irwin Publishing Inc., 1946.

VII The North

Text 1: *Collected Poems of Robert Service*, London, Ernest Benn Ltd., 1978. Reprinted by permission of Feinmann + Krasilovsky P. C., New York.

Text 2: Al Purdy, *North of Summer: Poems from Baffin Island*, Toronto, McClelland and Stewart, 1967.

Text 3: Duncan Campbell Scott *Selected Poetry*, ed. Glenn Clever, Ottawa, The Tecumseh Press, 1974. Reprinted by permission of John G. Aylen, Ottawa.

Text 4: *The World of Farley Mowat: A Selection from his Works*, ed. Peter Davison, Boston, Little, Brown and Company, 2nd printing, 1980.

Text 5: Yves Thériault, *Agaguk* (translated by Miriam Chapin). Copyright © The Ryerson Press, 1963.

Illustrations

Every effort has been made to contact copyright owners of illustration material used in this book. Should we have failed to inform anyone in any particular instance, we would welcome enquiries.

page 6–7: map from *Canada Past and Present*, Clarke, Irwin & Company Ltd., Toronto – page 14: photo courtesy C. N. R. – page 19: cartoon from *Language and Society*, Office of the Commissioner of Official Languages, Ottawa – page 31: from *Kurelek's Canada*, Pagurian Corporation LH, Toronto – page 34: painting by Michèle Lemieux – page 35 (bottom): painting by Eugène Hamel, Musée du Quebec – page 39: painting by Cornelius Krieghoff, Meridian Management, © 1971 by Hugues de Jouvancourt, Musson Book Company, 1973 – page 46: photo by G. Düsterhaus – page 59: Gilles Vigneault, Nouvelles Editions de l'Arc. Song text from *Gilles Vigneault*, Editions Pierre Seghers, Paris, 1969 – page 60: painting by Cornelius Krieghoff, *Merrymaking*, Beaverbrook Art Gallery, Fredericton, N.B. – page 63: cartoon from *The Montreal Star* – page 64: photo from Canadian Bureau for External Affairs – page 66: photo by Paul von Baich, Key Porter Books – page 68: Bett-Services, Chicago (r.) – page 74: National Film Board of Canada – page 75: photo by Paul von Baich, Key Porter Books – page 86: National Film Board of Canada – page 92: painting by William Kurelek from the Downstairs Gallery, Edmonton – page 98: painting by William Kurelek in *A Prairie Boy's Summer*, Tundra Books, Montreal – page 108: photo by G. Düsterhaus – page 109: photo by Menno Fieguth in *Saskatchewan*, Oxford University Press, Toronto – pages 110–112: photos by G. Düsterhaus – page 116: photo by Menno Fieguth (see above) – page 123: University of British Columbia Library, Special Collections Division – page 126: Information Canada Photothèque, photo by Doug Wilkinson – page 127: National Film Board of Canada – page 128: drawing by Jean Banks – page 132/134/138/141: National Film Board of Canada.